Guide to Tracing Your African Ameripean Civil War Ancestor

A Guide by an Experienced African Ameripean Family Historian and Military Researcher Who Traced Her Great-grandfather, Iverson Granderson, in the Union Navy (1863-1865)

Jeanette Braxton Secret

HERITAGE BOOKS
2007

HERITAGE BOOKS
AN IMPRINT OF HERITAGE BOOKS, INC.

Books, CDs, and more—Worldwide

For our listing of thousands of titles see our website
at
www.HeritageBooks.com

Published 2007 by
HERITAGE BOOKS, INC.
Publishing Division
65 East Main Street
Westminster, Maryland 21157-5026

Other Books by the Author:
Iverson Granderson, First Class "Colored" Boy, Union Navy (1863-1865)

International Standard Book Number: 978-0-7884-0672-0

To The Sons of Africa

To every thing there is a season, and
A time to every purpose under the heaven:
A time to be born, and a time to die;
A time to plant, and a time to pluck up that which is planted;

A time to kill, and a time to heal;
A time to break down, and
A time to build up;

A time to weep, and
A time to laugh;
A time to mourn, and
A time to dance;

A time to cast away stones, and
A time to gather stones together;
A time to embrace, and
A time to refrain from embracing;

A time to get, and
A time to lose;
A time to keep, and
A time to cast away;

A time to rend, and
A time to sew;
A time to keep silence, and
A time to speak;

A time to love, and
A time to hate;
A time of war, and
A time of peace

Ecclesiastes 19:9

Table of Contents

Acknowledgments

First, I would like to give honor to the Almighty who gave me the strength and perseverance to trace and locate my great-grandfather's military records, and pension records. Iverson Granderson was a sailor in the Union Navy from 1863-1865.

Locating Iverson Granderson's records would not have been possible without the family oral history passed down by his granddaughter, Alberta 'Dee Dee' Jones. Alberta 'Dee Dee' Jones was the oldest living family member of Iverson Granderson. Dee Dee was the family historian or known among most African tribes as a 'griot'. I am very grateful to Dee Dee for passing the family history torch to me.

A special thanks to James Smith, a self-taught African Ameripean Genealogist of Oakland, California, who found the illegible index (darker card) on microfilm listing information on Iverson Granderson. (General Index to Pension Files, 1861-1865). There were150 pages in Granderson's Pension File.

The author is particularly indebted to the following for assistance in various ways. Michael P. Musick and staff at the National Archives in Washington, D.C., and special thanks to Rebecca Livingston who sent me information on Granderson(s) whenever she came across the name.

I would like to express my appreciation to the National Archives and Records Administration for permission to reproduce pages from the "Tabular Analysis of the Records of the U.S. Colored Troops and their Predecessor Units in the National Archives of the United States-Special List No. 33,""NATF Form 80-National Archives Trust Fund Board," and "Military Service Records-National Archives Trust Fund Board-National Archives and Records Administration."

Also, I am grateful to the U.S. Dept. of Navy, Naval Historical Center for permission to reproduce pages from the Civil War Naval Chronology (1861-1865).

Finally, I am indebted to my significant other, Andrew Kirk (Red) Jones, for being so patient and supportive as I researched and wrote. Also, I am indebted to my mother, Mary Lee Martin, who taught me to respect my elders, and my dear sister, Beatrice 'Bea' Chatman, for the encouragement and support. Lastly, my children, Carmen Braxton-Gay, Colette Jones-Watts, Freddie Pierre Jones III, and their spouse Ralph Craig Gay, Charles Watts, and Djuana DeWalt-Jones with their devotion and belief in what I was working on.

Preface

"It seemed proper, also, that the memory of our forefathers should not be allowed to remain in longer obscurity, that it is fitting to recall their deeds of heroism, that all might know the sacrifice they made for freedom their descendants were so long denied from enjoying"

Joseph T. Wilson
The Black Phalanx

Introduction

Approximately 166 Negro regiments (45 infantries, seven cavalries, 12 heavy artilleries, one light artillery and one engineer), and approximately more than 180,000 free Negroes and former slaves were recruited and organized into the U.S. Colored Troops between June 30, 1863 to December 31, 1867.1

A total of 1,059 vessels was commissioned by the Navy from 1861 to 1865, and approximately more than 28,000 Negro seamen served in the Union Navy.2

With a combined total of approximately 200,000 African Ameripeans serving in the Union Civil War, it is very likely every African Ameripean had at least one ancestor that fought in the Civil War.

By beginning with family members born between the 1820s and1850s, possibly you can probably find a relative that fought in the Civil War. That family member might be a great-grandfather, a great-granduncle, a great-grandcousin, etc. who was a Federal trooper.

When you begin to trace a family member who might have been a soldier or seaman, start with the male's last name. Also, if you know the state that he lived and died in, it will serve as a great resource in locating your relative. Many former slaves changed their names after the Civil War. Their military war record lists both their original and new name and possible aliases.

In addition, if you do not have enough information to begin your family history research, war records and pension records information such as names of slave masters, locations of plantations, names of other family members and friends etc. could help in your family history research later.

The Indexes to the Compiled Service Records for the United States Colored Troops, Rendezvous Reports for Navy Enlistments, and Muster Rolls of the U.S. Marine Corps are embedded in the Military Service Records. It is a very difficult task locating those specific service records in the Military Service Records. The purpose of this book is to help you easily locate the Indexes to the Compiled Service Records for the U.S.C.T., Union Seamen, and U.S. Marine Corps in the Civil War.

The author only included Military Service Records' pages relating to the service records of volunteer Union soldiers who served with the United States Colored Troops, Navy Enlistments, and U.S. Marine Corps. Also, included are pages for the Veterans' Claims for Indexes to Pensions Files, Special Schedules of the Eleventh Census (1890) Enumerating Union Veterans and Widows of Union Veterans of the Civil War, and Selected Records Relating to Black Servicemen.

The author did not include pages for any service records for Confederate soldiers and sailors or service records for any other Wars other than the Civil War.

The author has used African Ameripean from the contemporary Africentric Model for African Americans. African Ameripean includes Americans of African, Native American, and European ancestry. Most African Americans have some Native American and European ancestors. Therefore, the author has used African Ameripean instead of African Americans to include all of the above ancestries.

The military records and pension records at the National Archives in Washington, D.C. are an untapped gold mine for African Ameripeans looking for their relatives who served in the Union Navy and U.S. Colored Troops.

A typical military record gives the soldier's name, rank, military unit, and dates of entry into the service and separation by discharge, desertion, or death. It may also show the soldier's age, place of birth, and residence at the time of enlistment.3

The pension records are equally valuable because they contain both historical and genealogical information.

The historical information in the pension records contained organization of military units, movement of troops, details of battles and campaigns. Also, activities of individuals obtained from application statements of veterans; from affidavits of witnesses, and from the muster roll, diary, order, or orderly books occasionally submitted as proof of service.4

If the pension records contain genealogical information on your ancestors, photocopy them: typical information of what may be found in applications for pension records.

A veteran's application typically shows veterans' name, rank, military unit, period of service, residence at time of mustering-in, residence at time of application, birthplace, age or date of birth, and when the claim was made on the basis of need, a list of property.

A widow's application shows most of the same information about the veteran noted above and the maiden name, date and place of marriage, and date and places of her husband's death.

A child or heir's application gives information about the veteran and his widow as noted above. Some information included on the child and heir's applications are the heir's name, heir's place and date of birth, residence at the time of application, and date of the mother's death.

In a veteran's application files, there are often supporting documents such as discharge papers, affidavits and deposition of witnesses, narrative of events during service (to prove that the veteran had served at a particular time although he might not have documentary evidence), marriage certificates, birth records, death certificates, pages from family Bibles, and other papers.5

The **Tabular Analysis of the Records of the U.S. Colored Troops and their Predecessor Units in the National Archives of the United States** is a good source for locating soldiers' regiments in the U.S. Colored Army.6

War records and pension records inquiries must be submitted on **NATF Form 80, Order for copies of Veterans Records.** Instructions for its use and an explanation of how orders are processed and printed on the form. When a pension claimfile is found, documents that normally contain the basic information of a personal nature about the veteran and his family will be selected and photocopied. Photo copies of the reproducible papers in the claimfile furnished for a moderate cost per page.7

Many veterans' discharge papers destroyed in home fires, carelessly misplaced, and/or lost when moving. Also, some veterans gave their discharge papers to dishonest carpetbaggers to file for veteran's benefits, but the carpetbaggers never seen again. Most African Ameripeans today do not have military papers of family members who served in the Civil War.

However, if you are fortunate enough to have copies of enlistment and/or discharge papers of a relative from the Civil War it is a priceless military service document.

If you want to locate military war records and pension records, these are the steps to follow for discovering and locating war records and pension records of family members and friends. Begin your search with a soldier in the U.S. Colored Troops (U.S.C.T.) because most Blacks served in the U.S. Colored Army during the Civil War.

Locate African Ameripean soldiers in the alphabetical card index in the compiled service records of volunteers Union soldiers who served with the United States Colored Troops.

M 589. 98 rolls. 16mm. DP.

Each index card gives the name of a solider, his rank, and the unit in which he served. There are cross-references for names that appear in the records under more than one spelling and for the service in more than one unit or organization.

To find the name **Granderson:**

Roll	Description
33	Go-Graw 8

Also, there are records of movements and activities of the U.S. Colored Troops (Record Groups 94 and 407), i.e.,

Roll	Description
	U.S. Colored Troops:
205	6th Heavy Artillery 8th-14th Heavy Artillery 1st Light Artillery 2nd Light Artillery Independent Battery, Light Artillery 1st Infantry 1st Infantry,1 year 1864. 9

Beginning in 1890, the War Department compiled histories of the volunteer military organizations that served during the Civil War. The compiled records for each organization are in jacket-envelopes bearing the title 'Record of Events' and giving the name of the unit.

Compiled service histories contain no information about individual soldiers. The abstract instead relates to the stations, movements, or activities of each unit or part of it. 10

In addition, there is a tabular list of regimental book records on the U.S. Colored Troops consisting mainly of copies letters received, registers of letters received, court-martial proceedings, and other miscellaneous records. 11

If you are unable to locate the war records of a serviceman in the U.S. Colored Troops that person might have served in the Union Navy.

Locate the African Ameripean seaman in the alphabetical index to Rendezvous Reports,Civil War,1861-1865.

T 1099. 31 rolls. 16mm.

Each card shows the name of the individual, rendezvous (place of enlistment or vessel on which enlisted); date of enlistment or return (the roll on which the name first appeared); and a space for a 'Record of Service'. Although the amount of information varies, the entry under reassignment or discharge, the names of vessels on which the individual served, or the date ofdeath.

To find the name Granderson:

Roll	Description
10	Girraty,John Hale,Sherman 12

Follow instructions and complete NATF FORM 80,Order for Copies of Veterans Records, and include all the detailed information from the alphabetical card index on the serviceman.13 The more information you provide, more likely the war records will be found.

On NATF Form 80, only check one box(military)in Number1. File To Be SEARCHED.

Locate the Pensioner's last name in the General Index to Pension Files,1861-1865.

T 288. 544 rolls. 16 mm.

This microfilm publication reproduces a general index to pension files, 1861-1934. The pension applications to which this index applies relate chiefly to Army, Navy, and Marine Corps service performed between 1861 and 1916. Most of the records relate to the Civil War Service.

Each card in the general index gives a veteran's name, rank, unit, and term of service, names of dependent(s), the filing date, the application number, the certification, and the state from which the claim filed. The darker cards relate to naval service.

To find the name Granderson:

Roll	Description
182	Gowner, Lewis-Green, Herman 14

5/ Miscellaneous Records relating to Veteran's Claims

There are other miscellaneous records relating to veteran's claims (Record Groups 29,94, and 407).

Locate the Civil War veteran's last name in the Special Schedules of the Eleventh Census (1890) enumerating Union Veterans and Widows of Union Veterans of the Civil War.

M123. 118 rolls.

An Act of March 1, 1889 gave the Superintendent of Census the authority to take the Eleventh Census on a Special Schedule. The Special Schedule forms included names, organizations, and length of service of those who had served in the Army, Navy or Marine Corps of the United States in the War of the Rebellion. Also, the Superintendent of Census included the survivors at the time of the inquiry, and the widows of soldiers, sailors, or marines.

Each entry showed the following information; the name of the veteran (or if he did not survive, the names of both the widow and her deceased husband). For example, the veteran's rank, company, regiment, or vessels, date of enlistment, date of discharge, and length of service in years, months, and days. Also, sometimes the entry included personal information such as the veteran's post office and address of each person listed, disability incurred by the veteran. In addition, remarks necessary for a complete statement of his term of service included in the entry.

All of Alabama through Kansas's Schedule for the States possibly destroyed by fire. Approximately half of the Schedule for the State of Kentucky appears destroyed, possibly by fire before the transfer of the remaining schedules to the National Archives in 1943.

The schedules arranged alphabetically by state or territory then by county and minor subdivision.

To find the name Granderson:

Roll	Description
Mississippi	
26	Entire State 15

6/ General correspondence of the Record and Pension Office, 1889-1920

Locate the pensioner's last name in the Index to General Correspondence of the Record and Pension Office, 1889-1920.

M 686. 385 rolls. 16mm DP.

The index cards on micro film list names of soldiers. Besides the names of the soldier, each card gives the organization in which he served, the name of the person or office who made the inquiry, the subject of the inquiry, and the file number. Other cards refer to names of volunteer organizational units, and of states. The military records and pension records to which these indexes refer are not available on microfilm.

To find the name Granderson:

Roll	Description
141	Grah-Grav 16

7/ Miscellaneous records Relating To Military Service

Lastly, there are Miscellaneous Records relating to military service. They are selected records relating to Black servicemen (Record Groups 94,107, and 153).

Locate the servicemen in the records relating to the Negro in the military service of the United States, 1639-1886.

M 858. 5 (five) rolls. DP.

Roll	Description
	Dates 1863
2	War of the Rebellion Military Employment Correspondence Relative to Civil Status, Labor, etc. Events, Battle Reports, etc.

This microfilm publication reproduces compiled records published by the Colored Troops Division of the Adjutant General's Office (AGO). This compilation, The Negro in the Military Service of the United States: A Compilation of Official Records, State Papers, Historical Extracts, etc., relating to military status and service, from the date of introduction into the British North American colonies, consisting principally of documents copied from published and unpublished primary sources.

In addition, there are a few original documents and extracts from secondary sources that cover periods of history for which primary sources were not readily available. The volumes are part of the Records of the Adjutant General's Office,1780-1917, Record Group 94.

The records in the compilation arranged into chapters corresponding roughly to 9 Periods, and separated into Sections by Subject. Those sections concerned with military employment and civil status are further divided between Confederate States and United States. On the last page of the compilation there is a heading "Statistical Tables"and a note state that the tables were too bulky to be placed with the copies of the records to be bound. Despite extensive searches there statistical tables have not been located. 17

Some description and roll numbers that have not been located, i.e.,

Roll	Description Dates 1861-62
1	War of the Rebellion Census Report Fugitive Slaves, Contraband of War, Laborers, etc. Military Employment Events, Battle Reports

Locate the selected documents relating to Blacks nominated for appointment to United States Military Academy During The19th Century,1870-1887.

M 1002. 21 rolls. D.P.

Roll	Description Dates
2	James Elias Rector Thomas Van Rensslear Gibbs Henry Ossian Flipper John Washington Williams William Henry Jarvis, Jr. William Henry White Whitefield McKinlay William Narcese Werles

This microfilm publication reproduces documents relating to27 Blacks nominated during the 19th Century. The documents include nomination and appointment papers, correspondence reports of examinations, consolidated weekly reports of class grades and conduct rolls, orders, and court-martial case files. No documents filmed relating to the military careers of nominees following their graduation from the Academy.

Of the 27 Black nominees, 21 were from Southern States. **Eleven** nominated by Black members of the U.S. House of Representatives from Florida, Louisiana, North Carolina, and South Carolina. **Five** of the 11 nominated by Representative Robert Smalls of South Carolina. The names of the nominees, the dates of their nominations, the Representatives who nominated them, and the congressional districts and states from which they nominated listed in the **Descriptive Pamphlet.** 18

Locate the documents relating to the Military and Naval Service of Blacks awarded the Congressional Medal of Honor from the Civil War to the Spanish-American War.

M 929. 4 rolls. DP. i.e.,

Roll	Description
	Civil War - U.S. Navy:
4	Landsman Aaron Anderson
	Landsman Robert Blake
	Landsman Willaim H. Brown
	Landsman Wilson Brown
	Landsman John Lawson
	Engineer's Cook James Mifflin
	Seaman Joachim Pease

Interim Period (1865-98) - U.S. Navy:

Ship's Cook Daniel Atkins
Ordinary Seaman John Davis
Seaman John Johnson
Cooper William Johnson
Seaman Joseph B. Noil
Seaman John Smith
Ordin. Seaman Robert A.Sweeney

Spanish-American War - U.S. Navy:

Fireman 1st Class, Robert Penn

On December 21,1861, President Lincoln approved the congressional bill establishing the Navy Medal of Honor given to noncommissioned officers and enlisted men of the Navy and, Marine Corps for extraordinary bravery. A joint resolution of Congress that authorized the preparation of 2,000 Medals of Honor presented to noncommissioned officers and privates of the Army and the Volunteer Forces for gallantry in action and other soldier-like qualities approved by President Lincoln on July 12, 1862.

The first Congressional Medal of Honor awarded to a Black enlisted man of the U.S. Navy announced in General Order 32, Navy Department, April16,1864. Not until April 6,1865, were Black privates and noncommissioned officers of the U.S. Colored Troops awarded the Congressional Medal of Honor.

The documents reproduced here consist mostly of copies of letters sent, letters received, and reports. Issuances and mostly court-martial case files and log entries included. The ranks and ratings shown respectively Army noncommissioned officers and privates and Navy enlisted, men are those held by the men at the time the medals awarded.

The documents microfilmed for the Navy Medal of Honor winners, including parts of ships' logs, relate only to the acts of bravery for which they were cited and to the award of the medals. The documents reproduced for the Army Medal of Honor winners, however, often provide other information relating to their military service. A few documents, less than 75 years old and relating to two Army Medal of Honor winners, have not been filmed because they contain medical information, the disclosure of which would constitute an invasion of personal privacy. 19

8/ National Archives and State Archives

The National Archives is a gold mine with published and unpublished military service documents relating to Black servicemen in the Civil War. Also, Black servicemen fought in other wars such as the Revolutionary War, War of 1812, Spanish-American War, etc. The National Archives can be used as a resource for African Ameripean's contributions to American history. Also, some of the military service records in the National Archives can provide useful information for African Ameripean family history research. If you don't have any information on your ancestors, the military service records might be the first place to begin searching for your relatives.

You don't have to go to Washington, D.C., to visit the National Archives. The National Archives has regional archives in or near Boston, Kansas City, Fort Worth, Denver, Los Angeles, San Francisco, Seattle, and Anchorage. They are national resources in local settings.

Each regional archives has historical records from Federal courts and from regional offices of Federal agencies in the geographic areas each serves. Records common to several regions are from the District Courts of the United States, the Bureau of Indian Affairs, Bureau of Customs, and Office of the Chief of Engineers.

The regional archives have extensive holdings of National Archives microfilm publications, which reproduce with introductions and annotations some of the most frequently requested records in National Archives custody. They contain basic documentation for the study of pre-Federal and early Federal history, U.S. Diplomacy, immigration, Indian affairs, the land and other natural resources, and war and military service. Of special interest are Federal population censuses for all states, 1790 to 1920.

- **National Archives-New England Region**
  380 Trapelo Road
  Waltham, Massachusetts 02154
  617-647-8100 archives@waltham.nara.gov
  Connecticut, Maine, Massachusetts, New Hampshire, Rhode Island, Vermont

- **National Archives-Pittsfield Region**
  100 Dan Fox Drive
  Pittsfield, Massachusetts 01201
  413-445-6885 archives@pittsfield.nara.gov
  Microfilm only

- **National Archives-Northeast Region**
  201 Varick Street
  New York, New York 10014
  212-337-1300 archives@newyork.nara.gov
  New Jersey, New York, Puerto Rico, the Virginia Islands

- **National Archives-Mid Atlantic Region**
  9th and Market Streets, Room 1350
  Philadelphia, Pennsylvania 19107
  215-597-3000 archives@philarch.nara.gov
  Delaware, Maryland, Pennsylvania, Virginia, West Virginia

- **National Archives-Southeast Region**
  1557 St. Joseph Avenue
  East Point, Georgia 30344
  404-763-7477 archives@atlanta.nara.gov
  Alabama, Florida, Georgia, Kentucky, Mississippi, North Carolina, South Carolina, Tennessee

- **National Archives-Great Lakes Region**
  7358 South Pulaski Road
  Chicago, Illinois 60629
  312-581-7816 archives@chicago.nara.gov
  Illinois, Indiana, Michigan, Minnesota, Ohio, Wisconsin

- **National Archives-Central Plains Region**
  2312 East Bannister Road
  Kansas City, Missouri 64131
  816-926-6272 archives@kansascity.nara.gov
  Iowa, Kansas, Missouri, Nebraska

- **National Archives-Southwest Region**
  501 West Felix Street, P.O. Box 6216
  Ft. Worth, Texas 76115
  817-334-5525 archives@ftworth.nara.gov
  Arkansas, Louisiana, New Mexico*, Oklahoma, Texas (*Most records from Federal agencies in New Mexico are at the Rocky Mountain Region.)

- **National Archives-Rocky Mountain Region**
  Building 48-Denver Federal Center
  Denver, Colorado 80225-0307
  303-236-0817 archives@denver.nara.gov
  Colorado, Montana, North Dakota, South Dakota, Utah, Wyoming, New Mexico (see * above)

- **National Archives-Pacific Southwest Region**
  24000 Avila Road
  Laguana Niguel, California 92656
  714-360-2641 archives@laguna.nara.gov
  Arizona, southern California, and Clark County, Nevada

- **National Archives-Pacific Sierra Region**
  1000 Commodore Drive
  San Bruno, California 94066
  415-876-9009 archives@sanbruno.nara.gov
  Northern California, Hawaii, Nevada (except Clark County), the Pacific Trust Territories, American Samoa

- **National Archives-Pacific Northwest Region**
  6125 Sand Point Way NE
  Seattle, Washington 98115
  206-526-6507 archives@seattle.nara.gov
  Idaho, Oregon, Washington

- **National Archives-Alaska Region**
  654 West Third Avenue
  Anchorage, Alaska 99501
  907-271-2441 archives@alaska.nara.gov
  Alaska

The regional archives are open for research weekdays, except Federal holidays, from 8 A.M. To 4 P.M. Contact individual regional archives for information on additional research hours.

In addition, one of your relatives might have served in the Confederate military service such as the 1st Native Guards, Militia from Louisiana, if they were free Negroes. [20] There is a "Rebel Archives" consisting of service records for confederate soldiers arranged by state or territory, by organizational regiment or independent battalion or company. Under each unit the military service records arranged alphabetically by surname.

Locate the confederate army volunteers in Microfilmed Indexes and compiled Military Service Records, i.e.

State	Index	Compiled Military Service Records
Consolidated	M253	----
Louisiana	M378	M320
Maryland	M379	M269
Mississippi	M382	M324
Virginia	M382	M324

Locate the consolidated Index to compiled service records of Confederate soldiers.

M 253. 535 rolls 16mm. DP., i.e.,

To find the name Granderson:

Roll	Description
183	Gracey-Granger [21]

Furthermore, you might locate military service records on the slave master which might assist you in your African Ameripean family history research.

Finally, the state archives are an excellent resource for tracing your Civil War and post Civil War ancestors. If your ancestor was not a serviceman in the Civil War, maybe your relative served in the State Militia. The Militia, a state-organized and controlled citizen army was segregated in the South. It is now known as the National Guard for the purpose of protecting the citizens and property of that state. 22

Another resource for locating your African Ameripean Civil War Ancestor, and White Officer of the U.S. Colored Troops is the African-American Civil War Memorial Freedom Foundation, Post Office Box 73517, Washington, D.C. 20009. Telephone Number (202)667-2667 and/or (202)667-6771 Fax.

More than 185,000 Colored soldiers and their White Officers who fought for freedom and to preserve the Union during the Civil War will be memorialized on a national monument for the U.S.C.T. Their names will be etched on a Civil War memorial monument in Washington, D.C.

In addition, after finding complete war records of your ancestors; female direct descendants can apply for membership in the **Daughters of Union Veterans of the Civil War, 1861-1865**, Park Lane Building, Suite 525, 2025 Pennsylvania Avenue, N.W., Washington, D.C. 20006.

All daughters, (grand-daughters, etc., direct descendants), **lineal descent only** of honorable discharge soldiers, sailors, and Marines who served in the Union Army or Navy during the Rebellion of 1861-1865 are eligible for membership.

The **Daughters of Union Veterans of Civil War, 1861-1865**, is the only Civil War lineal descent women's organization to perpetuate the memory, deeds, and loyalty of those ancestors who sacrificed so much in the struggle to establish freedom. It is the oldest and largest of all Civil War American women's organization genealogical based on lineal descent.

9/ Footnotes

1. Joseph B. Ross., compiled by, **Tabular Analysis of the Records of the U.S. Colored Troops and Their Predecessor Units in the National Archives of the United States, Special List. No. 33, National Archives and Records Service,** GSA, Washington: 1973.

2. Herbert Aptheker, **The Negro in the Union Navy,** Journal of Negro History, Vol. XXXII, No. 2, April 1947, Page 179.

3. **Military Service Records,** National Archives Trust Fund Board, National Archives and Records Administration, Washington, DC: 1985, Page 3.

4. Ibid., Page 233.

5. Ibid., Page 234.

6. Joseph B. Ross, compiled by, **Tabular Analysis of the Records of the U.S. Colored Troops and Their Predecessor Units in the National Archives of the United States, Special List No. 33,** National Archives and Records GSA, Washington: 1973.

7. **Military Service Records,** National Archives Trust Fund Board, National Archives and Records Administration, Washington, DC: 1985, Page 234.

8. Ibid., Pages 53-54.

9. Ibid., Page 83.

10. Ibid., Page 75.

11. Joseph B. Ross., compiled by, **Tabular Analysis of the Records of the U.S. Colored Troops and Their Predecessor Units in the National Archives of the United States, Special List No. 33,** National Archives and Records Service GSA, Washington: 1973.

12. **Military Service Records,** National Archives Trust Fund Board, National Archives and Records Administration, Washington, DC: 1985; Pages 226-227.

13. Ibid., Page 234.

14. Ibid., Pages 258-262.

15. Ibid., Pages 297-300.

16. Ibid., Pages 300-303.

17. Ibid., Pages 326-327.

18. Ibid., Pages 327-328.

19. Ibid., Page 328.

20. Benjamin Quarles, **The Negro In The Civil War,** DACapo Press, Inc., New York, 1953: Pages 35-41.

21. **Military Service Records,** National Archives Trust Fund Board, National Archives and Records Administration, Washington, D.C.: 1985; Pages 83-164.

22. Vernon Lane Wharton., **The Negro In Mississippi 1865-1890,** Harper Torch Books, New York, 1965: Pages 193-195.

(Appendix A)

Special List No. 33

Tabular Analysis of the Records of the U.S. Colored Troops and Their Predecessor units in the National Archives of the United States

Compiled by Joseph B. Ross

National Archives and Records Service
General Services Administration
Washington: 1973

Library of Congress Catalog Card No. 73-600083

Foreword

The General Services Administration, through the National Archives and Records Service, is responsible for administering the permanent noncurrent records of the Federal Government. These archival holdings, now amounting to more than 1 million cubic feet, date from the days of the First Continental Congress and consist of the basic records of the legislative, judicial, and executive branches of our Government: The Presidential libraries of Herbert Hoover, Franklin D. Roosevelt, Harry S. Truman, Dwight D. Eisenhower, John F. Kennedy, and Lyndon B. Johnson contain the papers of those Presidents and many of their associates in office. While many archival holdings document events of great moment in our Nation's history, most of them are preserved because of their continuing practical use in the ordinary processes of government, for the protection of private rights, and for research use of scholars and students.

To facilitate the use of the records and to describe their nature and content, archivists prepare various kinds of finding aids. The present work is one such publication. We believe that it will prove valuable to anyone who wishes to use the records it describes.

ARTHUR F. SAMPSON
Acting Administrator of General Services.

Preface

Special lists are published by the National Archives and Records Service (NARS) as part of its records description program. The special list describes in detail the contents of certain important records series; that is, units of records of the same form or that deal with the same subject or activity or that are arranged serially. Its form and style are not fixed but vary according to the nature of the records to which it relates. Its distinguishing characteristic is that it goes beyond the general description contained in a record group registration statement, a preliminary inventory, or an inventory and describes records in terms of individual record items.

In addition to lists and other finding aids that relate to particular record groups, NARS issues publications that give an overall picture of materials in its custody. A new comprehensive *Guide to the National Archives of the United States* and a revised and expanded *Guide to Materials on Latin America in the National Archives of the United States* were published in 1974. Reference information papers analyze records in the National Archives of the United States (hereafter called the Archives) on such subjects as transportation, small business, and the Middle East. Records of the Civil War are described in the *Guide to Federal Archives Relating to the Civil War* (1962), *Guide to the Archives of the Government of the Confederate States of America* (1968), and *Civil War Maps in the National Archives* (1964); those of *World War I in Handbook of Federal World War Agencies and Their Records,* 1917-1921 (1943); and those of World War II in the two-volume guide *Federal Records of the World War II* (1950-51). Genealogical records are described in *Guide to Genealogical Records in the National Archives* (1964). In the Archives are large quantities of audiovisual materials received from all sources: Government, private, and commercial. *The Guide to the Ford Film Collection in the National Archives* (1970) describes one of the largest private gift collections. The extensive body of maps and charts is described in the *Guide to Cartographic Records in the National Archives* (1971).

Many bodies of records of high research value have been microfilmed by NARS as a form of publication. Positive prints of these microfilm publications, many of which are described in the current Catalog of National Archives Microfilm Publications, are available for purchase. For other publications, see the most recent Select List of Publications of the National Archives and Records Service, General Information Leaflet No. 3.

JAMES B. RHOADS
Archivist of the United States

Introduction

The first regiment of U.S. Colored Troops was not mustered into Federal service until June 1863. Black troops were, however, organized to fight the Confederate forces prior to President Lincoln's Emancipation Proclamation of January 1, 1863, which was issued as War Department General Order 1 on January 2, 1863. Gen. David Hunter organized the 1st Regiment South Carolina Colored Volunteers in the spring and summer 1862, authorized President Lincoln to receive Blacks into the military service as soldiers, but on August 6, 1862, the President announced that he was still unready to enroll Blacks as soldiers in the Union Army.

Following the August 6th announcement, the 1st Regiment of South Carolina Colored Volunteers was disbanded by General Hunter only to be reorganized under Gen. Rufus Saxton with War Department authorization later in the same month. The 1st Regiment of Kansas Colored Volunteers was organized in August 1862 by Gen. James H. Lane without War Department approval but was not mustered into service until 1862, but, unlike the 1st Kansas Colored Volunteers, the 1st, 2d, and 3d Regiments of Louisiana Native Guards (later the Corps d'Afrique) were mustered into Federal service between September and November 1862.

The recruiting of Black soldiers by the War Department after the Emancipation Proclamation was slow until Secretary of War Edwin M. Stanton sent Adjutant General Lorenzo Thomas into the Mississippi Valley in March 1863 with the authority to recruit and organize free and contraband Blacks for service in the U.S. Volunteer service. The recruiting effort was successful, and on May 22, 1863, the War Department issued General Order 143, establishing the Colored Troops Bureau. This bureau was directly under the Adjutant General's Office, and Maj. Charles W. Foster was appointed chief with the title of Assistant Adjutant General. The bureau was made responsible for recruiting colored troops, commissioning officers to command them, organizing regiments, and maintaining the records of the various colored troop organizations. The first regiment of U.S. Colored Troops was mustered into the Federal service on June 30, 1863, at Washington, D.C.

The Corps d'Afrique and other State organizations were redesignated when they became part of the U.S. Colored Troops, with the exception of a few units raised in Massachusetts, Connecticut, and Louisiana. Approximately 166 regiments and 200,000 officers and men were recruited, commissioned, and organized into the U.S. Colored Troops from the federalizing of the first regiment on June 30, 1863, to December 31, 1867, when the last regiment was mustered out.

A tabular list has been compiled for the bound regimental books and the unbound regimental papers of the U.S. Colored Troops and their predecessor units. The records are a part of Records of the Adjutant General's Office, 1780's-1917, Record Group 94, and they amount to approximately 82 linear feet of bound records and 56 linear feet of unbound records.

The bound volumes of regimental book records consist mainly of copies of letters sent, registers of letters received, endorsements and memorandums, regimental and company order books, and regimental and company descriptive books. The volume containing the regimental descriptive book frequently contains such other records as guard reports, morning reports, court-martial proceedings, proceedings of regimental councils of administration, requisitions for clothing, camp, and garrison equipment, various account books, and other miscellaneous records. Copies of letters sent, registers of letters received, and endorsements and memorandums are usually bound in the same volume.

Most of these records were maintained as separate books by the regiments, but during the 1880's the books were bound together into the present volumes by the Adjutant General's Office. The number of volumes shown individual books contained therein.

Date spans have been provided in the table for some of the letters sent, registers of letters received, endorsements and memorandums, and general and special orders. Dates have not been provided for the remainder of the bound records since they often span the entire period of a regiment's existence. A list showing the dates of organization and muster-out for each regiment can be found in the appendix.

No distinction has been made between the separate order books maintained by the regimental headquarters and those kept by each company of the regiment, since both contain orders from regimental headquarters. Occasionally, orders issued by other commands have been copied into the regimental order book. Periods covered by the regimental and company order books sometimes vary, and the dates shown in the table for each type of order are the combined periods of coverage of both regimental and company order books.

Regimental and company descriptive books are shown in the tables as "R" and "C." From the regimental descriptive book of a typical U.S. Colored Troops unit, one can obtain the names and dates of appointment of the colonel commanding the regiment, the lieutenant colonel, major, adjutant, quartermaster, chaplain surgeon (and first and second assistant surgeons, if any), and the captains and lieutenants of each company. The company descriptive books list only the names and dates of appointment of the commissioned officers for each company. Both regimental and company descriptive books list and describe the noncommissioned officers and enlisted men of each company.

At the end of the regimental books are volumes containing descriptive lists of enlisted men mustered into service at Camp Nelson, Ky. (4 vols.), and Benton Barracks, Mo. (2 vols.), during 1864-65 and assigned to various U.S. Colored Troops regiments. These volumes are not indexed.

The unbound regimental papers consist primarily of letters and telegrams received; general, special, and court-martial orders; circulars; court-martial proceedings and sentences; and rosters. The unbound papers frequently include other records, such as morning reports, casualty lists, descriptive lists of deserters, lists of men detailed, recommendations for appointments, resignations, discharges, inspection reports, and other miscellaneous papers. For convenience, the unbound regimental papers have been grouped into three categories:letters received; issuances; and roster, reports lists, and other miscellaneous records. All three types of records are listed in chronological order.

Some of the letters have been recorded in the registers of letters received, but others have not. Filed at the end of the letters received for some units are a few copies of requests for information concerning enlisted men's service. These requests were received and completed by the Adjutant General's Office during the 1870's and 1880's, and copies were filed with the regimental papers. The issuances include orders and circulars from regimental headquarters as well as incomplete series of orders issued by other commands and received at regimental headquarters. Complete series of general and special orders issued by regimental headquarters are more likely to be found with the bound than with the unbound issuances.

The table includes names of predecessor units whose records have been found with records belonging to the regiment, and explanatory notes are provided for those regiments that underwent one or more consolidations and to identify any special arrangements or types of records.

Records relating to the U.S. Colored Troops can be found in other series of Records of the Adjutant General's Office, 1780's-1917 (Record Group 94). There are the records of the Colored Troops Division, 1863-89, which include a compilation of historical extracts and official papers concerning the military service of Blacks from the colonial period through the Civil War (published as Microfilm Publication M858). Information concerning the stations, movements, and battles participated in by units of the U.S. Colored Troops can be found in the regimental returns and muster rolls. There are compiled records showing service of U.S. Colored Troops units and other volunteer Union organizations (published as Microfilm Publication M594) and compiled service records of soldiers who served in the U.S. Colored Troops. Also in this record group are registers of sick and wounded, field hospital records, and other medical records of the U.S. Colored Troops.

Additional records pertaining to U.S. Colored Troops can be found in Records of the Bureau of Refugees, Freedmen, and Abandoned Lands, Record Group 105; Records of the Provost Marshal General's Bureau (Civil War), Record Group 110; Records of United States Army Continental Commands, 1821-1920, Record Group 393; and War Department collection of

Confederate Records, Record Group 109. The correspondence, issuances, and other records found in the regimental books and unbound papers of the U.S. Colored Troops are not likely to be found in U.S. War Department, *The War of the Rebellion: a Compilation of the Official Records of the Union and Confederate Armies* (Washington, 1880-1901).

Abbreviations used in the table and the appendix include the following: A.D. (African descent), Arty. (Artillery), Bn. (Battalion), Btry. (Battery), Cav. (Cavalry), C. D'Afr. (Corps d'Afrique), Inf. (Infantry), Hv. Arty. (heavy artillery), and Lt. Art. (Light artillery).

	Bound volumes													Unbound records		
Name of unit and predecessor unit(s) and No. of vols.	Letters sent	Endorsements and memorandums	Register of letters received	General orders	Special orders	Descriptive book	Guard reports	Morning reports	Court-martial proceedings	Proceedings of regt. council of administration	Req. for clothing, camp, and garrison equipage	Clothing account book for noncommissioned staff	Regt. Co. fund, account book, or band fund	Letters received	Issuances	Rosters, reports, lists, and misc. records
1st Cav. 6 vols.	Jan. 1864-Feb. 1866		Jan. 1864-Feb. 1866	Dec. 1863-Aug. 1866	Dec. 1863-Jan. 1866	R C	X	X						Jan. 1864-Feb. 1866 2 in.	Sept. 1863-July 1866 2 in.	Dec. 1863-Mar. 1866 3 in.
2d Cav. 4 vols.	Apr. 1865-Feb. 1866			Jan. 1864-Feb. 1866	Jan. 1864-Feb. 1866	C		X						Nov. 1863-Apr. 1866 5 in.	Dec. 1863-Apr. 1866 5 in.	Feb. 1864-Feb. 1866 6 in.
3d Cav. (1st Miss. Cav., A.D.) 6 vols.	Oct. 1863-Apr. 1865		June 1865-Jan. 1866	Oct. 1863-Jan. 1866	Oct. 1863-Jan. 1866	R C		X						Sept. 1863-Jan. 1866 2 in.	July 1864-Jan. 1866 1 in.	Feb. 1863-Jan. 1866 2 in.
4th Cav. (1st Cav., C. d'Afr.) 1 vol.							X							Oct. 1863-Mar. 1866 3 in.	Oct. 1863-Dec. 1866 1 in.	Nov. 1863-Mar. 1866 3 in.
5th Cav. 5 vols.	Oct. 1864-Mar. 1866[1]			Jan. 1864-Oct. 1865		R C	X	X		X	X	X	X	May 1864-June 1866	Nov. 1864-Mar. 1866	Aug. 1864-Apr. 1866
5th Mass. Cav. (Colored) 7 vols.		Sept. 1864-Mar. 1865		Jan. 1864-Oct. 1865		R C	X	X				X				
6th Cav. 5 vols.				Nov. 1864-Apr. 1866	Nov. 1864-Apr. 1866	R C	X	X					X	Oct. 1864-Apr. 1866 2 in.	Mar. 1865-Apr. 1866 1 in.	Mar. 1864-Apr. 1866 2 in.
1st Hv. Arty. 6 vols.	Feb. 1864-Mar. 1866	Jan. 1865-Mar. 1866	Feb. 1864-Dec. 1864	Mar. 1864-Mar. 1866	Mar. 1864-Mar. 1866	R C		X			X			Jan. 1864-Apr. 1866 2 in.	Apr. 1864-Mar. 1866 1 in.	Sept. 1863-June 1866 2 in.
3d Hv. Arty. (1st Tenn. Hv. Arty., A. D.; 2d U.S. Colored Hv. Arty.) 11 vols.	June 1863-Apr. 1866	Jan. 1864-Apr. 1866	Sept. 1863-Apr. 1866	June 1863-Apr. 1866	June 1863-Apr. 1866	R C	X	X		X			X	Dec. 1863-Apr. 1866 4 in.	Apr. 1863-Apr. 1866 8 in.	June 1863-Apr. 1866 1 in.
4th Hv. Arty. (2d Tenn. Hv. Arty., A.D.; 3d U.S. Colored Hv. Arty.) 5 vols.	June 1863-Feb. 1866	May 1864-Feb. 1866		June 1863-Feb. 1866	June 1863-Feb. 1866	R C		X		X		X		June 1863-Apr. 1866 1 in.	June 1863-Apr. 1866 2 in.	Dec. 1863-Jan. 1865 3 in.
5th Hv. Arty. (9th La. Inf., A.D.; 1st Miss. Hv. Arty., A.D.; 4th U.S. Colored Hv. Arty.) 10 vols.	Aug. 1863-May 1866		Jan. 1865-May 1866	Aug. 1863-May 1866	Sept. 1863-May 1866	R C		X					X	Aug. 1864-Dec. 1866 1 in.	Feb. 1864-May 1866 2 in.	Jan. 1863-May 1866 5 in.

	Bound volumes													Unbound records		
Name of unit and predecessor unit(s) and No. of vols.	Letters sent	Endorsements and memorandums	Register of letters received	General orders	Special orders	Descriptive book	Guard reports	Morning reports	Court-martial proceedings	Proceedings of regt. council of administration	Req. for clothing, camp, and garrison equipage	Clothingaccount book for noncommissioned staff	Regt. Co. fund, account book, or band fund	Letters received	Issuances	Rosters, reports, lists, and misc. records
6th Hv. Arty.[2] (2d Miss. Hv. Arty., A.D.; 5th U.S. Colored Hv. Arty.) 8 vols.				Oct. 1863-May 1866	Oct. 1863-May 1866	R C		X				X		Mar. 1864-May 1866 1 in.	Feb. 1864-June 1866 2 in.	Oct. 1863-Apr. 1866 1 in.
8th Hv. Arty. 5 vols.	June 1864-Feb. 1866	Oct. 1864-Jan. 1866	Sept. 1864-Dec. 1865	May 1864-Feb. 1866	May 1864-Feb. 1866	R C		X		X				Jan. 1864-June 1866 1 in.	Apr. 1864-Dec. 1865 1 in.	Apr. 1864-Apr. 1866 2 in.
9th Hv. Arty. 4 vols.				Nov. 1864-July 1865	Oct. 1864-July 1865	R C		X				X		Oct. 1864-Jan. 1866 1 in.	Dec. 1863-Jan. 1866 1 in.	Dec. 1863 Sept. 1866 5 in.
10th Hv. Arty.[3] (1st La. Hv. Arty., A.D.; 1st La. Hv. Arty., C. d'Afr.; 7th U.S. Colored Hv. Arty.) 1 vol.				Oct. 1865-Nov. 1866	Jan. 1866-Jan. 1867	C		X				X		Jan. 1864-Feb. 1867 3 in.	June 1863-Nov. 1866 3 in.	Nov. 1862-Oct. 1866 6 in.
11th Hv. Arty. (14th R.I. Hv. Arty., Colored; 8th U.S. Colored Hv. Arty.) 11 vols.	Aug. 1864-Sept. 1865	Mar. 1865-July 1865	Sept. 1863-Sept. 1865	Nov. 1863-Sept. 1865	Nov. 1863-Sept. 1865	R C	X	X						Aug. 1863-Dec. 1865 4 in.	July 1863-Apr. 1866 3 in.	Oct. 1863-Feb. 1866 6 in.
12 Hv. Arty. 8 vols.	Jan. 1865-Mar. 1866		Jan. 1865-Mar. 1865	Aug. 1864-Apr. 1866	Sept. 1864-Apr. 1866	R C		X		X			X	Sept. 1864-Apr. 1866 2 in.	Aug. 1864-June 1866 2 in.	July 1864-Oct. 1867 3 in.
13 Hv. Arty. 5 vols.	Aug. 1864-Mar. 1865	Aug. 1864-Sept. 1865	Aug. 1864-Sept. 1865	Nov. 1864-Sept. 1865	Aug. 1864-Nov. 1865	C		X						Aug. 1864-Feb. 1866 1 in.	Aug. 1864-Nov. 1865 1 in.	Feb. 1864-Feb. 1866 1 in.
14th Hv. Arty. (1st N.C. Hv. Arty., A.D.) 5 vols.	Aug. 1864-Nov. 1865	Sept. 1864-Dec. 1865	Aug. 1864-Oct. 1865	July 1864-Sept. 1865	July 1864-Nov. 1865	R C		X						Sept. 1864-Nov. 1865 1 in.	Oct. 1863-Dec. 1865 2 in.	Jan. 1864-May 1866 4 in.
2d Lt. Arty.[4] (1st Btry. Tenn. Lt. Arty., A.D.) Btry. A, 1 vol.	Apr. 1864-Aug. 1865		Aug. 1865-Nov. 1865	Apr. 1864-Nov. 1865	Apr. 1864-Jan. 1866	X		X			X	X	X	Jan. 1864-Jan. 1866 1 in.	Aug. 1863-July 1866 1 in.	Oct. 1863-Mar. 1866 3 in.
Btry. B 1 vol.				Jan. 1864-Jan. 1866	Dec. 1864-Feb. 1866	X		X				X				
Btry. C 1 vol.				Nov. 1864-Oct. 1865	Sept. 1863-Feb. 1865	X		X				X				

2d Lt. Arty. (con.) Btry. D 1 vol				Dec. 1863- Nov. 1865		X		X		X		X				
Btry. E 1 vol.				Dec. 1863- July 1865		X		X				X				
Btry. F[5] 1 vol.												X				
Btry. G 1 vol.					May 1864- Nov. 1864	X	X	X				X				
Btry. H 1 vol.				Mar. 1865- June 1865	June 1864- Feb. 1865	X		X				X				
Btry. I See Btry. F.							X					X				
Ind. Btry., Lt. Arty. (1st Btry., Kans. Lt. Arty., A.D.) 1 vol.						X						X				Apr. 1865- July 1865 7 items
1st Inf. 3 vols.				June 1863- Sept. 1865		R C		X						Jan. 1863- Oct. 1865 3 in.	Apr. 1863- Sept. 1865 3 in.	Jan. 1863- Oct. 1865 4 in.
2d Inf. 6 vols.	Aug. 1863 Jan. 1866	July 1863- Sept. 1865		July 1863- Dec. 1865	July 1863- Dec. 1865	R C		X	X	X		X		July 1863- Dec. 1865 2 in.	June 1863- Dec. 1865 2 in.	Mar. 1863- Dec. 1865 2 in.
3d Inf. 7 vols.	Aug. 1863- Oct. 1865	May 1864- July 1865		Sept. 1863- Oct. 1865	Aug. 1863- Oct. 1865	R C	X	X	X					Jan. 1863- Dec. 1865 2 in.	July 1863- Nov. 1865 1 in.	June 1863- Nov. 1865 2 in.
4th Inf. 6 vols.	Oct. 1863- Apr. 1866			Sept. 1863- Feb. 1866	July 1863- Apr. 1866	R C		X						July 1863- Dec. 1865 2 in.	Sept. 1863- Jan. 1865 1 in.	Nov. 1863- Sept. 1865 1 in.
5th Inf. 6 vols.	Oct. 1863- Mar. 1864		Mar. 1864- Sept. 1865	Sept. 1863- Sept. 1865	Nov. 1863- Dec. 1865	R C		X						Aug. 1863- Oct. 1865 2 in.	Oct. 1863- Sept. 1865 2 in.	Dec. 1863- Dec. 1865 1 in.
6th Inf. 6 vols.	Nov. 1863- Sept. 1865		Dec. 1863- July 1865	Sept. 1863- June 1865	Aug. 1863- Sept. 1865	R C	X	X						Nov. 1862- Nov. 1865 3 in.	Sept. 1863- Sept. 1865 3 in.	July 1863- Dec. 1865 3 in.
7th Inf. 8 vols.	Apr. 1864- Oct. 1866		Aug. 1865- Sept. 1866	Nov. 1863- Sept. 1866	Sept. 1863- Oct. 1866	R C	X	X		X				Mar. 1863- Dec. 1865 1 in.	Dec. 1863- Dec. 1865 1 in.	May 1863- Dec. 1865 4 in.
8th Inf. 4 vols.	Dec. 1863- Oct. 1865			Oct. 1863- Oct. 1865	Oct. 1863- Oct. 1865	R C	X	X						May 1863- Dec. 1865 1 in.	July 1863- Dec. 1865 1 in.	Dec. 1863 Dec. 1865 3 in.

Name of unit and predecessor Unit(s) and No. of vols.	Bound volumes: Letters sent	Endorsements and memorandums	Register of letters received	General orders	Special orders	Descriptive book	Guard reports	Morning reports	Court-martial proceedings	Proceedings of regt. council of administration	Req. for clothing, camp, and garrison equipage	Clothing account book for noncommissioned staff	Regt. Co. fund, account book, or band fund	Unbound records: Letters received	Issuances	Rosters, reports, lists, and misc. records
9th Inf. 8 vols.	June 1864- Nov. 1866	Oct. 1865- Nov. 1866		Nov. 1863- Oct. 1866	Nov. 1863- Nov. 1866	R C	X	X						Oct. 1863- Dec. 1865 2 in.	July 1863- Dec. 1865 5 in.	Nov. 1863- Dec. 1865 4 in.
10th Inf. 7 vols.	Oct. 1863- May 1866			Nov. 1863- Feb. 1866	Dec. 1863- Apr. 1866	R C		X						Aug. 1863- Dec. 1865 2 in.	Dec. 1863- Dec. 1865 1 in.	Apr. 1863- Dec. 1865 3 in.
11th Inf. (old)[6]														Oct. 1863- Apr. 1865 1 in.	Dec. 1863- June 1865 1 in.	Dec. 1864- Apr. 1865 1 in.
11th Inf. (new) (1st Ala. Siege Arty., A.D.; 6th and 7th U.S. Colored Hv. Arty.) 8 vols.	Mar. 1864- Nov. 1865		Mar. 1864- Dec. 1865	Feb. 1864- Dec. 1865	June 1863- Jan. 1866	R C	X	X		X				Jan. 1864- Dec. 1865 3 in.	Jan. 1864- Dec. 1865 3 in.	Dec. 1863- July 1865 1 in.
12th Inf. 6 vols.	Aug. 1863- Jan. 1866			Aug. 1863- Dec. 1865	Sept. 1863- Jan. 1866	R C	X	X						July 1863- Jan. 1866 3 in.	Aug. 1863- Jan. 1866 2 in.	Aug. 1863- Dec. 1865 3 in.
13th Inf. 5 vols.				Nov. 1863- Dec. 1865	Dec. 1863- Dec. 1865	R C		X						Dec. 1863- Dec. 1865 1 in.	Nov. 1863- July 1866 1 in.	Jan. 1864- Dec. 1865 2 in.
14th Inf. 6 vols.	Dec. 1863- Mar. 1866	Mar. 1864- Oct. 1865	Oct. 1864 Nov. 1865	Dec. 1863- Feb. 1866	Dec. 1863- Mar. 1866	R C	X	X						Apr. 1863- Apr. 1866 2 in.	July 1864- Mar. 1866 2 in.	Nov. 1863- Feb. 1865 2 in.
15th Inf. 5 vols.	Apr. 1864- Mar. 1866		Apr. 1864- Mar. 1866	Dec. 1863- Sept. 1865	Dec. 1863- Apr. 1866	C		X						Dec. 1863- Mar. 1866 1 in.	May 1863- Apr. 1866 1 in.	Dec. 1863- Apr. 1866 2 in.
16th Inf. 7 vols.	Jan. 1864- Apr. 1866		Feb. 1864- Apr. 1866	Dec. 1863- Mar. 1866	Dec. 1863- Apr. 1866	R C		X						Jan. 1863- Apr. 1866 2 in.	Aug. 1863- Apr. 1866 1 in.	Dec. 1863- Nov. 1865 2 in.
17th Inf. 7 vols.	Oct. 1864- Mar. 1866		Sept. 1864- Apr. 1866	Feb. 1864- Jan. 1866	Feb. 1864- Apr. 1866	R C		X						Aug. 1863- Sept. 1866 1 in.	Mar. 1864- Nov. 1866 1 in.	Jan. 1864- Feb. 1866 3 in.
18th Inf. 6 vols.	Sept. 1863- Feb. 1866[7]		Sept. 1865- Jan. 1866	May 1864- Feb. 1866	Jan. 1864- Feb. 1866	R C		X						Jan. 1864- Dec. 1867 3 in.	Feb. 1864- Apr. 1866 2 in.	Mar. 1864- Jan. 1866 2 in.

19th Inf. 8 vols.	Dec. 1863-Nov. 1866		Aug. 1865-Nov. 1866	Dec. 1863-Nov. 1866	Dec. 1863-Nov. 1866	R C	X	X						Nov. 1863-Jan. 1867 2 in.	Feb. 1863-Nov. 1866 7 in.	Dec. 1863-Apr. 1866 5 in.
20th Inf. 5 vols.	Apr. 1864-Oct. 1865		May 1865-Sept. 1865	Dec. 1863 Aug. 1865	Feb. 1864-Oct. 1865	R C		X						Dec. 1863-Oct. 1865 3 in.	Dec. 1863-Apr. 1866 4 in.	Jan. 1863-Feb. 1866 9 in.
21st Inf. (3d & 4th S.C. Inf., A.D.) 5 vols.	May 1863-June 1865		Apr. 1864-Mar. 1866	May 1863-Dec. 1864	May 1863-Apr. 1866	R C	X	X						Feb. 1863-June 1866 2 in.	Dec. 1863-May 1866 1 in.	Sept. 1863-May 1866 4 in.
22d Inf. 5 vols.	Jan. 1864-Feb. 1865		Feb. 1864-Sept. 1865	Jan. 1864-Aug. 1865	Jan. 1864-Sept. 1865	R C	X	X						Dec. 1863-Dec. 1865 2 in.	Jan. 1864-Dec. 1865 1 in.	Jan. 1863-Dec. 1865 4 in.
23d Inf. 5 vols.	Oct. 1864-Nov. 1865		Feb. 1865-Oct. 1865	Jan. 1864-Oct. 1865	Jan. 1864-Nov. 1865	R C	X	X						Dec. 1863-Nov. 1865 1 in.	Feb. 1864-Oct. 1865 2 in.	Jan. 1864-Nov. 1865 4 in.
24th Inf. 4 vols.	Dec. 1864-Sept. 1865[8]		June 1865-Aug. 1865	Jan. 1865-Sept. 1865	Apr. 1865-Sept. 1865	R C	X	X						Jan. 1864-Oct. 1865 1 in.	Jan. 1864-May 1865 1 in.	Jan. 1864-Oct. 1865 6 in.
25th Inf. 7 vols.	Feb. 1864-Dec. 1865		Aug. 1864-Dec. 1865	Jan. 1864-Nov. 1865	Feb. 1864-Dec. 1865	R C		X						Jan. 1864-Dec. 1865 3 in.	Jan. 1864-July 1866 2 in.	Jan. 1864-Dec. 1865 3 in.
26th Inf. 5 vols.	Apr. 1864-Aug. 1865		Mar. 1864-May 1865	Feb. 1864-Aug. 1865	Jan. 1864-Aug. 1865	R C		X						Jan. 1864-Oct. 1865 2 in.	Jan. 1864-Aug. 1865 2 in.	Jan. 1864-Oct. 1865 4 in.
27th Inf. 4 vols.				Mar. 1864-May 1865	Apr. 1864-Oct. 1865	R C	X	X						Jan. 1864-Oct. 1865 1 in.	May 1864-Mar. 1866 1 in.	Jan. 1864-Feb. 1866 3 in.
28th Inf. 4 vols.				Jan. 1865-Nov. 1865	Jan. 1865-Nov. 1865			X						Jan. 1864-Nov. 1865 1 in.	Aug. 1864-Nov. 1865 3 items	Feb. 1864-Oct. 1866 4 in.
29th Inf. 8 vols.	July 1865-Oct. 1865			Dec. 1863-Sept. 1865	Mar. 1864-Oct. 1865	R C		X						Sept. 1863-Nov. 1866 6 in.	May 1864-Oct. 1865 4 in.	Apr. 1864-Sept. 1865 3 in.
30th Inf. 4 vols.	Apr. 1864-Nov. 1865		June 1865-Nov. 1865	Feb. 1864-Dec. 1865	Mar. 1864-Dec. 1865	R C	X	X						Feb. 1864-Dec. 1865 1 in.	Feb. 1864-Dec. 1865 2 in.	Feb. 1864-Oct. 1865 2 in.
31st Inf. 5 vols.			Jan. 1865-Oct. 1865			R C	X	X						Jan. 1863-May 1866 3 in.	Nov. 1863-Mar. 1866 4 in.	Apr. 1863-Jan. 1866 4 in.
32d Inf. 4 vols.	Mar. 1864-July 1865		June 1864-July 1865	Sept. 1863-July 1865	Mar. 1864-Aug. 1865	R C		X						Feb. 1864-Sept. 1865 3 in.	Mar. 1864-Aug. 1865 2 in.	Feb. 1864-Aug. 1865 5 in.

	Bound volumes													Unbound records		
Name of unit and predecessor unit(s) and No. of vols.	Letters sent	Endorsements and memorandums	Register of letters received	General orders	Special orders	Descriptive book	Guard reports	Morning reports	Court-martial proceedings	Proceedings of regt. council of administration	Req. for clothing, camp, and garrison equipage	Clothing account book for noncommissioned staff	Regt. Co. fund, account book, or band fund	Letters received	Issuances	Rosters, reports, lists, and misc. records
33d Inf.[9] (1st S.C. Inf., A.D.) 6 vols.	Aug. 1864- July 1865		Nov. 1862- Oct. 1865		Dec. 1862- Feb. 1866	R C		X						Sept. 1862- Dec. 1865 2 in.	May 1863- Oct. 1865 1 in.	Sept. 1862- Dec. 1865 3 in.
34th Inf. (2d S.C. Inf., A.D.) 7 vols.	Apr. 1863- Mar. 1866		Nov. 1863- Oct. 1865	Apr. 1863- Sept. 1865	Jan. 1864- Feb. 1866	R C	X	X						June 1863- Dec. 1865 2 in.	Oct. 1863- Dec. 1865 1 in.	Oct. 1863- June 1865 1 in.
35th Inf. (1st N.C. Inf., A.D.) 7 vols.	Nov. 1863- May 1866		July 1864- Nov. 1864	June 1863- Dec. 1865	June 1863- May 1866	R C		X						June 1863- Dec. 1865 7 in.	Mar. 1863- Dec. 1865 4 in.	Oct. 1863- Dec. 1865 4 in.
36th Inf. (2d N.C. Inf., A.D.) 8 vols.	Aug. 1863- July 1866		July 1865- Oct. 1865	Aug. 1863- Aug. 1866	July 1863- Oct. 1866	R C		X						Sept. 1863- Dec. 1865 4 in.	Sept. 1863- Dec. 1865 6 in.	Jan. 1863- Nov. 1865 3 in.
37th Inf. (3d N.C. Inf., A.D.) 7 vols.	Jan. 1864 Feb. 1867		Apr. 1865- Jan. 1867	Feb. 1864- Dec. 1866	Feb. 1864- Feb. 1867	R C		X						June 1864- Dec. 1865 3 in.	Nov. 1863- Dec. 1865 4 in.	Jan. 1864- Mar. 1865 4 in.
38th Inf.[10] (1st Va. Colored Inf.) 9 vols.	June 1864- Jan. 1867		Jan. 1865- Jan. 1867	Dec. 1863- Jan. 1867	Dec. 1863- Jan. 1867	R C		X						Jan. 1864- Mar. 1867 6 in.	Dec. 1864- July 1865 2 items	Sept. 1864- July 1866 1 in.
39th Inf. 5 vols.				Mar. 1864- Aug. 1865	Mar. 1864- Dec. 1865	R C		X						Feb. 1864- Aug. 1866 1 in.	Mar. 1864- Jan. 1866 1 in.	Mar. 1864- Sept. 1865 2 in.
40th Inf.[11] 4 vols.	Nov. 1865- Apr. 1866	Oct. 1865- Mar. 1866	Jan. 1865- Apr. 1866	Jan. 1865- Feb. 1866	Apr. 1864- Apr. 1866	R C		X						Jan. 1864- Nov. 1866 4 in.	July 1864- June 1866 2 in.	Mar. 1865- Mar. 1866 1 in.
41st Inf. 6 vols.	Oct. 1864- Oct. 1865	Feb. 1865- Sept. 1865	Nov. 1864- Sept. 1865	Oct. 1864- Oct. 1865	Oct. 1864- Oct. 1865	R C	X	X	X					Jan. 1864- Oct. 1865 4 in.	Sept. 1864- Jan. 1866 4 in.	Sept. 1864- Jan. 1866 5 in.
42d Inf. 6 vols.	May 1864- Jan. 1866		June 1864- Jan. 1866	May 1864- Jan. 1866	May 1864- Jan. 1866	R C	X	X						Jan. 1864- Feb. 1866 2 in.	June 1864- Jan. 1866 3 in.	Mar. 1864- May 1865 1 in.
43d Inf. 4 vols.	Apr. 1864- Oct. 1865			Mar. 1864- Sept. 1865	Apr. 1864- Oct. 1865	R C	X	X						Apr. 1864- Oct. 1866 2 in.	Jan. 1864- Nov. 1865 1 in.	Feb. 1864- Nov. 1865 4 in.

44th Inf. 4 vols.	Nov. 1864- Mar. 1866		Oct. 1864- Apr. 1866	Oct. 1864- Feb. 1866	Oct. 1864- Apr. 1866	R C		X					X	Mar. 1864- Apr. 1866 2 in.	Apr. 1864- May 1866 2 in.	Feb. 1864- Apr. 1866 2 in.
45th Inf. 7 vols.	Aug. 1864- Sept. 1865			Sept. 1863- Oct. 1865	June 1864- Oct. 1865	R C		X	X	X			X	Mar. 1864- Oct. 1866 2 in.	June 1864- June 1866 2 in.	Mar. 1864- Oct. 1865 2 in.
46th Inf. (1st Ark. Inf., A.D.) 5 vols.	Sept. 1864- Jan. 1866		Nov. 1864- Jan. 1866	Sept. 1863- Dec. 1865	July 1863- Jan. 1866	R C	X	X	X					Aug. 1863- Jan. 1866 1 in.	Jan. 1863- Jan. 1866 2 in.	Apr. 1863- Jan. 1866 1 in.
47th Inf. (8th La. Inf., A.D.) 3 vols.				May 1863- Sept. 1865	June 1863- Sept. 1865	C		X						Oct. 1863- Dec. 1865 1 in.	Apr. 1863- Aug. 1865 1 in.	May 1863- Dec. 1865 1 in.
48th Inf. (10th La. Inf., A.D.) 4 vols.				June 1864- Nov. 1865	Dec. 1863- Nov. 1865	C		X						July 1863- Feb. 1866 1 in.	Apr. 1863- Sept. 1865 1 in.	Jan. 1863- Dec. 1865 1 in.
49th Inf. (11th La. Inf., A.D.) 8 vols.			Nov. 1863- Jan. 1866	June 1863- Jan. 1866	May 1863- Feb. 1866	R C		X			X	X		July 1863- Mar. 1866 1 in.	Apr. 1863- Mar. 1866 3 in.	Nov. 1864- Dec. 1865 1 in.
50th Inf. (12th La. Inf., A.D.) 6 vols.	Aug. 1863- Jan. 1865	Aug. 1864- Jan. 1865	July 1864- Jan. 1865	Oct. 1863- Jan. 1866	Sept. 1863 Mar. 1866	R C		X	X					Nov. 1863- Jan. 1866 1 in.	Nov. 1863- June 1866 1 in.	Dec. 1863- Sept. 1865 1 in.
51st Inf. (1st Miss. Inf., A.D.)														May 1863- May 1866 2 in.	May 1863- Apr. 1866 1 in.	July 1864- May 1866 1 in.
52d Inf. 2d Miss. Inf., A.D.) 6 vols.	June 1863- Apr. 1866			June 1863- Mar. 1866	June 1863- Mar. 1866	R C		X						Jan. 1863- July 1866 4 in.	June 1863- Dec. 1865 4 in.	Jan. 1863- Sept. 1865 2 in.
53d Inf. (3d Miss. Inf., A.D.) 4 vols.	June 1863- Feb. 1866			June 1863- Nov. 1865	Dec. 1863- Feb. 1866	R C	X	X						June 1863- Feb. 1866 3 in.	May 1863- May 1866 5 in.	July 1863- Jan. 1866 1 in.
54th Mass. Colored Inf. 7 vols.	June 1863- Aug. 1865		Apr. 1864- Aug. 1865	Mar. 1863- May 1865	Feb. 1863- Aug. 1865	R C		X								
54th Inf. (2d Ark. Inf., A.D.) 6 vols.	Apr. 1864- Sept. 1866		Sept. 1865- July 1866	Jan. 1864- Sept. 1866	Jan. 1864- Sept. 1866	C		X						Feb. 1863- Dec. 1865 1 in.	Dec. 1863- Aug. 1865 1 in.	Aug. 1863- Sept. 1865 1 in.
55th Mass. Colored Inf. 7 vols.	May 1863- June 1865		Dec. 1863- July 1865	May 1863- Aug. 1865	July 1863- July 1865	R C		X								
55th Inf. (1st Ala. Inf., A.D.) 8 vols.	June 1863- Nov. 1865		July 1863- Dec. 1865	May 1863- Dec. 1865	June 1863- Dec. 1865	R C	X	X						May 1863- Dec. 1865 2 in.	Apr. 1863- Dec. 1865 2 in.	June 1863- Dec. 1865 1 in.

Name of unit and predecessor unit(s) and No. of vols.	Bound volumes													Unbound records		
	Letters sent	Endorsements and memorandums	Register of letters received	General orders	Special orders	Descriptive book	Guard reports	Morning reports	Court-martial proceedings	Proceedings of regt. council of administration	Req. for clothing, camp, and garrison equipage	Clothing account book for noncommissioned staff	Regt. Co. fund, account book, or band fund	Letters received	Issuances	Rosters, reports, lists, and misc. records
56th Inf. (3d Ark. Inf., A.D.) 7 vols.	Nov. 1863-Sept.,1866			Aug. 1863-Sept. 1866	Aug. 1863-Sept. 1866	R C		X					X	July 1863-Dec. 1865 5 in.	Feb. 1863-Dec. 1865 2 in.	Sept. 1863-Dec. 1865 7 items
57th Inf. (4th Ark. Inf., A.D.) 5 vols.	Oct. 1864-Dec. 1866		Oct. 1864-Dec. 1866	Sept. 1863-Oct. 1866	Sept. 1863 Dec. 1866	R C		X						Aug. 1863-Dec. 1865 5 in.	Feb. 1863-Dec. 1865 6 in.	Sept. 1863-Dec. 1865 2 in.
58th Inf. (6th Miss. Inf., A.D.) 5 vols.	Apr. 1865-Apr. 1866		Apr. 1864-Apr. 1866	Sept. 1863-Apr. 1866	Sept. 1863-Apr. 1866	R C		X						Aug. 1863-Jan. 1866 8 in.	Feb. 1863-Dec. 1865 3 in.	Sept. 1863-Dec. 1865 2 in.
59th Inf. (1st Tenn. Inf., A.D.) 7 vols.		Oct. 1863-Jan. 1866	Oct. 1863-Jan. 1866	Sept. 1863 Dec. 1865	Oct. 1863-Jan. 1866	R C		X						Aug. 1863-Jan. 1866 10 in.	Apr. 1863-Jan. 1866 7 in.	Jan. 1864-Oct. 1865 2 in.
60th Inf. (1st Iowa Inf., A.D.) 5 vols.	Oct. 1863-Oct. 1865	Jan. 1864-June 1865		Oct. 1863-Dec. 1865	Sept. 1863-Oct. 1865	R C		X		X				Sept. 1863-Oct. 1865 4 in.	Apr. 1863-Feb. 1866 9 in.	Mar. 1864-Oct. 1865 1 in.
61st Inf. (2d Tenn. (W. Tenn.) Inf., A.D.) 4 vols.	July 1863-Mar. 1865	Feb. 1864-Sept. 1864	June 1864-Mar. 1865	July 1863-July 1865	July 1863-Oct. 1865	R C		X						May 1863-Jan. 1866 3 in.	Jan. 1864-Dec. 1865 2 in.	Feb. 1864-Dec. 1865 1 in.
62d Inf. (1st Mo. Inf., A.D.) 5 vols.	Dec. 1863-Mar. 1866			Dec. 1863-Mar. 1866	Dec. 1863-Mar. 1866	C		X						Dec. 1863-Apr. 1866 2 in.	Oct. 1863-Jan. 1866 1 in.	Dec. 1863-Jan. 1866 2 in.
63d Inf. (9th La. Inf., A.D.) 4 vols.				Oct. 1863-Dec. 1865	Oct. 1863-Dec. 1865	R C		X						Apr. 1863-Dec. 1865 2 in.	Oct. 1863-Feb. 1866 2 in.	Nov. 1863-May 1865 1 in.
64th Inf. (7th La. Inf., A.D.) 6 vols.	Nov. 1864-Feb. 1866		Oct. 1864-Feb. 1866	Dec. 1863-Feb. 1866	Nov. 1863-Mar. 1866	R C		X						Jan. 1864-Mar. 1866 2 in.	Nov. 1863-Mar. 1866 2 in.	Dec. 1863-Mar. 1866 1 in.
65th Inf.[12] (2d Mo. Inf., A.D.) 7 vols.	Jan. 1864-Aug. 1866		Jan. 1864-Oct. 1866	Jan. 1864-Nov. 1866	Jan. 1864-Dec. 1866	C		X						Dec. 1863-Dec. 1866 3 in.	Dec. 1863-Jan. 1867 1 in.	Jan. 1864-July 1866 4 in.
66th Inf. (4th Miss. Inf., A.D.) 7 vols.	Jan. 1864-Feb. 1866	Jan. 1865-Feb. 1866	Jan. 1864-Mar. 1865	Jan. 1864-Mar. 1866	Mar. 1864-Feb. 1866	R C	X	X						Nov. 1863-Feb. 1866 6 items	Feb. 1863-Jan. 1867 4 in.	Mar. 1864-Mar. 1866 4 items

67th Inf.[13] (3d Mo. Inf., A.D.) 6 vols.	Mar. 1864-Aug. 1865		Jan. 1864-Aug. 1865	Jan. 1864-July 1865	Feb. 1864-Aug. 1865	R C	X	X						Feb. 1864-Oct. 1866 2 in.	Sept. 1864-Apr. 1866 1 in.	Feb. 1864-Dec. 1865 1 in.
68th Inf. (4th Mo. Inf., A.D.) 3 vols.			Apr. 1864-Dec. 1864	Apr. 1864-Jan. 1866	Mar. 1864-Jan. 1866	C		X						Mar. 1864-Jan. 1866 1 in.	Oct. 1863-Sept. 1865 1 in.	Feb. 1864-Jan. 1866 3 in.
69th Inf.[14] 3 vols.				Sept. 1864 June 1865	Aug. 1864-Aug. 1865	C		X						Mar. 1864-Jan. 1866 1 in.	Apr. 1864-Oct. 1865 1 in.	Jan. 1864-Sept. 1865 1 in.
70th Inf.[15] 6 vols.	May 1864-Feb. 1866		May 1864-Feb. 1866	May 1864-Feb. 1866	Apr. 1864-Feb. 1866	R C		X						Nov. 1865-June 1866 1 in.	Mar. 1864-Feb. 1866 1 in.	June 1864-June 1865 1 in.
71st Inf.[15] 1 vol.						C								Mar. 1864-Sept. 1864 8 items	Aug. 1864-Sept. 1865 2 items	May 1864-Oct. 1864 1 in.
72d Inf. 2 vols.				Feb. 1864-June 1866	Oct. 1864-June 1865	R								June 1864-July 1866 1 in.	July 1864-Aug. 1865 1 in.	July 1864-July 1865 1 in.
73d Inf.[16] (1st La. Native Guards, Hv. Arty., A.D.; 1st Inf., C. d'Afr.) 1 vol.						C								Jan. 1863-Oct. 1865 4 in.	Apr. 1864-Dec. 1865 1 in.	Sept. 1862-Sept. 1865 1 in.
74th Inf.[17] (2d La. Native Guards, A.D.; 2d Inf., C. d'Afr.) 3 vols.				Oct. 1862-Sept. 1865	Jan. 1863-Oct. 1865	C		X						July 1863-Nov. 1865 2 in.	Feb. 1863-Dec. 1865 1 in.	Oct. 1862-Dec. 1865 3 in.
75th Inf. (3d La. Native Guards, A.D.; 3d Inf., C. d'Afr.) 3 vols.				Dec. 1863-Nov. 1865	Nov. 1863-Nov. 1865	C		X						Jan. 1863-Nov. 1865 1 in.	Feb. 1863-June 1866 1 in.	Nov. 1862-Sept. 1865 2 in.
76th Inf. (4th La. Native Guards, A.D.; 4th Inf., C. d'Afr.) 1 vol.					Jan. 1865-Dec. 1865									Feb. 1863-Jan. 1866 1 in.	Mar. 1863-Jan. 1866 1 in.	Mar. 1863-Jan. 1866 2 in.
77th Inf.[18] (5th Inf., C. d'Afr.)														Aug. 1863-Jan. 1867 3 in.	May 1864-Jan. 1866 1 in.	Dec. 1863-Sept. 1865 2 in.
78th Inf.[19] (6th Inf., C. d'Afr.)														Feb. 1863-Feb. 1866 3 in.	Aug. 1865-Jan. 1866 1 in.	Sept. 1863-Sept. 1866 3 in.
79th Inf. (old) (7th Inf., C. d'Afr.)														Aug. 1863-June 1864 1 in.	Apr. 1863-Mar. 1864 1 in.	Jan. 1863-Aug. 1864 1 in.
79th Inf. (new) (1st Kans. Inf., A.D.) 4 vols.				Jan. 1863-Oct. 1865	Jan. 1863-Oct. 1865	C		X						Dec. 1862-Oct. 1865 2 in.	Feb. 1863-Sept. 1865 1 in.	Aug. 1863-Mar. 1866 2 in.

Name of unit and predecessor unit(s) and No. of vols.	Bound volumes													Unbound records		
	Letters sent	Endorsements and memorandums	Register of letters received	General orders	Special orders	Descriptive book	Guard reports	Morning reports	Court-martial proceedings	Proceedings of regt. council of administration	Req. for clothing, camp, and garrison equipage	Clothing account book for noncommissioned staff	Regt. Co. fund, account book, or band fund	Letters received	Issuances	Rosters, reports, lists, and misc. records
80th Inf. (8th Inf., C. d'Afr.)														July 1863-Nov. 1866 2 in.	Dec. 1863-July 1866 1 in.	Aug. 1863-Sept. 1866 2 in.
81st Inf. (9th Inf., C. d'Afr.) 1 vol.														July 1863-Jan. 1867 3 in.	July 1863-Oct. 1865 1 in.	Sept. 1863-Jan. 1867 3 in.
82d Inf. (10th Inf., C. d'Afr.) 2 vols.				Apr. 1863-Jan. 1866	May 1863-June 1866	C		X						Aug. 1863-Aug. 1866 1 in.	Jan. 1866-Aug. 1866 1 in.	Aug. 1863-Apr. 1866 1 in.
83d Inf. (old) (11th Inf., C. d'Afr.)														Sept. 1863-Dec. 1864 1 in.	Aug. 1864-Dec. 1865 5 items	Aug. 1863-July 1864 1 in.
83d Inf. (new) (2d Inf., Kans. Colored Volunteers) 6 vols.	Sept. 1864 Oct. 1865		Oct. 1863-Oct. 1865	Nov. 1863-Aug. 1865	Oct. 1863-Oct. 1865	R C		X						June 1863-Dec. 1865 2 in.	Sept. 1863-Oct. 1865 3 in.	Apr. 1864-Apr. 1865 1 in.
84th Inf. (12th Inf., C. d'Afr.) 4 vols.				Sept. 1863-Jan. 1866	Sept. 1863-Feb. 1866	C		X						Sept. 1863-Mar. 1866 3 in.	Apr. 1864-Jan. 1866 1 in.	Oct. 1863-Feb. 1866 2 in.
85th Inf.[20] (13th Inf., C. d'Afr.)														Nov. 1863-June 1864 6 items		Dec. 1863-Sept. 1864 7 items
86th Inf. (14th Inf., C. d'Afr.) 1 vol.				Oct. 1863-Aug. 1864	Sept. 1864-June 1865			X						Dec. 1863-May 1866 1 in.	Mar. 1864- 1 item	Sept. 1863-Feb. 1865 1 in.
87th Inf. (old)[21] (16th Inf., C. d'Afr.)														Oct. 1863-Oct. 1865 1 in.	Dec. 1863- 7 items	Oct. 1863-Aug. 1865 1 in.
87th Inf. (new)[22] 3 vols.				Dec. 1864-Aug. 1865	Dec. 1864-Aug. 1865	C		X						Jan. 1865-Aug. 1865 1 in.	Sept. 1864-Jan. 1866 5 items	Jan. 1865-Aug. 1865 1 in.
88th Inf. (old) (17th Inf., C. d'Afr.)														Oct. 1863-Dec. 1863 3 items	Nov. 1863-Sept. 1864 4 items	Sept. 1863-Feb. 1865 1 in.

88th Inf. (new)[23] 6 vols.	May 1865- Dec. 1865	Apr. 1865- Dec. 1865	Feb. 1865- Dec. 1865	Mar. 1965- Dec. 1865	Aug. 1865- Dec. 1865	R C	X	X						Oct. 1863- Oct. 1865 2 in.	Mar. 1865- Dec. 1865 7 items	Feb. 1865- Sept. 1866 6 items
89th Inf. (18th Inf., C. d'Afr.) 4 vols.				Sept. 1863- June 1864	Sept. 1863- Aug. 1864	C		X						Nov. 1863- Aug. 1864 4 items		Oct. 1863- May 1866 3 in.
90th Inf. (19th Inf., C. d'Afr.)														Sept. 1863- July 1865 1 in.		Nov. 1863- Aug. 1864 1 in.
91st Inf.[24] (20th Inf. C. d'Afr.) 1 vol.								X						May 1862- June 1864 1 in.		Oct. 1863- June 1864 1 in.
92d Inf. (22d Inf., C. d'Afr.) 1 vol.				Nov. 1863- May 1865	Jan. 1864- Dec. 1865	C								Oct. 1863- Jan. 1866 2 in.	Jan. 1865- Mar. 1866 1 in.	Oct. 1863- Jan. 1866 2 in.
93d Inf. (25th Inf., C. d'Afr.) 3 vols.				Oct. 1863- June 1865	Oct. 1863- June 1865	C		X						Oct. 1863- June 1865 1 in.	Sept. 1864- Mar. 1865 4 items	Jan. 1864- June 1865 2 in.
95th Inf.[25] (1st & 3d Engineers, C. d'Afr.)														June 1863- July 1864 1 in.	June 1863- Dec. 1864 4 items	June 1863- Aug. 1864 1 in.
96th Inf. (2d Engineers, C. d'Afr.)														Aug. 1863- Apr. 1866 2 in.	July 1863- Feb. 1866 1 in.	Sept. 1863- Jan. 1866 2 in.
97th Inf. (3d Engineers, C. d'Afr.)														Nov. 1863- Apr. 1866 2 in.	Jan. 1866 1 item	Dec. 1863- June 1865 1 in.
98th Inf.[26] (4th Engineers, C. d'Afr.)														Oct. 1863- July 1865 1 in.	Sept. 1864- Aug. 1865 7 items	Dec. 1863- Aug. 1865 1 in.
99th Inf. (15th Inf., C. d'Afr.) 4 vols.				Aug. 1863- Sept. 1865	Aug. 1863- Sept. 1865	C		X						Aug. 1863- Apr. 1866 2 in.	Oct. 1864- Apr. 1866 1 in.	Sept. 1863- July 1865 2 in.
100th Inf. 4 vols.				June 1864- Dec. 1865	June 1864- Dec. 1865	C		X						July 1864- Jan. 1866 2 in.	Feb. 1864- Dec. 1865 2 in.	July 1864- Dec. 1865 4 in.
101st Inf. 4 vols.	June 1864- Aug. 1865		Aug. 1864- Nov. 1865	Aug. 1865- Dec. 1865	July 1864- Dec. 1865	R C		X						Apr. 1864- Feb. 1866 2 in.	Jan. 1864- Jan. 1866 3 in.	June 1864- July 1865 1 in.
102d Inf. (1st Mich. Inf., A.D.) 5 vols.		May 1865- July 1865		Apr. 1864- July 1864	Apr. 1864- Sept. 1865	R C	X	X						Jan. 1864- Oct. 1865 2 in.	Dec. 1863- Dec. 1865 1 in.	Apr. 1864- Aug. 1865 2 in.

Name of unit and predecessor unit(s) and No. of vols.	Bound volumes													Unbound records		
	Letters sent	Endorsements and memorandums	Register of letters received	General orders	Special orders	Descriptive book	Guard reports	Morning reports	Court-martial proceedings	Proceedings of regt. council of administration	Reg. for clothing, camp, and garrison equipage	Clothing account book for noncommissioned staff	Regt. Co. fund, account book, or band fund	Letters received	Issuances	Rosters, reports, lists, and misc. records
103d Inf. 4 vols.	Mar. 1865-Apr. 1866			Apr. 1865-Sept. 1865	Mar. 1865-Apr. 1866	R C	X	X						Feb. 1865-May 1866 1 in.	Feb. 1865-Apr. 1866 1 in.	Apr. 1865-May 1866 1 in.
104th Inf. 4 vols.			Aug. 1865-Sept. 1865	Apr. 1865-Jan. 1866	Apr. 1865-Jan. 1866	C	X	X						June 1865-Feb. 1866 1 in.	June 1865-Dec. 1865 1 in.	July 1864-Dec. 1865 1 in.
106th Inf.[27] (4th Ala. Inf., A.D.) 1 vol.				July 1865 (only one)	Sept. 1864-July 1865	C		X						July 1864-Oct. 1865 7 items	Apr. 1864-June 1865 3 items	July 1864-June 1865 1 in.
107th Inf. 6 vols.	July 1864-Oct. 1866	Aug. 1864-Aug. 1866	July 1864-Oct. 1866	July 1864-Oct. 1866		R C		X						Jan. 1864-Dec. 1866 5 in.	June 1864-Mar. 1867 7 in.	Sept. 1864-Oct. 1866 1 in.
108th Inf. 6 vols.	July 1864-Dec. 1865		July 1864-Jan. 1866	July 1864-Mar. 1866	Sept. 1865-Dec. 1865	R C		X						Jan. 1864-Mar. 1866 6 in.	Apr. 1863-Apr. 1866 4 in.	Jan. 1864-Mar. 1866 2 in.
109th Inf. 4 vols.			June 1864-Dec. 1865	June 1864-Jan. 1866	June 1864-Jan. 1866	R C		X						Jan. 1864-Mar. 1866 1 in.	July 1864-Feb. 1866 1 in.	July 1864-Mar. 1866 1 in.
110th Inf. (2d Ala. Inf., A.D.) 4 vols.			Apr. 1865-Jan. 1866	Feb. 1865-Dec. 1865	Feb. 1865-Feb. 1866	R C	X	X						Mar. 1864-Jan. 1866 1 in.	Jan. 1864-Jan. 1866 2 in.	July 1863-Dec. 1865 1 in.
111th Inf. (3d Ala. Inf., A.D.) 4 vols.			Jan. 1865-Apr. 1866	Jan. 1864-Apr. 1866	Mar. 1864-Mar. 1866	R C		X						Jan. 1865-June 1866 1 in.	Nov. 1864-Nov. 1866 1 in.	Mar. 1865-July 1867 1 in.
112th Inf.[28] 2 vols.				Apr. 1864-Feb. 1865	May 1864-May 1865	R C		X						May 1864-May 1865 5 items	Apr. 1864-May 1865 2 in.	Apr. 1864-Mar. 1865 1 in.
113th Inf. (old)[29] (6th Ark. Inf., A.D.)	Mar. 1864-Apr. 1865	Jan. 1864-Apr. 1865		Jan. 1864-Apr. 1865										Oct. 1864-Aug. 1865 1 in.	Jan. 1865-Feb. 1865 7 items	July 1864-June 1865 1 in.
113th Inf. (new)[30] 5 vols.	Apr. 1865-Apr. 1866	May 1865-Mar. 1866	June 1865-Mar. 1866	Apr. 1865-Apr. 1866	Apr. 1865-Apr. 1866	R C		X						Apr. 1865-Aug. 1866 1 in.	Feb. 1865-Apr. 1866 2 in.	Jan. 1865-Jan. 1866 2 in.

114th Inf. 6 vols.	Nov. 1864- Jan. 1867	1865-66 (gaps)		Sept. 1864- Mar. 1867	Mar. 1865- Mar. 1867	R C		X						July 1864- May 1867 4 in.	July 1864- Apr. 1867 7 in.	Oct. 1864- Jan. 1867 4 in.
115th Inf. 5 vols.	Jan. 1865- May 1865			July 1864- Jan. 1866	July 1864- Feb. 1866	R C		X						July 1864- Mar. 1866 1 in.	Jan. 1864- Jan. 1866 1 in.	Mar. 1863- Jan. 1866 1 in.
116th Inf. 8 vols.	Sept. 1864- Jan. 1867			July 1864- Nov. 1866	July 1864- Dec. 1866	R C	X	X						July 1864- June 1867 2 in.	July 1864- Oct. 1867 2 in.	Dec. 1863- Oct. 1866 3 in.
117th Inf. 6 vols.	July 1864- Aug. 1867		Jan. 1865- Dec. 1866	Aug. 1864- Aug. 1867	July 1864- Aug. 1867	R C		X						July 1864- July 1867 1 in.	Oct. 1864- July 1867 1 in.	Sept. 1864- July 1867 2 in.
118th Inf. 5 vols.	Sept. 1864- Jan. 1866		Sept. 1864- Dec. 1865	Sept. 1864- Jan. 1866	Aug. 1864- Feb. 1866	R C	X	X						Aug. 1864- Jan. 1867 4 in.	Feb. 1864- Oct. 1866 1 in.	Oct. 1864- Jan. 1866 1 in.
119th Inf.[31] 6 vols.	Sept. 1864- Apr. 1866	Oct. 1864- Jan. 1866 (telegrams)	June 1865- Apr. 1866	Sept. 1864- Apr. 1866	Mar. 1865- Apr. 1866	R C	X	X					X	Sept. 1864- May 1866 4 in.	July 1864- May 1866 2 in.	Apr. 1865- Dec. 1865 1 in.
120th Inf. 1 vol.						C		X				X		Mar. 1865- Aug. 1867 1 in.	Apr. 1865- Nov. 1865 1 in.	Mar. 1865- Oct. 1865 1 in.
121st Inf. 2 vols.				Mar. 1865- Apr. 1865	Jan. 1865- Aug. 1865	C						X		July 1864- Oct. 1864 3 items	June 1865- Aug. 1865 3 items	N.d. 1 in.
122d Inf.[32] 5 vols.	Oct. 1864- Feb. 1866		Sept. 1864- Jan. 1866	Oct. 1864- Dec. 1865	Oct. 1864- Jan. 1866	R C	X	X						Sept. 1864- Mar. 1866 1 in.	Jan. 1864- Feb. 1866 1 in.	Jan. 1864- Apr. 1866 3 in.
123d Inf. 4 vols.	Jan. 1865- Sept. 1865		Oct. 1864- Oct. 1865	Jan. 1865- Sept. 1865	Oct. 1864- Oct. 1865	R C		X						Sept. 1864- Nov. 1865 1 in.	Jan. 1864- Jan. 1866 1 in.	Jan. 1865- Sept. 1865 1 in.
124th Inf. 4 vols.	Jan. 1865- Oct. 1865		Mar. 1865- Sept. 1865	Jan. 1865- Sept. 1865	Jan. 1865- Oct. 1865	R C		X						Dec. 1864- Jan. 1866 1 in.	Nov. 1864- Apr. 1866 1 in.	Jan. 1865- June 1865 1 in.
125th Inf. 8 vols.	Aug. 1865- Dec. 1867		Dec. 1865- Dec. 1867	June 1865- Dec. 1867	Apr. 1865- Dec. 1867	R C		X						Jan. 1865- Dec. 1867 6 in.	Feb. 1865- Dec. 1867 8 in.	Dec. 1864- Mar. 1867 3 in.
127th Inf.[33] 4 vols.	Oct. 1864- Sept. 1865			Sept. 1864- Oct. 1865	Sept. 1864- Sept. 1865	R		X						Aug. 1864- Dec. 1865 1 in.	Aug. 1864- Nov. 1865 1 in.	Aug. 1864- June 1865 2 in.
128th Inf. 4 vols.	Mar. 1865- Aug. 1866		May 1865- Mar. 1866	Apr. 1865- Sept. 1866	Apr. 1865- Oct. 1866	R C	X	X						Mar. 1865- Dec. 1866 1 in.	Mar. 1865- Oct. 1866 1 in.	Apr. 1865- July 1866 5 in.

Name of unit and predecessor unit(s) and No. of vols.	Bound volumes													Unbound records		
	Letters sent	Endorsements and memorandums	Register of letters received	General orders	Special orders	Descriptive book	Guard reports	Morning reports	Court-martial proceedings	Proceedings of regt. council of administration	Req. for clothing, camp, and garrison equipage	Clothing account book for noncommissioned staff	Regt. Co. fund, account book, or band fund	Letters received	Issuances	Rosters, reports, lists, and misc. records
135th Inf. 4 vols.				Apr. 1865-Sept. 1865 (2 orders)	June 1865-Sept. 1865	R C		X						Jan. 1865-Jan. 1866 1 in.	Mar. 1865-Oct. 1865 1 in.	Aug. 1865-Nov. 1865 1 in.
136th Inf. 4 vols.	July 1865-Dec. 1865			July 1865-Dec. 1865	July 1865-Dec. 1865	R C		X						Sept. 1865-Dec. 1867 1 in.	May 1865-Oct. 1865 1 in.	Aug. 1865-Nov. 1867 1 in.
137th Inf. 4 vols.	June 1865-Aug. 1865			June 1865-Jan. 1865	June 1865-Jan. 1866	R C		X							June 1865-Dec. 1865 1 in.	May 1865-June 1865 1 in.
138th Inf. 4 vols.	Sept. 1865 (5 letters)			July 1865-Sept. 1865	July 1865-Nov. 1865	R C		X						Sept. 1865-Oct. 1865 2 items	Aug. 1865- 1 item	July 1865 1 in.
Unattached Co. A (Va. Colored Guards) 1 vol.						X		X				X				
Pioneer Co., 1st Div. 16th Army Corps 1 vol.						X		X				X				
Capt. Powell's Regt.,[34] Inf.															Nov. 1864 1 item	
Unassigned men														Apr. 1864-May 1865 4 in.	May 1864-Jan. 1865 2 in.	Jan. 1865 4 items
Troops enlisted at Camp Nelson, Ky. 4 vols.						X										
Troops enlisted at Benton Barracks, Mo. 2 vols.						X										

Notes

1 Includes letters received and endorsements. There are telegrams received for June-July 1865.
2 Records also include a register showing the residences and names of former owners of enlisted men of the regiment.
3 Consolidated with the 77th U.S. Colored Infantry on October 1, 1865.
4 All regimental papers for batteries A through I have been interfiled under 2d U.S. Colored Light Artillery.
5 Consolidated with the 3d U.S. Colored Heavy Artillery on December 28, 1865.
6 Consolidated with the 112th U.S. Colored Infantry and 113th U.S. Colored Infantry (old) on April 1, 1864, to form the 113th U.S. Colored Infantry (new). Records of the 11th U. S. Colored Infantry (old) are with those of the 113th U.S. Colored Infantry (new).
7 Includes letters sent by Headquarters, 18th Infantry, Corps d'Afrique, from September 1863 to March 1864 and letters sent by Headquarters, 89th U.S. Colored Infantry, from April to July 1864.
8 Earlier letters were sent from Camp William Penn, Pa., prior to the official date of organization of the regiment.
9 Includes records of the 1st South Carolina Infantry, A. D., following the assumption of command by Col. Thomas Wentworth Higginson in November 1862.
10 Includes orders issued by headquarters of the Department of Virginia and North Carolina, the 18th Army Corps, and the 25th Army Corps from December 1863 to January 1866.
11 Consolidated with the 106th U.S. Colored Infantry on November 7, 1865.
12 Consolidated with the 67th U.S. Colored Infantry on July 12, 1865.
13 Consolidated with the 65th U.S. Colored Infantry on July 12, 1865.
14 Discontinued on September 20, 1865, and officers and men transferred to 63d and 64th U.S. Colored Infantry.
15 Four companies of the 70th U.S. Colored Infantry were organized from April 23 to October 1, 1864. The organization of the regiment was completed on November 8, 1864, by consolidation with the 71st U.S. Colored Infantry, which had been organized from March 3 to August 13, 1864.
16 Consolidated with the 96th U.S. Colored Infantry on September 27, 1865.
17 Consolidated with the 91st U.S. Colored Infantry on July 7, 1864.
18 Consolidated with the 85th U.S. Colored Infantry on May 24, 1864, and with the 10th U.S. Colored Heavy Artillery on October 1, 1865.
19 Consolidated with the 98th U.S. Colored Infantry on August 26, 1865.
20 Consolidated with the 77th U.S. Colored Infantry on May 24, 1864.

21 Consolidated with the 95th U.S. Colored Infantry on November 26, 1864, to form the 81st U.S. Colored Infantry (new), which subsequently became the 87th U.S. Colored Infantry (new).
22 Consolidated with the 84th U.S. Colored Infantry on August 14, 1865.
23 Consolidated with 3d U.S. Colored Heavy Artillery on December 16, 1865.
24 Consolidated with the 74th U.S. Colored Infantry on July 7, 1864.
25 Consolidated with the 87th U.S. Colored Infantry on November 26, 1864, to form the 81st U.S. Colored Infantry (new), which subsequently became the 87th U.S. Colored Infantry (new).
26 Consolidated with the 78th U.S. Colored Infantry on August 26, 1865.
27 Consolidated with the 40th U.S. Colored Infantry on November 7, 1865.
28 Consolidated with the 11th U.S. Colored Infantry (old) and the 113th U. S. Colored Infantry (old) to form the 113th U.S. Colored Infantry (new) on April 1, 1865.
29 Records of the 113th U.S. Colored Infantry (old) and 113th U.S. Colored Infantry (old) and 113th U.S. Colored Infantry (new) have been bound together. Records of the 11th U.S. Colored Infantry (old) can be found with those of the 113th U.S. Colored Infantry (new).
30 Organized on April 1, 1865, by a consolidation of the 11th U.S. Colored Infantry (old), the 112th U.S. Colored Infantry (old), and the 113th U.S. Colored Infantry (old).
31 There are two pages in a small volume on which are listed the names of wives and the number of children of enlisted men of this regiment.
32 Consolidated into a battalion of three companies on January 17, 1866.
33 Consolidated into a battalion of three companies on September 11, 1865.
34 This company was organized pursuant to Special Order No. 322, HQ, 16th Army Corps, Memphis, Tenn., on December 16, 1863, and mustered out of service on November 27, 1865, at Montgomery, Ala.

APPENDIX

Dates of Organization and Muster-Out of U.S. Colored Troops Units
{From U.S. War Department, *Official Army Register of the Volunteer Force of the United States Army, 1861-65*, part VII (Washington, 1867)}

Unit	Date or period of organization	Date of muster-out
1st Cav.	Dec. 22, 1863	Feb. 4, 1866
2d Cav.	Dec. 22, 1863-Jan 8, 1864	Feb. 12, 1866
3d Cav.	Oct. 9, 1863-Mar. 1, 1864, as 1st Miss. Ca. (A.D.)	Jan. 26, 1866
4th Cav.	Sept. 12, 1863-July 19, 1864, as 1st Cav., C. d'Afr.	Mar. 20, 1866
5th Cav.	Oct. 24-30, 1864	Mar. 16, 1866
6th Cav.	Nov. 1, 1864-June 21, 1865	Apr. 15, 1866
5th Mass. Colored Cav.	Jan. 9-May 5, 1864	Oct. 31, 1865
1st Hv. Arty.	Feb. 20-Nov. 12, 1864	Mar. 31, 1866
3d Hv. Arty	June 5-Dec. 22, 1863 as 1st Tenn. Hv. Arty. (A. D.)	Apr. 30, 1866
4th Hv. Arty.	June 16, 1863-Apr. 19, 1864, as 2d Ten. Hv. Arty. (A. D.)	Feb. 25, 1866
5th Hv. Arty.	Aug. 7, 1863-Jan. 17, 1864, as 9th La. Volunteers (A. D.)	May 20, 1866
6th Hv. Arty.	Sept. 12, 1863-Jan. 21, 1864, as 2d Miss. Hv. Arty. (A.D.)	May 13, 1866
8th Hv. Arty.	Apr. 26-Oct. 13, 1864	Feb. 10, 1866
9th Hv. Arty.	Oct. 8-Nov. 1, 1864	Broken up May 5, 1865
10th Hv. Arty.	Nov. 29, 1862-Nov. 8, 1864, as 1st Regt., La. Hv. Arty.	Feb. 22, 1867

Unit	Date or period of organization	Date of muster-out
11Th Hv. Arty.	Aug. 28, 1863-Jan. 25, 1864, as 14th R.I. Colored Hv. Arty.	Oct. 2, 1865
12Th Hv. Arty.	July 15, 1864-July 15, 1865	Apr. 24, 1866
13th Hv. Art.	June 23, 1865	Nov. 18, 1865
14th Hv. Art.	Mar. 14, 1864-Apr. 30, 1865 As 1st N.C. Hv. Arty. (Colored)	Dec. 11, 1865
2d Lt. Arty. Btry. A.	Apr. 30, 1864	Jan. 13, 1866
Btry. B	Jan. 8-Feb. 27, 1864	Mar. 17, 1866
Btry. C	Nov. 6, 1863, as 1st Btry., La. Arty. (A. D.)	Dec. 28, 1865
Btry. D	Dec. 21, 1863, as 2d Btry., La. Lt. Arty. (A. D.)	Dec. 28, 1865
Btry. E	Dec. 1, 1863, as 3d Btry., La. Arty. (A. D.)	Sept. 26, 1865
Btry. F	Nov. 23, 1863, as Memphis Lt. Btry.	Dec. 28, 1865
Btry. G	May 24, 1864	Aug. 12, 1865
Btry. H	June 4, 1864, as 1st Ark. Colored Btry.	Sept. 15, 1865
Btry. I	Apr. 19, 1864	Jan. 10, 1866
Indep. Btry.	Dec. 23, 1864	July 22, 1865
1St Inf.	May 19-June 30, 1863	Sept. 29, 1865
2d Inf.	June 23-Nov. 11, 1863	Jan. 5, 1866
3d Inf.	Aug. 3-10, 1863	Oct. 31, 1865
4th Inf.	July 15-Sept. 1, 1863	May 4, 1866

Unit	Date or period of organization	Date of muster-out
5th Inf.	Aug. 6, 1863-Jan. 15, 1864	Sept. 20, 1865
6th Inf.	July 28-Sept. 12, 1863	Sept. 20, 1865
7th Inf.	Sept. 26-Nov. 12, 1863	Oct. 13, 1866
8th Inf.	Sept.22-Dec. 4, 1863	Nov. 10, 1865
9th Inf.	Nov. 11-30, 1863	Nov. 26, 1866
10th Inf.	Nov. 18, 1863-Sept. 23, 1864	May 17, 1866
11th Inf.	Dec. 19, 1863-Sept. 23, 1864	Consolidated with 113th Regt., Apr. 22, 1865
11th Inf. (New)	June 20, 1863-Apr. 2, 1864 as 1st Ala. Siege Arty. (A. D.)	Jan. 12, 1866
12th Inf.	July 24-Aug. 14, 1863	Jan. 16, 1866
13th Inf.	Nov. 19, 1863	Jan. 10, 1866
14th Inf.	Nov. 16, 1863-Jan. 8, 1864	Mar. 26, 1866
15th Inf.	Dec. 2, 1863-Mar. 11,1864	Apr. 7, 1866
16th Inf.	Dec. 4, 1863-Feb. 13, 1864	Apr. 30, 1866
17th Inf.	Dec. 12-21, 1863	Apr. 25, 1866
18th Inf.	Feb. 1-Sept. 28, 1864	Feb. 21, 1866
19th Inf.	Dec. 25, 1863-Jan. 16, 1864	Jan. 15, 1867
20th Inf.	Feb. 9, 1864	Oct. 7, 1865
21st Inf.	June 19, 1853-Oct. 1, 1864	Apr. 25, 1866
22d Inf.	Jan. 10-29, 1864	Oct. 16, 1865
23d Inf.	Nov. 23, 1863-June 30, 1864	Nov. 30, 1865
24th Inf.	Jan. 30-Mar. 30, 1865	Oct. 1, 1865

Unit	Date or period of organization	Date of muster-out
25th Inf.	Jan. 13-Feb. 12, 1864	Dec. 6, 1865
26th Inf.	Feb. 27, 1864	Aug. 28, 1865
27th Inf.	Jan. 16-Aug. 6, 1864	Sept. 21, 1865
28th Inf.	Dec. 24, 1865-Mar. 31, 1864	Nov. 8, 1865
29th Inf.	6 companies organized Apr. 24, 1864; 4 companies organized Oct. 23, 1864-Jan. 1, 1865	Nov. 6, 1865
30th Inf.	Feb. 12-Mar. 18, 1864	Dec. 10, 1865
31st Inf.	Apr. 29-Nov. 14, 1864, as 30th Conn. Colored Volunteers	Nov. 7, 1865
32d Inf.	Feb. 17-Mar. 7, 1864	Aug. 22, 1865
33d Inf.	Jan. 31, 1863, as 1st S.C. Volunteers	Jan. 31, 1866
34th Inf.	May 22, 1863-Dec. 31, 1864, as 2d S.C. Colored Volunteers	Feb. 28, 1866
35th Inf.	June 30, 1863, as 1st N.C. Volunteers	June 1, 1866
36th Inf.	Oct. 28, 1863, as 2d N.C. Colored Volunteers	Oct. 28, 1866
37th Inf.	Jan. 30-Sept. 19, 1864, as 3d N.C. Volunteers	Feb. 11, 1867
38th Inf.	Jan. 23, 1864-Mar. 30, 1865	Jan. 25, 1867
39th Inf.	Mar. 22-31, 1864	Dec. 4, 1865
40th Inf.	Feb. 29, 1864-May 6, 1865	Apr. 25, 1866
41st Inf. (Bn. Of)	Sept.30-Dec. 7, 1864	Dec. 10, 1865
42d Inf.	April 20, 1864-July 6, 1865	Jan. 31, 1866
43d Inf.	Mar. 12-June 3, 1864	Oct. 20, 1865

Unit	Date or period of organization	Date of muster-out
44th Inf.	Apr. 7-Sept. 16, 1864	Apr. 30, 1866
45th Inf.	June 13-Aug. 19, 1864	Nov. 4, 1865
46th Inf.	May 1, 1863, as 1st Ark. Volunteers (A. D.)	Jan. 30, 1866
47th Inf.	May 5, 1863. As 8th La. Volunteers (A. D.)	Jan. 5, 1866
48th Inf.	May 6-Aug. 8, 1863, as 10th La. Volunteers (A. D.)	Jan. 4, 1866
49th Inf.	May 23-Aug. 22, 1863, as 11th La. Volunteers (A. D.)	Mar. 22, 1866
50th Inf.	July 11-27, 1863, as 12th La. Volunteers (A. D.)	Mar. 20, 1866
51st Inf.	May 16, 1863-Mar. 7, 1864, as 1st Miss. Volunteers (A. D.)	June 16, 1866
52d Inf.	July 27-Dec. 22, 1863 as 2d Miss. Volunteers (A. D.)	May 5, 1866
53d Inf.	May 19, 1863, as 3d Miss. Volunteers (A. D.)	Mar. 8, 1866
54th Inf.	Sept. 4-Dec. 24, 1863, as 2d Ark. Volunteers (A. D.)	Dec. 31, 1866
55th Inf.	May 21, 1863, as 1st Ala. Volunteers (A. D.)	Dec. 31, 1866
56th Inf.	Aug. 12-Sept. 29, 1863, as 3d Ark. Volunteers (A. D.)	Sept. 15, 1866
57th Inf.	Dec.2, 1863-Mar. 1, 1864, as 4th Ark. Volunteers (A. D.)	Dec. 13, 1866
58th Inf.	Aug. 27, 1863, as 6th Miss. Volunteers (A. D.)	Apr. 30, 1866
59th Inf.	June 6-27, 1863, as 1st Tenn. Volunteers (A. D.)	Jan. 31, 1866

Unit	Date or period of organization	Date of muster-out
60th Inf.	Oct. 15-Dec. 4, 1863, as 1st Iowa Volunteers (A. D.)	Oct. 15, 1865
61st Inf.	June 30-Aug. 8, 1863, as 2d Tenn. Volunteers (A. D.)	Dec. 30, 1865
62d Inf.	Dec. 7-14, 1863, as 1st Mo. Volunteers (A. D.)	Mar. 31, 1866
63d Inf.	Nov. 19-Dec. 14, 1863, as 9th La. Volunteers (A. D.)	Jan 9, 1866
64th Inf.	Dec. 1, 1863-Feb. 1, 1864 as 7th La. Volunteers (A. D.)	Mar. 13, 1866
65th Inf.	Dec. 18, 1863-Jan. 16, 1864 as 2d Mo. Volunteers (A. D.)	Jan. 8, 1867
66th. Inf.	Dec. 11, 1863-Jan. 11, 1864 as 4th Miss. Volunteers (A. D.)	Mar. 20, 1866
67th Inf.	Jan. 19-Feb. 13, 1864 3d Mo. Volunteers (A. D.)	July 12, 1865
68th Inf.	Mar. 8-Apr. 23, 1864, as 4th Mo. Volunteers (A. D.)	Feb. 5, 1866
69th Inf.	Dec. 14, 1864-Mar. 17, 1865	Discontinued Sept. 20, 1865
70th Inf.	Apr. 23-Oct. 1, 1864	Mar. 7, 1866
71st Inf.	Mar. 3-Aug. 13, 1864	Nov. 8, 1864
72d Inf.	Apr. 18-22, 1865	Discontinued May 3, 1865
73d Inf.	Sept. 27, 1862, as La. Native Guards (A. D.)	Mustered-out when terms of service expired
74th Inf.	Oct. 12, 1862, as 2d La. Native Guards (A. D.)	Oct. 11, 1865

Unit	Date or period of organization	Date of muster-out
75th Inf.	Nov. 24, 1862, as 3d La. Native Guards (A. D.)	Nov. 25, 1865
76th Inf.	Feb. 10-Mar. 6, 1863, as 4th La. Native Guards (A. D..)	Dec. 31, 1865
77th Inf.	Dec. 8, 1863, as 5th Inf., C. d'Afr.	Consolidated with 10th U. S. Colored Hv. Arty., Oct. 1, 1865
78th Inf.	Sept. 4, 1863, as 6th Inf., C. d'Afr.	Jan. 6, 1866
79th Inf. (Old)	Aug. 31, 1863, as 7th Inf. C. d'Afr.	Broken up July 28, 1864
79th Inf. (new)	Jan. 13-May 2, 1863, as 1st Kans. Colored Volunteers	Oct. 1, 1865
80th Inf.	Sept. 1, 1863, 8th Inf., C. d'Afr.	Mar. 1, 1867
81st Inf.	Sept. 2, 1863, as 9th Inf., C. d'Afr.	Nov. 30, 1866
82d Inf.	Sept. 1, 1863, as 10th Inf., C. d'Afr.	Sept. 10, 1866
83d Inf. (old)	Aug. 17, 1863, as 11th Inf., C. d'Afr.	Broken up July 28, 1864
83d Inf. (new)	Aug. 11-Oct. 17, 1863, as 2d Kans. Colored Volunteers	Oct. 9, 1865
84th Inf.	Sept. 24-Oct. 16, 1863 as 12th Inf., C. d'Afr.	Mar. 14, 1866
85th Inf.	Mar. 11, 1864, as 13th Inf., C. d'Afr.	Consolidated with 77th U.S. Colored Inf., May 24, 1864
86th Inf.	Aug. 12-Sept. 3, 1863, as 14th Inf., C. d'Afr.	Apr. 10, 1866

Unit	Date or period of organization	Date of muster-out
87th Inf. (old)	Oct. 8-16, 1863, as 16th Inf., C. d'Afr.	Subsequently changed to 87th U.S. Colored Inf., (new), Dec. 19, 1864
87th Inf. (new)	Nov. 26, 1864, as 81st U.S. Colored Inf. (new); designated 87th U.S. Colored Inf. (new) on Dec. 19, 1864	Consolidated with 84th U.S. Colored Inf., Aug. 14, 1865
88th Inf. (old)	Sept. 24, 1863, as 17th Inf., C. d'Afr.	Broken up July 18, 1864
88th Inf. (new)	Feb. 20-Aug. 10, 1865	Consolidated with 3d U.S.Colored Hv. Art., Dec. 16, 1865
89th Inf.	Oct. 9-Nov. 8, 1863, as 18th Inf., C. d'Afr.	Broken up July 28, 1864
90th Inf.	Feb. 11, 1864, as 19th Inf., C. d'Afr.	Broken up July 28, 1864
91st Inf.	Sept. 1, 1863, as 20th Inf. C. d'Afr.	Consolidated with 74th., July 7, 1864
92d Inf.	Sept. 30-Oct. 24, 1863, as 22d Inf., C. d'Afr.	Dec. 31, 1865
93d Inf.	Nov. 21, 1863, as 25th Inf., C. d'Afr.	Broken up June 23, 1865
95th Inf.	Apr. 28, 1863, as 1st Engineers, C. d'Afr.	Consolidated with 87th.,U.S. Colored Inf. to form 81st U.S. Colored Inf., Nov. 26, 1864
96th Inf.	Aug. 15, 1863, as 2d Engineers, C. d'Afr.	Jan. 29, 1866
97th Inf.	Aug. 26, 1863, as 3d Engineers, C. d'Afr.	Apr. 6, 1866

Unit	Date or period of organization	Date of muster-out
98th Inf.	Sept. 3, 1863-Mar. 3, 1864, as 4th Engineers, C. d'Afr.	Consolidated with 78th Regt., Aug. 26, 1865
99th Inf (Bn. of)	Aug. 27, 1863, as 15th Inf., C. d'Afr.	Apr. 23, 1866
100th Inf.	May 3-June 1, 1864	Dec. 26, 1865
101st Inf.	Sept. 16, 1864-Aug. 5, 1865	Jan. 21, 1866
102d Inf.	Feb. 17, 1864, as 1st Mich. Colored Volunteers	Sept. 30, 1865
103d Inf.	Mar. 10, 1865	Apr. 15-20, 1866
104th Inf.	Apr. 28-June 25, 1865	Feb. 5, 1866
106th Inf.	Mar. 31-Aug. 10, 1864, as 4th Ala. Inf. (A. D.)	Consolidated with 40th U.S. Colored Inf., Nov. 7, 1865
107th Inf.	May 3-Sept. 15, 1864	Nov. 22, 1866
108th Inf.	June 20-Aug. 22, 1864	Mar. 21, 1866
109th Inf.	July 5, 1864	Feb. 6, 1866
110th Inf.	Nov. 20, 1863-Jan. 14, 1864, as 2d Ala. Volunteers (A. D.)	Feb. 6, 1866
111th Inf.	Jan. 13-Apr. 5, 1864 as 3d Regt., Ala. Volunteers (A. D.)	Apr. 30, 1866
112th Inf.	Apr. 23-Nov. 8, 1864	Consolidated with 11th U.S. Colored Inf. (Old) to form 113th U.S. Colored Inf. (new) Apr. 1, 1865

Unit	Date or period of organization	Date of muster-out
113th Inf. (old)	Mar. 1-June 20, 1864 , as 6th Ark. Volunteers (A. D.)	Consolidated with 11th U.S. Colored Inf. And 112th U.S. Colored Inf. to form 113th U.S. Colored Inf. (new) on Apr. 1, 1865
113th Inf. (new)	Apr. 1, 1865, by consolidation of the 11th (old), 112th, and 113th (old) U.S. Colored Infantries	Apr. 9, 1866
114th Inf.	July 4, 1864	Apr. 2, 1867
115th Inf.	July 15-Oct. 21, 1864	Feb. 10, 1866
116th Inf.	June 6-July 12, 1864	Jan. 17, 1867
117th Inf.	July 18-Sept.. 27, 1864	Aug. 10, 1867
118th Inf.	Oct. 19, 1864	Feb. 6, 1866
119th Inf.	Jan. 18-May 16, 1865	Apr. 27, 1866
120th Inf.	Nov. 1864-June 1865	Discontinued June 21, 1865
121st Inf	Oct 8, 1864-May 31, 1865	Discontinued June 30, 1865
122d Inf.	Dec 31, 1864	Feb. 8, 1866
123d Inf	Dec 2, 1864	Oct. 16, 1865
124th Inf.	Jan. 1-Apr. 27, 1865	Oct. 24, 1865
125th Inf.	Feb. 13-June 2, 1865	Oct. 31, 1867-Dec. 20, 1867
127th Inf. (Bn.)	Aug. 23-Sept. 10, 1864	Oct. 20, 1865

Unit	Date or period of organization	Date of muster-out
128th Inf.	Apr. 23-29, 1865	Oct. 10, 1866
135th Inf.	Mar. 28, 1865	Oct. 23, 1865
136th Inf.	July 15, 1865	Jan. 4, 1866
137th Inf.	Enrolled Apr. 8, 1865; mustered into U.S. Service June 1, 1865	Jan. 15, 1866
138th Inf.	July 15, 1865	Jan. 6, 1866
54th Mass. Colored Inf.	Mar. 30-May 13, 1863	Aug. 20, 1865
55th Mass. Colored Inf.	May 31-June 22, 1863	Aug. 29, 1865
29th Conn. Colored Inf.	Mar. 8, 1864	Oct. 24, 1865
6th La. Colored Inf. (60 days)	July 4, 1863	Aug. 13, 1863
7th La. Colored Inf.	July 10, 1863	Aug. 6, 1863
Company A, unassigned (1 year)	Sept. 28, 1864	July 29, 1865
Independent Company A (100 days)	July 20, 1864	Nov. 14, 1864

(Appendix B)

NATIONAL ARCHIVES ORDER FOR COPIES OF VETERANS RECORDS

Dear Researcher,

Before completing the form, please read both sides of this page for ordering instructions and general information about the types of records that can be ordered with this form. Mail order photocopying service by using this form is available ONLY from ***General Reference Branch (NNRG-P), National Archives and Records Administration, 7th and Pennsylvania Avenue NW., Washington, DC 20408.*** For more information, please write to us at the address above.

IMPORTANT INFORMATION ABOUT YOUR ORDER

The success of our search depends on the completeness and accuracy of the information you provide in blocks 3-18 on this form. Please note that each NATF Form 80 is handled separately. When you send more than one form at a time, you may not receive all of your replies at the same time.

Military service records rarely contain family information. Pension application files generally are most useful to those who are doing genealogical research and contain the most complete information regarding a man's military career. We suggest that you first request copies of a man's pension file. You should request copies of a bounty-land warrant file or a military record only when no pension file exists. If the veteran's service was during the Revolutionary War, bounty-land warrant applications have been consolidated with pension application papers. You can obtain both files by requesting the pension file only.

We will copy complete compiled military service and bounty-land application files. When we are unable to provide copies of all pension documents because of the size of a pension application file, we will send copies of the documents we think will be most useful to you for genealogical purposes. Many of the documents in these files are repetitive or administrative in nature. You may order copies of all remaining documents in a file by making a specific request. We will notify you of the cost of the additional copies.

Do NOT use this form to request photocopies of records relating to service in World War I or II, or subsequent service. Write to: *National Personnel Records Center (Military Records), NARA, 9700 Page Boulevard, St. Louis, MO 63132.*

INSTRUCTIONS FOR COMPLETING THIS FORM

Use a separate NATF Form 80 for each file that you request. Remove this instruction sheet. You must complete blocks 3-7 or we cannot search for the file. Print your name (last, first, middle) and address in the block provided at the bottom of the form, which is your mailing label. The information must be legible on all copies. Keep the PINK copy of the form for your records. Mail the remaining three pages of the form to: *General Reference Branch (NNRG-P), National Archives and Records Administration, 7th and Pennsylvania Avenue NW., Washington, DC 20408.* **DO NOT SEND PAYMENT WITH THIS FORM.** When we search your order, we will make photocopies of records that relate to your request. For credit card orders, we will mail the copies immediately. For other types of orders, we will invoice you for the cost of these copies and hold them until we receive your payment.

SEE THE REVERSE OF THIS PAGE FOR DESCRIPTIONS OF THE TYPES OF RECORDS THAT CAN BE ORDERED WITH THIS FORM.

TYPES OF RECORDS THAT CAN BE ORDERED WITH THIS FORM

PENSION APPLICATION FILES

Pension application files, based on Federal (not State) service before World War I, usually include an official statement of the veteran's military service, as well as information of a personal nature. Pensions based on military service for the Confederate States of America were authorized by some Southern States but not by the Federal Government until 1959. Inquiries about State pensions should be addressed to the State archives or equivalent agency at the capital of the veteran's State of residence after the war.

BOUNTY-LAND WARRANT APPLICATION FILES

Bounty-land warrant application files are based on Federal (not State) service before 1856. Documents in a bounty-land warrant application file are similar to those in a pension application file. In addition, these files usually give the veteran's age and place of residence at the time the application was made.

MILITARY SERVICE RECORDS

Military service records are based on service in the UNITED STATES ARMY (officers who served before June 30, 1917, and enlisted men who served before October 31, 1912); NAVY (officers who served before 1903 and enlisted men who served before 1886); MARINE CORPS (officers who served before 1896 and enlisted men who served before 1905); and CONFEDERATE ARMED FORCES (officers and enlisted men, 1861-65). In addition to persons who served in regular forces raised by the Federal Government, volunteers fought in various wars chiefly in the Federal Government's interest from the Revolutionary War through the Philippine Insurrection, 1775-1902.

Compilations of information concerning most military service performed by individuals in volunteer organizations during the 19th and early 20th centuries are available, but such records were not compiled for Regular Army officers who served before 1863 and for Regular Army enlisted men and Navy and Marine Corps personnel who served during most of the 19th century. Records pertaining to such service are scattered among many files and generally contain few details concerning a man's service. We cannot undertake the research necessary to locate all such documents. If you request a military service record, we will copy the documents that best summarize the veteran's service.

The record of an individual's service in any one organization is entirely separate from his record of service in another organization. We are unable to establish accurately the identity of individuals of the same name who served in different organizations. If you know that an individual served in more than one organization and you desire copies of all of the military service records, submit a separate form for the service record in each organization.

Discharge certificates are not usually included as a part of a compiled military service record. Before 1944, Army regulations allowed the preparation of an original discharge certificate only, which was given to the soldier. Confederate soldiers in service at the time of surrender did not receive discharge certificates. They were given paroles, and these paroles became the property of the soldier.

NATIONAL ARCHIVES
ORDER FOR COPIES OF VETERANS RECORDS

(See Instructions page before completing this form)

DATE RECEIVED IN NNRG

INDICATE BELOW THE TYPE OF FILE DESIRED AND THE METHOD OF PAYMENT PREFERRED.

1. FILE TO BE SEARCHED *(Check one box only)*

☐ PENSION

☐ BOUNTY-LAND WARRANT APPLICATION *(Service before 1856 only)*

☐ MILITARY

2. PAYMENT METHOD *(Check one box only)*

☐ CREDIT CARD *(VISA or MasterCard) for IMMEDIATE SHIPMENT of copies*

Account Number: Exp. Date:

Signature: Daytime Phone:

☐ **BILL ME** *(No Credit Card)*

REQUIRED MINIMUM IDENTIFICATION OF VETERAN - MUST BE COMPLETED OR YOUR ORDER CANNOT BE SERVICED

3. VETERAN *(Give last, first, and middle names)*

4. BRANCH OF SERVICE IN WHICH HE SERVED ☐ ARMY ☐ NAVY ☐ MARINE CORPS

5. STATE FROM WHICH HE SERVED

6. WAR IN WHICH, OR DATES BETWEEN WHICH, HE SERVED

7. IF SERVICE WAS CIVIL WAR, ☐ UNION ☐ CONFEDERATE

PLEASE PROVIDE THE FOLLOWING ADDITIONAL INFORMATION, IF KNOWN

8. UNIT IN WHICH HE SERVED *(Name of regiment or number, company, etc, name of ship)*

9. IF SERVICE WAS ARMY, ARM IN WHICH HE SERVED ☐ INFANTRY ☐ CAVALRY ☐ ARTILLERY *If other, specify:*

Rank ☐ OFFICER ☐ ENLISTED

10. KIND OF SERVICE ☐ VOLUNTEERS ☐ REGULARS

11. PENSION/BOUNTY-LAND FILE NO.

12. IF VETERAN LIVED IN A HOME FOR SOLDIERS, *GIVE LOCATION (City and State)*

13. PLACE(S) VETERAN LIVED AFTER SERVICE

14. DATE OF BIRTH

15. PLACE OF BIRTH *(City, County, State, etc.)*

16. DATE OF DEATH

17. PLACE OF DEATH *(City, County, State, etc.)*

18. NAME OF WIDOW OR OTHER CLAIMANT

NATIONAL ARCHIVES TRUST FUND BOARD NATF Form 80 (rev. 10-93)

DO NOT WRITE BELOW - SPACE IS FOR OUR REPLY TO YOU

☐ **NO--We were unable to locate the file you requested above. No payment is required.**

DATE SEARCHED | SEARCHER

☐ REQUIRED MINIMUM IDENTIFICATION OF VETERAN WAS NOT PROVIDED. Please complete blocks 3 (give full name), 4, 5, 6, and 7 and resubmit your order.

☐ A SEARCH WAS MADE BUT THE FILE YOU REQUESTED ABOVE WAS NOT FOUND. When we do not find a record for a veteran, this does not mean that he did not serve. You may be able to obtain information about him from the archives of the State from which he served.

☐ See attached forms, leaflets, or information sheets.

☐ **YES--We located the file you requested above. We have made copies from the file for you. The cost for these copies is $10.**

DATE SEARCHED | SEARCHER

FILE DESIGNATION

Make your check or money order payable to NATIONAL ARCHIVES TRUST FUND. Do not send cash. Return this form and your payment in the enclosed envelope to:

NATIONAL ARCHIVES TRUST FUND
P.O. BOX 100221
ATLANTA, GA 30384-0221

PLEASE NOTE: We will hold these copies awaiting receipt of payment for only 45 days from the date completed, which is stamped below. After that time, you must submit another form to obtain photocopies of the file.

THIS IS YOUR MAILING LABEL. PRESS FIRMLY.

NAME (Last, First, MI)

STREET

CITY, STATE

ZIP CODE

A291531

INVOICE/REPLY COPY - DO NOT DETACH

NATIONAL ARCHIVES
ORDER FOR COPIES OF VETERANS RECORDS

DATE RECEIVED IN NNRG

INDICATE BELOW THE TYPE OF FILE DESIRED AND THE METHOD OF PAYMENT PREFERRED.

1. **FILE TO BE SEARCHED**
(Check one box only)
PENSION
BOUNTY-LAND WARRANT APPLICATION
(Service before 1856 only)
MILITARY

REQUIRED MINIMUM IDENTIFICATION OF VETERAN - MUST BE COMPLETED OR YOUR ORDER CANNOT BE SERVICED

3. VETERAN *(Give last, first, and middle names)*
4. BRANCH OF SERVICE IN WHICH HE SERVED ☐ ARMY ☐ NAVY ☐ MARINE CORPS
5. STATE FROM WHICH HE SERVED
6. WAR IN WHICH, OR DATES BETWEEN WHICH, HE SERVED
7. IF SERVICE WAS CIVIL WAR, ☐ UNION ☐ CONFEDERATE

PLEASE PROVIDE THE FOLLOWING ADDITIONAL INFORMATION, IF KNOWN

8. UNIT IN WHICH HE SERVED *(Name of regiment or number, company, etc, name of ship)*
9. IF SERVICE WAS ARMY, ARM IN WHICH HE SERVED ☐ INFANTRY ☐ CAVALRY ☐ ARTILLERY *If other, specify:*
Rank ☐ OFFICER ☐ ENLISTED
10. KIND OF SERVICE ☐ VOLUNTEERS ☐ REGULARS
11. PENSION/BOUNTY-LAND FILE NO.
12. IF VETERAN LIVED IN A HOME FOR SOLDIERS, *GIVE LOCATION (City and State)*
13. PLACE(S) VETERAN LIVED AFTER SERVICE
14. DATE OF BIRTH
15. PLACE OF BIRTH *(City, County, State, etc.)*
16. DATE OF DEATH
17. PLACE OF DEATH *(City, County, State, etc.)*
18. NAME OF WIDOW OR OTHER CLAIMANT

NATIONAL ARCHIVES TRUST FUND BOARD NATF Form 80 (rev. 10-93)

THESE ARE THE COPIES YOU ORDERED FROM THE FILE IDENTIFIED ABOVE.

DO NOT SEND ADDITIONAL PAYMENT.

DATE SEARCHED	SEARCHER
FILE DESIGNATION	

To inquire about this order, please write to the address below or telephone 202-501-5170.

NATIONAL ARCHIVES AND RECORDS ADMINISTRATION
GENERAL REFERENCE BRANCH (NNRG-P)
7TH AND PENNSYLVANIA AVENUE, NW
WASHINGTON, DC 20408

SEND TO:
NAME (Last, First, MI)
STREET
CITY, STATE *ZIP CODE*

MAILROOM COPY - DO NOT DETACH

NATIONAL ARCHIVES
ORDER FOR COPIES OF VETERANS RECORDS

DATE RECEIVED IN NNRG

INDICATE BELOW THE TYPE OF FILE DESIRED AND THE METHOD OF PAYMENT PREFERRED.

1. FILE TO BE SEARCHED
(Check one box only)
- PENSION
- BOUNTY-LAND WARRANT APPLICATION *(Service before 1856 only)*
- MILITARY

REQUIRED MINIMUM IDENTIFICATION OF VETERAN - MUST BE COMPLETED OR YOUR ORDER CANNOT BE SERVICED

3. VETERAN *(Give last, first, and middle names)*

4. BRANCH OF SERVICE IN WHICH HE SERVED
ARMY NAVY MARINE CORPS

5. STATE FROM WHICH HE SERVED

6. WAR IN WHICH, OR DATES BETWEEN WHICH, HE SERVED

7. IF SERVICE WAS CIVIL WAR,
UNION CONFEDERATE

PLEASE PROVIDE THE FOLLOWING ADDITIONAL INFORMATION, IF KNOWN

8. UNIT IN WHICH HE SERVED *(Name of regiment or number, company, etc. name of ship)*

9. IF SERVICE WAS ARMY, ARM IN WHICH HE SERVED
INFANTRY CAVALRY ARTILLERY *If other, specify:*
Rank
OFFICER ENLISTED

10. KIND OF SERVICE
VOLUNTEERS REGULARS

11. PENSION/BOUNTY-LAND FILE NO.

12. IF VETERAN LIVED IN A HOME FOR SOLDIERS, *GIVE LOCATION (City and State)*

13. PLACE(S) VETERAN LIVED AFTER SERVICE

14. DATE OF BIRTH

15. PLACE OF BIRTH *(City, County, State, etc.)*

16. DATE OF DEATH

17. PLACE OF DEATH *(City, County, State, etc.)*

18. NAME OF WIDOW OR OTHER CLAIMANT

NATIONAL ARCHIVES TRUST FUND BOARD NATF Form 80 (rev. 10-93)

DO NOT WRITE BELOW - SPACE IS FOR OUR REPLY TO YOU

NO--We were unable to locate the file you requested above. No payment is required.

DATE SEARCHED SEARCHER

REQUIRED MINIMUM IDENTIFICATION OF VETERAN WAS NOT PROVIDED. Please complete blocks 3 (give full name), 4, 5, 6, and 7 and resubmit your order.

A SEARCH WAS MADE BUT THE FILE YOU REQUESTED ABOVE WAS NOT FOUND. When we do not find a record for a veteran, this does not mean that he did not serve. You may be able to obtain information about him from the archives of the State from which he served.

See attached forms, leaflets, or information sheets.

YES--We located the file you requested above. We have made copies from the file for you. The cost for these copies is $10.

DATE SEARCHED SEARCHER

FILE DESIGNATION

Make your check or money order payable to NATIONAL ARCHIVES TRUST FUND. Do not send cash. Return this form and your payment in the enclosed envelope to:

NATIONAL ARCHIVES TRUST FUND
P.O. BOX 100221
ATLANTA, GA 30384-0221

PLEASE NOTE: We will hold these copies awaiting receipt of payment for only 45 days from the date completed, which is stamped below. After that time, you must submit another form to obtain photocopies of the file.

THIS IS YOUR MAILING LABEL. PRESS FIRMLY.

NAME (Last, First, MI)

STREET

CITY, STATE *ZIP CODE*

NNRG FILE COPY - DO NOT DETACH

DATE RECEIVED IN NNRG

NATIONAL ARCHIVES
ORDER FOR COPIES OF VETERANS RECORDS

INDICATE BELOW THE TYPE OF FILE DESIRED AND THE METHOD OF PAYMENT PREFERRED.

1. FILE TO BE SEARCHED *(Check one box only)*

☐ PENSION

☐ BOUNTY-LAND WARRANT APPLICATION *(Service before 1856 only)*

☐ MILITARY

2. PAYMENT METHOD *(Check one box only)*

☐ CREDIT CARD *(VISA or MasterCard) for IMMEDIATE SHIPMENT of copies*

☐ **BILL ME** *(No Credit Card)*

REQUIRED MINIMUM IDENTIFICATION OF VETERAN - MUST BE COMPLETED OR YOUR ORDER CANNOT BE SERVICED

3. VETERAN *(Give last, first, and middle names)*

4. BRANCH OF SERVICE IN WHICH HE SERVED ☐ ARMY ☐ NAVY ☐ MARINE CORPS

5. STATE FROM WHICH HE SERVED

6. WAR IN WHICH, OR DATES BETWEEN WHICH, HE SERVED

7. IF SERVICE WAS CIVIL WAR, ☐ UNION ☐ CONFEDERATE

PLEASE PROVIDE THE FOLLOWING ADDITIONAL INFORMATION, IF KNOWN

8. UNIT IN WHICH HE SERVED *(Name of regiment or number, company, etc, name of ship)*

9. IF SERVICE WAS ARMY, ARM IN WHICH HE SERVED ☐ INFANTRY ☐ CAVALRY ☐ ARTILLERY *If other, specify:*

Rank ☐ OFFICER ☐ ENLISTED

10. KIND OF SERVICE ☐ VOLUNTEERS ☐ REGULARS

11. PENSION/BOUNTY-LAND FILE NO.

12. IF VETERAN LIVED IN A HOME FOR SOLDIERS, *GIVE LOCATION (City and State)*

13. PLACE(S) VETERAN LIVED AFTER SERVICE

14. DATE OF BIRTH

15. PLACE OF BIRTH *(City, County, State, etc.)*

16. DATE OF DEATH

17. PLACE OF DEATH *(City, County, State, etc.)*

18. NAME OF WIDOW OR OTHER CLAIMANT

NATIONAL ARCHIVES TRUST FUND BOARD NATF Form 80 (rev. 10-93)

IMPORTANT INFORMATION ABOUT YOUR ORDER

We can only search for a record based on the information you provided in blocks 3-18. The success and accuracy of our search is determined by the information you provide. Often there are many files for veterans of the same or nearly the same name. If there are five or fewer files for men with the same name as the individual in whom you are interested, we will examine all the relevant files and compare their contents with the information that you have provided us. If the veteran's identity seems obvious, we will furnish you a copy of the file we think is the correct one.

If there are more than five files, we will not make a file-by-file check to see if the information in the numerous files matches that provided for the veteran in whom you are interested. In such cases, we suggest that you visit the National Archives and examine the various files, or hire a professional researcher to examine the files for you. We do not maintain a list of persons who do research for a fee; however, many researchers advertise their services in genealogical periodicals, usually available in libraries.

PLEASE NOTE: This mail order photocopying service is available **ONLY** from ***General Reference Branch (NNRG-P)*** at the address below. Please address all inquiries about your order to the General Reference Branch at this address or call us at 202-501-5170. When you send more than one form at a time, each form is handled separately. Therefore, you may not receive all of your replies at the same time. Allow a minimum of 8 to 10 weeks for processing your order. More information about the availability of records pertaining to military service or family histories may be found in our free genealogical information leaflets and forms. You may request these, as well as order additional copies of this form, by writing to:

General Reference Branch (NNRG)
National Archives and Records Administration
7th and Pennsylvania Avenue NW.
Washington, DC 20408

A291521

THIS IS YOUR MAILING LABEL.

NAME (Last, First, MI)

STREET

CITY, STATE *ZIP CODE*

CUSTOMER COPY - KEEP FOR YOUR RECORDS

(Appendix C)

MILITARY SERVICE RECORDS

A Select Catalog of National Archives Microfilm Publications

National Archives Trust Fund Board • National Archives and Records Administration

This catalog is one in a series that describes National Archives microfilm publications related to specific subjects of high research interest. Each catalog is compiled through an extensive review of microfilmed records to locate relevant publications. The catalogs contain descriptions of the records and roll-by-roll listings for each publication. The six catalogs in this series of **Select Catalogs of National Archives Microfilm Publications** are:

American Indians, published 1984
Black Studies, published 1984
Genealogical and Biographical Research, published 1983
Immigrant and Passenger Arrivals, published 1983
Military Service Records, published 1985
Diplomatic Records, expected publication date 1986

Other available microfilm catalogs are:
Comprehensive Catalog of National Archives Microfilm Publications, expected publication date, 1986
1910 Federal Population Census on Microfilm
1900 Federal Population Census on Microfilm
1790-1890 Federal Population Censuses on Microfilm

This publication was not printed at taxpayer expense.

The cover photograph (165-PF-7) of Brig. Gen. Fred C. Ainsworth (1852-1934) is from Record Group 165, Records of the War Department General and Special Staff.

Ainsworth was placed in charge of the newly created Record and Pension Division (later the Record and Pension Office) of the War Department in July 1889. He began the system of compiling abstract cards and index cards of military service records as an aid in evaluating Civil War pension applications. These cards, many of which are now on microfilm, are used extensively to research a veteran's military service record.

Introduction

The National Archives and Records Administration (NARA) is the official repository for records of military personnel who have been discharged from the U.S. Air Force, Army, Marine Corps, and Navy. Those records available for public examination at the National Archives are a valuable source of information about an individual's military service, family, and medical history. These records can also be used to study military and social history.

Because of their research value, NARA has microfilmed many of these records, primarily those created before 1900. This catalog is organized by type of record; similar types of records are arranged chronologically. Brief descriptions of the records are followed by roll-by-roll listings of the contents. The catalog does not reproduce the records, however.

The first section explains *compiled military service records* of volunteer soldiers who fought for the United States in various wars and conflicts from the Revolutionary War through the Philippine Insurrection—1775 to 1902. During the 1890's, the War Department abstracted these records from such original records as muster rolls, returns, and medical and prison registers. The records usually show a soldier's presence or absence on certain dates, his rank and military organization, and the term of service. Sometimes they also show age, place of enlistment, and place of birth. These records are of value for proving military service, but generally don't have other genealogical information.

The second section of the catalog describes *records relating to service in the regular U.S. Army or Navy.* The War Department began to maintain personnel files for Regular Army officers in 1863 and for enlisted men in 1912. Records relating to service before those dates are scattered among many different series of War Department records—registers of enlistments, post and regimental returns, and correspondence. Similarly, records for naval officers and enlisted men were not compiled until after 1885 (after 1903 for enlisted men). Sources for earlier service consist of indexes to rendezvous reports, Marine Corps muster rolls, abstracts of service of naval officers, indexes to officers' records, and records of general courts-martial.

The third section treats records of veterans' *claims for bounty land and pensions.* Between 1776 and 1855, the Federal Government granted bounty land warrants entitling veterans to free land in specific areas of the public domain as an inducement to enter military service. Applications for these bounty land warrants and pension files may contain a great deal of personal information about a veteran and his family. The files may show the veteran's name, age, and residence at the date of the application; the names of his wife and children; and dates of births, marriages, and deaths within the family. Pension records also document the veteran's military service by indicating his unit and the dates of his service.

The final section of the catalog describes *miscellaneous records that relate to military service:* additional records relating to Revolutionary War pay, settlement of accounts, and pensions; records relating to Confederates; records relating to the U.S. Military Academy cadets and U.S. Naval Academy midshipmen; and selected records relating to black servicemen.

Records relating to the following groups of military personnel are at the *National Personnel Records Center* in St. Louis, MO:

- U.S. Army officers and enlisted personnel completely separated after 1956. Personnel jackets of officers separated between 30 June 1917 and 1956 were destroyed by fire in 1972, as were jackets of enlisted men separated between 30 October 1912 and 1956.
- U.S. Air Force officers and enlisted men completely separated after 1956. Earlier jackets of the Army Air Corps and the U.S. Air Force were destroyed by fire in 1972.
- U.S. Navy officers completely separated after 1902 and enlisted men completely separated after 1885.
- U.S. Coast Guard officers completely separated after 1928 and enlisted personnel completely separated after 1914.

Requests for information about veterans should be submitted to the National Personnel Records Center (MPR), 9700 Page Blvd., St. Louis, MO 63132, using Standard Form 180, Request Pertaining to Military Records. This form is available from the St. Louis Center, the Government Printing Office, Federal Information Centers, local Veterans Administration offices, veterans service organizations, and the Reference Services Branch (NNIR), National Archives and Records Administration, Washington, DC 20408.

For additional information you may wish to refer to other NARA publications: *Military Service Rec-*

ords in the National Archives of the United States (General Information Leaflet 7); *Genealogical Research in the National Archives* (General Information Leaflet 5); and *Guide to Genealogical Research in the National Archives.*

Other related catalogs of microfilm publications of interest are: *Immigrant and Passenger Arrivals, Genealogical and Biographical Research, American Indians, Black Studies,* and *1790–1890 Federal Population Censuses.* These catalogs of microfilm publications do not reproduce the records, but briefly describe the records and tell what records are available on microfilm.

The records listed in this catalog are from the following record groups:

Record Group	*Title*
15	Records of the Veterans Administration
18	Records of the Army Air Forces
24	Records of the Bureau of Naval Personnel
29	Records of the Bureau of the Census
39	Records of the Bureau of Accounts (Treasury)
45	Naval Records Collection of the Office of Naval Records and Library
49	Records of the Bureau of Land Management
53	Records of the Bureau of the Public Debt
92	Records of the Office of the Quartermaster General
94	Records of the Adjutant General's Office, 1780s–1917
107	Records of the Office of the Secretary of War
109	War Department Collection of Confederate Records
125	Records of the Judge Advocate General (Navy)
127	Records of the United States Marine Corps
153	Records of the Judge Advocate General (Army)
217	Records of the United States General Accounting Office
391	Records of the United States Regular Army Mobile Units, 1821–1942
393	Records of the United States Army Continental Commands, 1821–1920
395	Records of the United States Army Overseas Operations and Commands, 1898–1942
405	Records of the United States Naval Academy
407	Records of the Adjutant General's Office, 1971–

This catalog was compiled by Cynthia G. Fox and Contance Potter with the assistance of Beverly Bagge and Mary Ryan. Jan Danis edited the final manuscript.

Roll	Description
3	Cam–Cor
4	Cos–D
5	E–Ge
6	Gh–Ha
7	He–J
8	K–Lp
9	Lu–Mon
10	Moo–Peq
11	Per–Roo
12	Rop–So
13	Sp–Va
14	Ve–Z

Index to Compiled Service Records of Volunteer Union Soldiers Who Served in Organizations From the State of Virginia. M394. 1 roll. 16mm. DP.

The compiled service records to which this index applies are reproduced on M398.

Index to Compiled Service Records of Volunteer Union Soldiers Who Served in Organizations From the Territory of Washington. M558. 1 roll. 16mm. DP.

Index to Compiled Service Records of Volunteer Union Soldiers Who Served in Organizations From the State of West Virginia. M507. 13 rolls. 16mm. DP.

The compiled service records to which the index applies are reproduced on M508.

Roll	Description
1	A–Bon
2	Boo–Ch
3	Ci–De
4	Di–F
5	G–Ha
6	He–J
7	K–L
8	M–Me
9	Mg–Pa
10	Pe–Ro
11	Ru–Spe
12	Sph–V
13	W–Z

Index to Compiled Service Records of Volunteer Union Soldiers Who Served in Organizations From the State of Wisconsin. M559. 33 rolls. 16mm. DP.

Roll	Description
1	A–Bak
2	Bal–Be
3	Bh–Bre
4	Bri–Cah
5	Cai–Cli
6	Clo–Cro
7	Crs–Dh
8	Di–Ek
9	El–Fj
10	Fl–Ga
11	Ge–Gr
12	Gs–Har
13	Has–Hi
14	Ho–Hy
15	I–Ka
16	Ke–Ko
17	Kr–Len
18	Leo–Mal
19	Man–McI
20	McJ–Mj
21	Mo–Ne
22	Ni–O
23	P–Pj
24	Pl–Reh
25	Rei–Ros
26	Rot–Schu
27	Schw–Sj
28	Sk–Sta
29	St. C–Ta
30	Tc–Ty
31	U–Wa
32	We–Wilk
33	Will–Z

Index to Compiled Service Records of Volunteer Union Soldiers Who Served with United States Colored Troops. M589. 98 rolls. 16mm. DP.

In May 1863 the War Department authorized the formation of the United States Colored Troops (U.S.C.T.). Most of the soldiers served in the infantry, but some served in the cavalry, engineer units, and in light and heavy artillery batteries. The Corps d'Afrique and other State organizations were redesignated when they became part of the U.S.C.T., with the exception of a few units raised in Massachusetts, Connecticut, and Louisiana.

Nearly all of the U.S.C.T. officers were white. Although the War Department imposed a stringent examination of all applicants, it discouraged blacks from applying. Only 75 to 100 black officers were appointed, and three-quarters of those served in Gen. Benjamin Butler's Department of Louisiana.

The soldiers of the U.S.C.T. met with varying reactions and treatment. In the trans-Mississippi West, the troops saw combat, while in the Department of Tennessee and in the South they were assigned fatigue work. In the East, they drew both combat and fatigue duty. In addition, they received unequal pay, poor equipment, and inadequate medical attention. In July 1864, Congress acted to remedy the pay inequality by authorizing equal pay, retroactive to January 1, 1864, for all who had been free as of April 19, 1861.

This microfilm publication reproduces an alphabetical card index to the compiled service records of volunteer Union soldiers who served with the U.S. Colored Troops. Each index card gives the name of a soldier, his rank, and the unit in which he served. There are cross-references for names that appear in the records under more than one spelling and for service in more than one unit or organization.

The compiled military service records to which this index refers are not microfilmed.

Roll	Description
1	A–Alk
2	All–Ande
3	Andl–Az
4	B–Baq
5	Bar–Bat
6	Bau–Ben
7	Beo–Blai

Roll	Description
8	Blak-Bor
9	Bos-Brag
10	Brah-Broo
11	Bros-Brown, J.
12	Brown, K.-Buf
13	Bug-Bus
14	But-Cam
15	Can-Car
16	Cas-Che
17	Chi-Cl
18	Co-Com
19	Con-Cot
20	Cou-Cr
21	Cs-Dau
22	Dav-Daz
23	De-Dic
24	Did-Dov
25	Dow-Dy
26	E-El
27	Em-Fa
28	Fe-Fl
29	Fo-Fran
30	Frap-Gak
31	Gal-Gh
32	Gi-Gn
33	Go-Graw
34	Gray-Gref
35	Greg-Gy
36	H-Ham
37	Han-Harris, K.
38	Harris, L.-Haw
39	Hax-Heno
40	Henr-Hik
41	Hil-Holl
42	Holm-Hoz
43	Hu-Hy
44	I-Jackson, I.
45	Jackson, J.-Jay
46	Je-Johnson, C.
47	Johnson, D.-Johnson, M.
48	Johnson, N.-Jom
49	Jon-Jont
50	Joo-Ke
51	Kh-Lah
52	Lai-Laz
53	Le-Lev
54	Lew-Loc
55	Lod-Ly
56	M-Marr
57	Mars-Mat
58	Mau-McD
59	McE-Mel
60	Mem-Mil
61	Mim-Moon
62	Moor-Morr
63	Mors-My
64	N-Ni
65	No-O
66	P-Pas
67	Pat-Pes
68	Pet-Pi
69	Pl-Pre
70	Pri-Ram
71	Ran-Ree
72	Ref-Ric
73	Rid-Robe
74	Robi-Rok
75	Rol-Ry
76	S-Scl
77	Sco-Se
78	Sh
79	Si-Sme
80	Smi-Smith, J.
81	Smith, K.-So
82	Sp-Steu
83	Stev-Sty
84	Su-Tax
85	Tay-Thol
86	Thom-Thomp
87	Thoms-To
88	Tr-Ty
89	U-V
90	W-Ward
91	Ware-Wash
92	Wass-Wem
93	Wen-White
94	Whitf-Williams, E.
95	Williams, F.-Williams, T.
96	Williams, V.-Wils
97	Wilt-Wo
98	Wr-Z

Index to Compiled Service Records of Volunteer Union Soldiers Who Served in the Veteran Reserve Corps. M636. 44 rolls. 16mm. DP.

This microfilm publication reproduces an alphabetical card index to the compiled service records of volunteer Union soldiers who served in the Veteran Reserve Corps. The compiled military service records to which this index refers are not microfilmed.

The Veteran Reserve Corps was composed of deserving officers and enlisted men who were unfit for active field service because of wounds or disease contracted in the line of duty, but who were still capable of performing garrison duty. The Corps also included officers and enlisted men borne on the Army rolls who were absent from duty and in hospitals, in convalescent camps, or otherwise under the control of medical officers, but who were capable of serving as cooks, nurses, clerks, or orderlies at hospitals and as guards for hospitals or other public buildings. When the Corps was first authorized on April 28, 1863, it was known as the "Invalid Corps." Its name was changed to the Veteran Reserve Corps on March 18, 1864.

Roll	Description
1	A
2	Ba
3	Be-Bla
4	Ble-Bri
5	Bro-Bur
6	Bus-Ca
7	Ce-Cok
8	Col-Coz
9	Cr-Dau
10	Dav-Dom
11	Don-Dy
12	E
13	F-Fl

Roll	Description
14	Fo-Gal
15	Gam-Go
16	Gr-Gy
17	H-Har
18	Has-He
19	Hi-Hos
20	Hot-I
21	J-Ka
22	Ke-Ki
23	Kl-La
24	Le-Lo
25	Lu-Mat
26	Mau-Mcl
27	McK-Me
28	Mi-Mor
29	Mos-Ni
30	No-Pap
31	Par-Pi
32	Pl-Re
33	Re-Ri
34	Ro-Ry
35	S-Sc
36	Se-Sh
37	Si-Sn
38	So-Sti
39	St.J-Sz
40	T-To
41	Tr-V
42	W-Wel
43	Wem-Wil
44	Wim-Z

Compiled Service Records

Compiled Service Records of Volunteer Union Soldiers Who Served in Organizations From the State of Alabama. M276. 10 rolls. 16mm. DP.

The compiled service records reproduced in this microfilm publication are indexed on M263.

Roll	Description
1	1st Cavalry
	A-Br
2	Bu-C
3	D-Go
4	Gr-H
5	I-L
6	M-Ne
7	Ni-Rh
8	Ri-Sp
9	St-V
10	W-Z
	Miscellaneous Card Abstracts Personal Papers

Compiled Service Records of Volunteer Union Soldiers Who Served in Organizations From the State of Arkansas. M399. 60 rolls. 16mm. DP.

The compiled service records reproduced in this microfilm publication are indexed on M383.

Roll	Description
1	1st Cavalry
	A-Bod
2	Bog-Cl
3	Co-D
4	E-Gl
5	Go-Hi
6	Ho-Joh
7	Jon-Le
8	Li-McC
9	McD-N
10	O-Re
11	Rh-Sl
12	Sm-Ta
13	Te-We
14	Wh-Z
15	2d Cavalry
	A-Bo
16	Br-Cr
17	Cu-F
18	G-Ho
19	Hu-Mas
20	Mat-My
21	N-Ram
22	Ran-So
23	Sp-Wa
24	We-Y
	3d Cavalry
	A-Ba
25	Be-Ch
26	Cl-Fe
27	Fi-Ham
28	Han-Ji
29	Jo-Mat
30	Mau-Pas
31	Pat-Sa
32	Sc-U
33	V-Y
	4th Cavalry
	A-An
34	Ar-Br
35	Bu-Da
36	De-G
37	Ha-Je
38	Jo-Me
39	Mi-Poi
40	Pol-So
41	Sp-Wa
42	We-Y
	1st Battery, Light Artillery
	A-He
43	Hi-Y
	1st Infantry
	A-Al
44	An-B
45	C-Do
46	Dr-He
47	Hi-Le
48	Li-M
49	N-Ro
50	Ru-Sti
51	Sto-Wh
52	Wi-Y
	1st Battalion, Infantry
	A-K
53	L-Y
	2d Infantry
	A-Bo
54	Br-Da
55	De-I
56	J-Mc

Roll	Description
41	Br–Cod
42	Cok–Di
43	Do–Gl
44	Gl–Hol
45	Hoo–Ki
46	Kl–L
47	M–Mi
48	Mo–Pa
49	Pe–Rod
50	Rol–Sp
51	St–T
52	V–Z
6th U.S. Volunteers:	
53	A–Bo
54	Br–Coo
55	Cop–E
56	F–G
57	H
58	I–L
59	M–Mi
60	Mo–Q
61	R–Se
62	Sh–St
63	Su–Wh
64	Wi–Y
Personal papers:	
65	A–Z

Records of Movements and Activities of Volunteer Union Organizations (Record Groups 94 and 407)

Beginning in 1890, the War Department compiled histories of the volunteer military organizations that served during the Civil War. The compiled records for each organization are in jacket-envelopes bearing the title "Record of Events" and giving the name of the unit. Many of the envelopes contain abstracts of the information found in the record-of-events section of the original muster rolls and returns. Also included are some cards showing the exact captions of the muster-in and muster-out rolls and the certifications by the mustering officers verifying the accuracy of the rolls. The jacket-envelopes for a few units contain no documents but only references to other units with which these units were merged.

Compiled service histories contain no information about individual soldiers. The abstracts instead relate to the stations, movements, or activities of each unit or part of it. Frequently there is information about the unit's organization or composition, strength and losses, and disbandment. Sometimes the cards also show the names of commanding officers, the dates the unit was called into service and mustered out, the terms of service, and similar information.

Compiled Records Showing Service of Military Units in Volunteer Union Organizations. M594. 225 rolls. DP.

This microfilm publication reproduces the compiled records that give histories of military units in volunteer Union organizations. Most of the records are arranged alphabetically by State or Territory, thereunder by type of unit (cavalry, artillery, or infantry), followed by militia, reserve, sharpshooter, and other organizations. Whenever possible, the units are arranged numerically within each type, for example, the 1st Cavalry, 1st Veteran Cavalry, 1st Mounted Rifles, and 2d Cavalry of New York.

The records for units from States and Territories are followed by the records of units that were not limited to any one State or Territory, such as the U.S. Colored Troops, U.S. Volunteers, and U.S. Veteran Reserve Corps.

Roll	Description
Alabama:	
1	1st Cavalry
Arizona:	
	1st Infantry
Arkansas:	
	1st–4th Cavalry
	1st Battalion, Light Artillery
	1st Battalion, Infantry, 3 months, 1862
	1st Infantry
	2d Infantry
	4th Infantry
California:	
2	1st Cavalry
	1st Battalion, Native Cavalry
	2d Cavalry
	1st Infantry
	1st Battalion, Mountaineers, Infantry
	2d Infantry
3	3d–8th Infantry
	Mounted Detachment, Infantry, 3 months, 1861
Colorado:	
4	1st Cavalry
	2d Cavalry
	McLain's Independent Battery, Light Artillery
	2d Infantry
	3d Infantry
	Denver City Home Guards, 6 months, 1861–62
Connecticut:	
5	1st Cavalry
	1st Heavy Artillery
	2d Heavy Artillery
	1st–3d Independent Battery, Light Artillery
	1st Infantry, 3 months, 1861–3d Infantry
	5th Infantry
	6th Infantry
6	7th–11th Infantry
7	12th–17th Infantry
8	18th Infantry
	20th–28th Infantry
	Garrison Guard, Infantry
Dakota Territory:	
9	1st Battalion, Cavalry
Delaware:	
	1st Battalion, Cavalry
	Capt. Milligan's Independent Cavalry
	Capt. Ahl's Independent Battery, Heavy Artillery
	Capt. Nields' Independent Battery, Light Artillery
	1st–9th Infantry

Roll	Description
195	1st Light Artillery
	1st Infantry
	1st Veteran Infantry
	2d Veteran Infantry
	4th–7th Infantry
196	9th–15th Infantry
	17th Infantry
	Co. A, Independent Exempts, Infantry
	Independent Co. B (Capt. West's), Infantry
Wisconsin:	
197	1st–4th Cavalry
	1st Heavy Artillery
	1st Independent Battery, Light Artillery
	2d Independent Battery, Light Artillery
198	3d–10th Independent Battery, Light Artillery
	12th Independent Battery, Light Artillery
	13th Independent Battery, Light Artillery
	1st–3d Infantry
	5th Infantry
199	6th–11th Infantry
200	12th–18th Infantry
201	19th–25th Infantry
202	26th–32d Infantry
203	33d–53d Infantry
U.S. Colored Troops:	
204	1st–5th Cavalry
	5th Massachusetts Cavalry
	6th Cavalry
	1st Heavy Artillery
	3d–5th Heavy Artillery
205	6th Heavy Artillery
	8th–14th Heavy Artillery
	1st Light Artillery
	2d Light Artillery
	Independent Battery, Light Artillery
	1st Infantry
	1st Infantry, 1 year, 1864
206	2d Infantry
	3d Infantry
	3d Tennessee Infantry
	4th–11th Infantry
207	12th–21st Infantry
208	22d–29th Infantry
	29th Connecticut Infantry
	30th–33d Infantry
209	34th–43d Infantry
210	44th–52d Infantry
211	53d–58th Infantry
212	59th–72d Infantry
213	73d–82d Infantry
214	83d–95th Infantry
215	96th–104th Infantry
	106th–108th Infantry
216	109th–118th Infantry
217	119th–125th Infantry
	127th Infantry
	128th Infantry
	135th–138th Infantry
	Capt. Powell's Regiment, Infantry
	Co. A, Unassigned, Infantry
	Co. A, Southord Infantry, Pa., 100 days, 1864
	Pioneer Corps, Cavalry Division, 16 Army Corps (A.D.)
	Pioneer Co., 1st Division, 16 Army Corps, Infantry (A. D.)
	Brigade Band, No. 1
	Brigade Band, No. 2
	Brigade Band, No. 1, Corps d'Afrique
	Brigade Band, No. 2, Corps d'Afrique

Roll	Description
	Quartermaster Detachment, Infantry
U.S. Volunteers:	
218	1st Sharp Shooters
	2d Sharp Shooters
	Signal Corps
	1st Veteran Volunteers, Engineers
	1st–9th Veteran Volunteers, Infantry (1 Army Corps)
219	1st–6th Volunteers
	1st Independent Co., Volunteers
	1st Co., Pontoniers, Volunteers
	Capt. Stufft's Independent Co., Indian Scouts, Volunteers (Indian Expedition to the Upper Missouri, 1864)
U.S. Veteran Reserve Corps:	
	1st–4th
220	5th–14th
221	15th–24th
222	1st Battalion
	2d Battalion
	1st–49th Co.
223	50th–107th Co.
224	108th–174th Co.
225	1st–7th Independent Co.
	Unassigned Detachments
Other U.S. organizations:	
	Brigade Bands
	Departmental Corps, Department of the Monongahela
	1st Indian Home Guards
	2d Indian Home Guards
	3d Indian Home Guards
	4th & 5th Indian Home Guards
	1st Battalion, Cavalry, Mississippi Marine Brigade
	Light Battery, Mississippi Marine Brigade
	1st Infantry, Mississippi Marine Brigade
	Marine Regiment, U.S. Volunteers
	General and Staff, Mississippi Marine Brigade
	Signal Corps Detachment, Mississippi Marine Brigade
	Ram Fleet, Mississippi Marine Brigade
	Battalion, Pioneer Brigade (Army of the Cumberland)

Records of Confederate Soldiers Who Served During the Civil War (Record Group 109)

In April 1865, during the final days of the Civil War, as the Confederate Government evacuated Richmond, its archives were shipped south, burned, or abandoned. Some of the military records passed into the hands of Union Army officers and were sent to the War Department in Washington. There the Adjutant General in July 1865 established a bureau in his office for the "collection, safekeeping, and publication of Rebel Archives." In 1903 the Secretary of War persuaded the Governors of most Southern States to lend the War Department the

Roll	Description
506	R347-R357
507	R359-R383
508	R384-R402
509	R403-R443
510	R445-R494
511	R499-R515
512	S1-S107
513	S109-S168
514	S169-S213
515	S217-S288
516	S289-S369
517	S371-S410
518	S411-T37
519	T40-T82
520	T96-T159
521	T168-V44
522	V46-W83
523	W86-W208
524	W210-W265
525	W267
526	W274-W287
527	W290-Z6

Name and Subject Index to the Letters Received by the Appointment, Commission, and Personal Branch of the Adjutant General's Office, 1871–1894. M1125. 4 rolls. DP.

This microfilm publication reproduces an alphabetical card index to the letters received by the Appointment, Commission, and Personal Branch of the AGO, 1871–94. The index is principally to names, but it also includes a limited number of subject references. Staff members of the National Archives and Records Administration compiled the index to facilitate research in the AGO records.

The correspondence files to which this index refers are not currently available on microfilm. The index may prove useful, however, in searching for information relating to Regular Army officers.

Roll	Description
1	A–Do
2	Dr–Kl
3	Kn–Rh
4	Ri–Z

Records Relating to Service in the U.S. Navy and U.S. Marine Corps (Record Groups 24, 125, and 127)

Records relating to service in the American Navy in the Revolutionary War, 1775–83; in the U.S. Navy for officers, 1798–1902, and for enlisted men, 1789–1885; and in the U.S. Marine Corps, 1798–1895, are held by the National Archives. Naval service records of the Revolutionary War are fragmentary, showing only such information as the serviceman's name and rank, the name of the vessel on which he served, and the dates of his service or the dates he was paid.

Records relating to the service of commissioned officers in the Navy after the Revolutionary War but before 1846 give each officer's name, rank, State of birth, sometimes age or date of birth, date of residence, and dates of service. Records for 1846 and later contain the above information and occasionally give the date and place of an officer's death in service or the date of his retirement.

Records relating to a Navy enlisted man's service before 1846 usually give only his name and rating, the names of the vessels on which he served, and the dates of his service. Later records also give an enlisted man's age and place of birth and occasionally place of enlistment.

Records of commissioned officers in the Marine Corps usually show each officer's name and rank and the date of his appointment or acceptance of a commission. They may also give his age and residence. Service records for enlisted marines usually show the man's name and age, and the date, place, and term of enlistment.

The National Personnel Records Center in St. Louis holds the individual personnel records (jackets) of Navy commissioned officers separated after 1902, Navy enlisted personnel separated after 1885, and Marine Corps enlisted personnel separated after 1905.

Indexes to Rendezvous Reports

Indexes to Rendezvous Reports (Navy Enlistments) Through 1884

The following microfilm publications reproduce alphabetical name indexes to the U.S. Navy rendezvous reports (enlistments), 1846–84. The indexes were filmed by the U.S. Navy before transferring the records to the National Archives. The Navy filmed the cards for the Civil War, 1861–65, separately.

Each card shows the name of the individual; rendezvous (place of enlistment or vessel on which enlisted); date of enlistment or return (the roll on which the name first appeared); and a space for a "Record of Service." Although the amount of information varies, the entry under "Record of Service" may provide the date of reassignment or discharge, the names of vessels on which the individual served, or the date of death.

The records to which these indexes refer are not on microfilm, but they are open to researchers at the National Archives.

Index to Rendezvous Reports, Before and After the Civil War (1846–1861, 1865–1884). T1098. 32 rolls. 16mm.

Roll	Description
1	A. Bon–Bailey, Sam'l
2	Bailey, Sam'l–Benson, Benjamin
3	Benson, Bernard–Bronson, Harry
4	Bronson, William–Burns, M.E.
5	Burns, M.H.–Cervenka, Jos.
6	Cervenka, Jos.–Cooly, Patrick
7	Coomadt, Andrew–Darineil, Jno.
8	Davy, H.T.–Dow, Austin
9	Dow, Benjamin–Fenarty, Thos.
10	Fenderson, Jno.–Foley, John
11	Foley, John–Goddard, N.P.
12	Goddard, N.P.–Greif, William
13	Greig, John–Hawley, Chas.
14	Hawley, Chas. P.–Hook, Fred
15	Hook, Fred'k–Jones, Daniel
16	Jones, Daniel–Jyttropsen, R.D.
17	Kaack, Heinrich–Lavery, William
18	Lavery, William–Lundberg, Thomas
19	Lundburg, Adolph–McMillan, Angus
20	McMillan, Angus–Meanol, Adam
21	Meany, Francis A.–Mulholland, James
22	Mulholland, John–Obre, Edward
23	O'Brien, Edwards–Pettyjohn, James H.
24	Petukin, Chas. L.–Redding, M.
25	Redding, Martin–Rudinos, Santiago
26	Rupell, Charles–Sharpe, Charles
27	Sharpe, Frederick–Smith, Wm.
28	Smith, Wm.–Sturtevant, W.P.
29	Sturtevent, Wm. P.–Townsend, T.
30	Townsend, Treadwell–Washington, Corbin
31	Washington, Corbin–William, Thos.
32	William, Thos.–Zylinicke, Alfons

Index to Rendezvous Reports, Civil War, 1861–1865. T1099. 31 rolls. 16mm.

Roll	Description
1	Abaling, Louis–Barth, Theodore
2	Barthel, Eugene A.–Bowen, William
3	Bowen, William–Burns, Jno.
4	Burns–Champ, Samuel
5	Champion, Chris–Coveliers, Albert
6	Covell, Almeron–Day, Thos. P.
7	Day, Vandewater–Duskin, William
8	Duson, Albert–Fitzgerald, John
9	Fitzgerald, John–Girraty, John
10	Girraty, John–Hale, Sherman
11	Hale, Sherman–Hewit, Benjamin
12	Hewit, John–Ingersoll, Hiram
13	Ingersoll, Jas.–Justin, William H.
14	Kaab, William–Langen, Thomas
15	Langen, Thomas–Lowd, William
16	Lowden, Frances–McGarth, Christopher
17	McGarth, Christopher–McGuire, Peter
18	McGuire, Peter–Maney, Patrick
19	Maney, Richard–Moore, Charles W.
20	Moore, Cicero–Muller, Jno. Philip
21	Muller, Julius–O'Keefe, Patrick
22	O'Keefe, Robert–Peterson, Chas.
23	Peterson, Charles–Richards, Frank W.
24	Richards, Geo.–Ryan, Daniel
25	Ryan, Dan'l–Sloane, John
26	Sloane, John M.–Stanton, Robert
27	Stanton, Robert–Thompson, Robert
28	Thompson, Robert–Wallace, John
29	Wallace, John–William, John
30	Williams, John–Yerry, Edward
31	Yerkes, Henry–Zwicker, Frank

Indexes to World War I and Later Rendezvous Reports

The following microfilm publications reproduce finding aids to records that are in the custody of the National Personnel Records Center. Requests for information about Navy officers separated since 1902, Navy enlisted men separated since 1885, Marine Corps officers separated after 1895, and Marine Corps enlisted men separated after 1905 should be made on Standard Form 180, "Request Pertaining to Military Records." Send these requests to Military Personnel Records, 9700 Page Boulevard, St. Louis, MO 63132.

Index to Rendezvous Reports, Armed Guard Personnel, 1917–1920. T1101. 3 rolls. 16mm.

The index card shows the name of the individual, the name of the vessel on which he served and dates of service, and the place where the records and accounts were held. The index sometimes indicates the individual's assigned job.

Roll	Description
1	Abbott, Henry J.–Luebke, Charles
2	Luke, Wilmer L.–Visnow, Norman S.
3	Visocky, William M.–Zwick, Walter

Index to Rendezvous Reports, Naval Auxiliary Service, 1917–1918. T1100. 1 roll. 16mm.

The index cards, arranged alphabetically, show the name, the date of enlistment, and the name of the vessel on which the individual served and the dates he was assigned and left the vessel.

Other Records

Muster Rolls of the U.S. Marine Corps, 1789–1892. T1118. 123 rolls.

This microfilm publication reproduces the U.S. Marine Corps muster rolls for 1789–1892. There is some duplication of roll numbers. Most volumes are indexed by the name of the vessel or the station. The roll list below is arranged by the inclusive dates, not by the roll number.

The muster rolls were filmed chronologically as they appeared in bound volumes. They are monthly, quarterly, or in some cases annual lists of individuals serving in the U.S. Marine Corps either at land stations or on board vessels. Entries on the lists are arranged by rank. While the amount of information varies, muster rolls generally show for an individual Marine name and rank, the name of the station or vessel on which he served, the date of enlistment, and term of enlistment. A separate column for

VETERANS' CLAIMS

Military Bounty Land Warrants and Pensions (Record Groups 15, 49, and 217)

Bounty Land Warrants

Military *bounty land warrants* were certificates giving eligible veterans rights to free land in the public domain. Congress used bounty land warrants to encourage enlistments during the Revolutionary War. From 1781 until 1855 the Federal Government continued to issue bounty land warrants to veterans or their heirs as a reward for service. A succession of administrative units of the War Department processed the applications for warrants. In 1849 responsibility was transferred to the Department of the Interior.

The National Archives has bounty land warrant application files based on service in wartime between 1775 and 1855. The majority of the bounty land applications available on microfilm relate to service during the Revolutionary War.

For additional information on land records, see *Genealogical and Biographical Research: A Select Catalog of Microfilm Publications.*

Pension Records

The National Archives has *pension applications* and *records of pension payments* for veterans, their widows, and other heirs. They are based on service in the Armed Forces of the United States between 1775 and 1916 but not to duty in the service of the Confederate States of America, 1861–65. In a few cases, the Federal Government assumed responsibility for pensions based on service in State military organizations, and records of these pensions are also in the National Archives. Most pension records are found among the Records of the Veterans Administration (Record Group 15).

The Federal Government provided three principal types of pensions:

- Disability or invalid pensions were awarded to servicemen for physical disabilities incurred in the line of duty.
- Service pensions were awarded to women and children whose husbands or fathers had served in wartime for specified periods.
- Widows' pensions were awarded to women and children whose husbands or fathers had served for specified periods or had been killed in war.

Pension legislation during the Revolutionary War was designed to encourage enlistment and acceptance of commissions and to prevent desertion and resignation. After the war, pensions became a form of reward for services rendered. Both during and after the Revolution, the States, as well as the Federal Government, awarded pensions based on participation in the conflict. The records reproduced in these microfilm publications pertain only to pensions granted or paid pursuant to public and private acts of the U.S. Government. Public acts, under which the majority of such pensions were authorized, encompassed large classes of veterans or their dependents who met common eligibility requirements. Private acts concerned specific individuals whose special services or circumstances merited consideration, but who could not be awarded pensions under existing public acts.

The records contain both historical and genealogical information. Historical information pertaining to the organization of military units, movement of troops, details of battles and campaigns, and activities of individuals, may be obtained from application statements of veterans; from affidavits of witnesses; and from the muster roll, diary, order, or orderly books that were occasionally submitted as proof of service and were not sent by the Bureau of Pensions to another Government Department or Agency. Naval and privateer operations are documented by applications, affidavits, and orders in some files based on service at sea. A few files contain letters written to or by soldiers and sailors during the Revolutionary War, which give firsthand accounts of military, naval, and civil events and conditions. Furloughs, passes, pay receipts, enlistment papers, commissions, warrants, and other original records of the period 1775–83 are also in some of the files.

Generally, the records were not microfilmed unless they contain genealogical information.

The following information is typical of what may be found in applications for pensions or bounty land warrants based on a veteran's service at any period. *A veteran's application* typically shows the veteran's name, rank, military unit, period of service, residence at time of mustering-in, residence at time of application, birthplace, age or date of birth, and, when the claim was made on the basis of need, a list of property. *A widow's application* shows most of the same information about the veteran noted above as well as the widow's name, age, residence at time of application, maiden name, date and place of marriage, and date and place of her husband's death. *An application of a child or heir* shows the information about the veteran and widow noted above, the heir's name, heir's place and date of birth, residence at the time of application, and date of the mother's death.

In application files, there are often supporting documents such as discharge papers, affidavits and deposition of witnesses, narratives of events during service (to prove that the veteran had served at a particular time although he might not have documentary evidence), marriage certificates, birth records, death certificates, pages from family Bibles, and other papers.

Requests for Records

Inquiries about pension and bounty land claims should be submitted on NATF Form 80, "Order for Copies of Veterans Records." Instructions for its use and an explanation of how orders are processed are printed on the form. When a pension claim file is found, documents that normally contain the basic information of a personal nature about the veteran and his family will be selected and photocopied. The selected documents generally contain the basic information in the pension file; the remaining documents rarely contain any additional genealogical data. Photocopies of the reproducible papers in the claim file can be furnished for a moderate cost per page.

Revolutionary War Bounty Land Warrant Applications and Pensions

During the Revolutionary War, Congress used pension legislation and the promise of free land to encourage enlistment and the acceptance of commissions. After the war, such legislation constituted a reward for service already rendered. Pension and bounty land warrant applications are based on the participation of American military, naval, and marine officers, and enlisted personnel in the Revolutionary War.

A bounty land warrant application file contains documents relating to claims for bounty lands: an application by the veteran or his widow for a warrant, sometimes a discharge certificate submitted by the veteran or his heirs as evidence of service, and a jacket showing whether the claim was approved or disapproved.

The pension records are arranged in alphabetical order by surname of the veteran. When two or more veterans have the same surname and given name, the further arrangement of the files is generally alphabetical by the State or organization in which a veteran served, or by the words "Continental," "Navy," or some other designation. Within each file, the records are unarranged.

Several types of pension files exist: survivors, widows, rejected, and pre-1800 disability. A fire in the War Department in 1800 destroyed Revolutionary War pension applications and related papers submitted before that date. Consequently, if a veteran applied for a disability or invalid pension before 1800, his file will show his name, the State or organization in which he served, and a file symbol.

Selected Records From Revolutionary War Pension and Bounty Land Warrant Application Files, 1800–1900. M805. 898 rolls. DP.

This publication reproduces records of interest to genealogists selected from the 80,000 pension and bounty land warrant application files. The complete pensions are reproduced on M804.

For a copy of the DP that lists the microfilm available on M805, write Publications Sales Branch (NEPS), Room 505, National Archives, Washington, DC 20408.

Revolutionary War Pension and Bounty Land Warrant Application Files, 1800–1900. M804. 2,670 rolls. DP.

This microfilm publication reproduces in their entirety the 80,000 pension and bounty land warrant application files. The records are arranged in alphabetical order. The names of most of the servicemen for whom a pension or bounty land warrant application files is reproduced in this publication are listed in *Index of Revolutionary War Pension Applications*, by Max E. Hoyt *et. al.*, (Washington, D.C., 1966).

Roll	*Description*
1	Aaron, William–Abbot, Ezra
2	Abbot, George–Abbot, William
3	Abbott, Aaron–Abbott, Moses
4	Abbott, Nathaniel–Abell, Thomas
5	Aber, Israel–Abston, John
6	Acart, Frederick–Ackler, Leonard
7	Ackley, Abraham–Acres, George
8	Acron, Gabriel–Adams, Bryant
9	Adams, Daniel–Adams, Ezekiel
10	Adams, Francis–Adams, Issacher
11	Adams, Jacob–Adams, Joel
12	Adams, John
13	Adams, Jonas–Adams, Luke
14	Adams, Mark–Adams, Phinehas
15	Adams, Reuben–Adams, Shubael
16	Adams, Silas–Adams, Titus

Roll	Description
86	Smit–Smith, R.
87	Smith, S.–Spe
88	Spi–Step
89	Ster–Sto
90	Str–Sy
91	T–Thi
92	Tho–Tim
93	Tin–Turb
94	Turc–Vanr
95	Vans–Walk
96	Wall–Wats
97	Watt–Wes
98	Wet–Wie
99	Wig–Willi
100	Willk–Won
101	Woo–Wr
102	Wu–Z

Indexes to Pensions Including Civil War and Later Service

Old War Index to Pension Files, 1815–1926. T316. 7 rolls. 16mm.

This microfilm publication reproduces a card index to the "Old Wars" series of pension files, 1815–1926. These files relate chiefly to claims based on death or disability incurred in service in the Regular Army, Navy, or Marine Corps between the end of the Revolutionary War in 1783 and the outbreak of the Civil War in 1861.

Each card shows the name of a veteran; the name and class of dependent, if any; the service unit; the application, file, and certificate number; and the State from which the claim was filed.

Roll	Description
1	Aaron, Wm.–Brinson, Zebulon
2	Briscoe, Wm.–Duncan, Alexander
3	Duncan, Daniel C.–Herrin, Lemuel
4	Herring, Charles–McDonnell, James
5	McDonnell, John–Porter, Thomas J.
6	Porter, W.C.B.S.–Sullivan, Dennis
7	Sullivan, Eugene–Zeuinge, Anton

General Index to Pension Files, 1861–1934. T288. 544 rolls. 16mm.

This microfilm publication reproduces a general index to pension files, 1861–1934. The pension applications to which this index applies relate chiefly to Army, Navy, and Marine Corps service performed between 1861 and 1916. Most of the records relate to Civil War service; some relate to earlier service by Civil War veterans; others relate to service in the Spanish-American War, the Philippine Insurrection, the Boxer Rebellion, and the Regular Establishment. There are no records of service in Confederate forces. Confederate pensions were granted by Southern States after the war, and the files are State, not Federal, records. For more information, contact the Museum of the Confederacy, 1201 East Clay Street, Richmond, Va. 23219.

Each card in the general index gives a veteran's name, rank, unit, and term of service; names of dependent(s); the filing date; the application number; the certificate number; and the State from which the claim was filed. The darker cards relate to naval service.

Roll	Description
1	Aab–Ackerman, Garrett
2	Ackerman, George–Adams, Lige
3	Adams, Lincoln–Ah, Her Saw
4	Ah, Qua Rah–Aldrich, Walter
5	Aldrich, Warren–Allen, Clarence
6	Allen, Clarence–Allen, William
7	Allen, William–Americas, Edward
8	Ames, Alge–Anderson, James
9	Anderson, Jas.–Andrews, Dan
10	Andrews, Daniel–Appenfelder, Frederick
11	Appenfelder, Frederick–Armstrong, James
12	Armstrong, James–Arthurs, Abraham
13	Arthur, Robert–Atkinson, Felix
14	Atkinson, Francis–Axe, Lorenzo
15	Axe, Peter–Bacon, Lester
16	Bacon, Levi–Bailey, Samuel
17	Bailey, Samuel O.–Baker, Jacob
18	Baker, Jacob–Baldwin, Julius
19	Baldwin, Justin R.–Bangert, Geo.
20	Bangert, Henry–Barentzen, Lauritz
21	Barepole, Charley–Barnes, James
22	Barnes, James–Barre, Lucius
23	Barre, Onesime–Bartlett, Charles F.
24	Bartlett, Charles G.–Batchelor, Geo.
25	Batchelor, Henry–Baumgardner, Christian
26	Baumgardner, Daniel–Beamen, James
27	Beamenderfer, John H.–Bechtol, George
28	Bechtol, Henry–Beekman, Arthur
29	Beekman, Chancey–Bell, James R.
30	Bell, James R.–Benford, John H.
31	Benford, Joseph–Benning, John
32	Benning, Charles–Bernard, Dennis
33	Bernard, Dennis–Bettman, Alfred
34	Bettman, Gotleib–Biggs, Elijah
35	Biggs, Elisha–Birk, Gottfield
36	Birk, Jacob–Black, John W.
37	Black, John W.–Blair, John W.
38	Blair, Jonas–Blase, Wm. F.
39	Blasedell, Joseph–Bluit, Anthony
40	Bluitt, Lyman–Bogue, Silas
41	Bogue, Stephen–Boner, Peter
42	Boner, Peter–Boreman, Jacob
43	Boreman, Thomas–Boulson, Kenneth
44	Boult, Frank–Bowles, Daniel
45	Bowles, Daniel–Boyo, Wm. H.
46	Boyd, Wm. H.–Bradford, James
47	Bradford, James–Braisted, Wm.
48	Braisure, Amos–Branum, Charles
49	Branum, Charles–Brennan, Jeremiah
50	Brennan, Jeremiah–Brewer, Katie
51	Brewer, Lafayette–Brileya, Peter
52	Brilhart, Hiram–Brockway, Stephen
53	Brockway, Stephen–Brophy, Wm.
54	Brophy, Wm.–Brown, Dennis
55	Brown, Dennis–Brown, James B.
56	Brown, James B.–Brown, Oscar
57	Brown, Oscar–Browne, Byron
58	Browne, Charles–Brussard, Eugen
59	Brusse, Henry–Buck, Haven
60	Buck, Harvey–Bull, James R.
61	Bull, Jefferson–Burd, Wm.
62	Burd, Wm.–Burke, Thomas

Roll	Description
63	Burke, Thomas-Burns, Hiram
64	Burns, Hiram-Burt, Lucius
65	Burt, Luther-Butcher, Jesse
66	Butcher, John-Buzan, Wm.
67	Buzan, Wm.-Cager, Robert
68	Cagg, Andrew-Callahan, John
69	Callahan, John-Campbell, Geo.
70	Campbell, Geo. S.-Canfield, Lewis
71	Canfield, Lewis-Carkhuff, John
72	Carkhuff, Samuel-Carpenter, Harry
73	Carpenter, Harry-Carroll, James
74	Carroll, James-Carter, Lewis
75	Carter, Lewis-Case, Henry O.
76	Case, Henry W.-Castle, Wm. D.
77	Castle, Wm.-Chadwick, Adel
78	Chadwick, Albert-Chance, Wm. T.
79	Chance, Wm. W.-Chappel, Robert
80	Chappel, Robert C.-Cheney, Isaiah
81	Cheney, Ithamar-Chrisman, Lorenzo
82	Chrisman, Luke-Clammer, Jacob
83	Clamor, Engracio-Clark, Hiland
84	Clark, Hinman H.-Clark, Vincent B.
85	Clark, Vincent E.-Cleveland, Albert B.
86	Cleaveland, Albert H.-Cline, Wm.
87	Cline, Wm.-Cobb, Oliver
88	Cobb, Oliver-Coggin, Wm. T.
89	Coggins, Anthony-Cole, Robert H.
90	Cole, Robert M.-Collins, Berta
91	Collins, Bertrand-Colton, Edward
92	Colton, Edward H.-Conger, Alex.
93	Conger, Anson-Connolly, Bart
94	Connolly, Bernard-Cook, Christopher
95	Cook, Christopher-Cooley, Nathan L.
96	Cooley, Nathan M.-Cooper, Wyley
97	Cooper, Youle-Cornelius, Gust.
98	Cornelius, Hardin-Cotter, Michael
99	Cotter, Michael-Cowan, Theodore
100	Cowan, Theodore-Coyle, James J.
101	Coyle, James J.-Crandall, James R.
102	Crandall, James S.-Crays, Andrew
103	Crays, David-Crockett, Francis M.
104	Crockett, Francis T.-Crosser, Adam
105	Crosser, Harrison-Crumrine, Bishop
106	Crumrine, Boyd-Cummins, Oliver
107	Cummins, Orange S.-Curry, Michael
108	Curry, Michael-Dabney, Clark
109	Dabney, Cornelius-Danforth, Clarence
110	Danforth, Clarence-Daniels, Isaiah
111	Daniels, J. S.-Davenport, Alfred
112	Davenport, Alfred-Davis, Decon
113	Davis, Dewey-Davis, John P.
114	Davis, John P.-Davison, Isaiah
115	Davison, Jacob-Dean, Charles B.
116	Dean, Charles B.-Decook, Henry
117	Decook, Peter-Delap, Joseph
118	Delap, Joseph-Dennewitz, Conrad
119	Denney, Abram-Deschler, Maurice
120	Deschler, Valentine-Dewitt, Geo. W.
121	Dewitt, Geo. W.-Dickson, Benjamin
122	Dickson, Benjamin-Dillon, John F.
123	Dillon, John F.-Dixon, Joseph C.
124	Dixon, John-Dohn, Adam
125	Dohn, Andrew-Donnely, William
126	Donnely, William-Doss, Charles

Roll	Description
127	Doss, Charles W.-Dow, Francis R.
128	Dow, Frank-Doyle, Cornelius
129	Doyle, James-Doyle, Jacob
130	Doyle, James-Drinkwater, Alpheus
131	Drinkwater, Charles-Duff, James W.
132	Duff, James W.-Duncan, Joseph
133	Duncan, Joseph-Dunn, Thomas
134	Dunn, Thomas B.-Dutton, Edward
135	Dutton, Edward-Earl, Robert R.
136	Earl, Robert W.-Eberling, Wm.
137	Eberly, Albert M.-Edmonds, John
138	Edmonds, John A.-Eggers, Emil
139	Eggers, Peter-Eliott, Halbert
140	Eliott, James-Ellis, John B.
141	Ellis, John C.-Emerson, James P.
142	Emerson, James R.-Engstrom, John
143	Engstrom, John-Erb, George
144	Erb, Harvey-Estover, George
145	Estrada, Antonio-Evans, Wm. T.
146	Evans, Wm. T.-Failing, Charles
147	Failing, Cornelius-Farmer, Thompson
148	Farmer, Traais-Faunce, George
149	Faunce, Martin-Fennen, Henry
150	Fenner, Albert C.-Fesler, Benjamin
151	Fesler, Cassius A.-Filey, Wm. H.
152	Filley, Wm. H.-Fish, Thomas S.
153	Fish, Thomas J.-Fitch, John A.
154	Fitch, John A.-Flanders, Samuel
155	Flanders, Samuel B.-Flew, William
156	Flewallen, Alfred-Foglesang, Eli W.
157	Foglesang, Nathaniel-Ford, John B.
158	Ford, John-Foster, Aaron
159	Foster, Aaron-Fowler, Olin N.
160	Fowler, Oliver-Francisco, Juan
161	Francisco, Levi-Frech, Henry
162	Frech, Hubert-French, John
163	French, John-Frost, Benjamin
164	Frost, Benjamin-Fuller, John W.
165	Fuller, John W.-Furneisen, H.
166	Furneld, George-Callagher, Jas. H.
167	Gallagher, James H.-Garcelon, W.
168	Garch, Joseph-Garnier, John
169	Garnier, Joseph-Gaston, James
170	Gaston, James W.-Gee, Charles R.
171	Gee, Christopher C.-Gehris, Wilson
172	Gehrike, Albert-German, Linsey
173	German, Littleton-Gibson, James L.
174	Gibson, James M.-Gilbert, John B.
175	Gilbert, John C.-Gilliam, Peter
176	Gilliam, Primus-Givier, Edwin
177	Givier, George-Glidden, Arno
178	Glidden, Augustus-Golden, Andrew
179	Golden, Andrew-Goodrich, Bertrand
180	Goodrich, Bethuel-Gorham, William
181	Gorham, Wm. E.-Gowman, Wm.
182	Gowner, Lewis-Grane, Herman
183	Grane, Mikal O.-Gray, Edward
184	Gray, Edward-Green, David L.
185	Green, David M.-Greenberger, B.
186	Greenburgh, Samuel-Gresh, Henry
187	Gresh, Samuel-Griggs, Albert P.
188	Griggs, Alexander-Gross, Daniel
189	Gross, Daniel-Guest, John W.
190	Guest, Joseph-Gutline, Ethru F.

Roll	Description
191	Gutling, Wm.–Haffner, W.
192	Hafford, B.–Halbert, Silas
193	Halbert, Smith–Hall, Ivory
194	Hall, Ivory A.–Halliman, Thomas
195	Halliman, Wm.–Hamilton, Robert
196	Hamilton, Robert–Hanchett, John
197	Hanchett, Joseph–Hannefin, J.
198	Hanneford, Wm.–Hardin, Robert
199	Hardin, Ruburtus–Harmer, Alfred
200	Harmer, Amos–Harrington, Michael
201	Harrington, Michael B.–Harris, Stephen
202	Harris, Stephen–Hart, Jacob
203	Hart, Jacob–Harvey, Adam
204	Harvey, Albert–Hatch, David G.
205	Hatch, David O.–Haw, William
206	Haw, William–Hayes, Charles W.
207	Hayes, Charles W.–Hazel, Jack
208	Hazel, James H.–Heck, Theodore
209	Hechinger, Clifford–Heiple, Henry
210	Heiple, Henry F.–Henderson, Charles
211	Henderson, Charles–Hennessy, Michael
212	Hennessey, Michael–Hepler, Andrew
213	Hepler, Clarence–Hershey, Isaac
214	Hershey, Isaac–Hibbard, Harris
215	Hibbard, Harry–Higgins, Jason
216	Higgins, Jasper–Hill, Henry H.
217	Hill, Henry H.–Hiltman, Abraham
218	Hiltman, John–Hirschfeld, Emanuel
219	Hirschfeld, Ernest–Hockman, Wm. W.
220	Hockman, Wm. W.–Hoffman, Werner L.
221	Hoffman, Wesley R.–Holder, Edward
222	Holder, Eleano–Holly, Daniel
223	Holly, Daniel W.–Holverson, Frank
224	Holverson, Halver–Hopes, J. Solomon
225	Hopes, Thomas W.–Horney, Joseph
226	Horney, Joseph M.–Houghton, Geo. W.
227	Houghton, Geo. W.–Howard, John
228	Howard, John–Howland, Herbert V.
229	Howland, Herman–Hudon, Louis
230	Hudon, Ombro–Hughes, George
231	Hughes, Geo. W.–Humbell, John
232	Humber, Carroll–Hunt, William
233	Hunt, William–Hurd, Thomas W.
234	Hurd, Thomas–Hutchinson, Mathias
235	Hutchinson, Mayheir–Imfeld, Ferd.
236	Imfeld, Franz–Irvine, Robert W.
237	Irvine, Samuel–Jackson, Charles F.
238	Jackson, Charles F.–Jackson, Wm. A.
239	Jackson, William A.–James, William
240	James, W.–Jauslin, Joseph
241	Jauss, Christian–Jenkins, John
242	Jenkins, John–Jewett, Charles A.
243	Jewett, Charles A.–Johnson, Chris
244	Johnson, Chris–Johnson, James
245	Johnson, James–Johnson, Ogden
246	Johnson, Okey M.–Johnson, Wm. P.
247	Johnson, Wm. Q.–Jones, Chesley
248	Jones, Chesley–Jones, James W.
249	Jones, James. W.–Jones, Smith
250	Jones, Smith E.–Jordan Wm. O.
251	Jordan, William P.–Kaf Fes Sah
252	Kaffey, Martin–Kauble, Benjamin
253	Kauble, Benjamin F.–Keeley, John
254	Keeley, John–Kell, Nathaniel

Roll	Description
255	Kell, Noah–Kellum, Daniel F.
256	Kellum, Edward M.–Kelter, Daniel
257	Keltner, Dion B.–Kennedy, Richard
258	Kennedy, Richard–Kerney, Timothy
259	Kerney, Whit–Keys, Southey
260	Keys, Stephen W.–Kimball, Chas.
261	Kimball, Chas. C.–King, Harry
262	King, Harry–Kinley, Jacob
263	Kinley, James–Kurkendall, Rich.
264	Kirkendall, Robert–Kleinhans, M.
265	Kleinhays, Wm.–Knapp, Zero
266	Knappe, Adolph–Knowlton, Daniel
267	Knowlton, Daniel–Kooner, Thos.
268	Koones, Albert–Kriege, William
269	Kriegel, Emil F.–Kurtz, John
270	Kurtz, John–LaGraff, John B.
271	LaGraff, Michael–LaMont, John
272	Lamont, John–Lane, John M.
273	Lane, John M.–Lapay, Pedro
274	Lape, Aamon–Lathbury, John
275	Lathe, Abner P.–Lawrence, Edward
276	Lawrence, Edward–Leach, James
277	Leach, James M.–Lee, Dwight, M.
278	Lee, Earl–Leger, William
279	Legere, Andrew–Lennon, Edward
280	Lennon, Francis–Levan, Obediah
281	Leven, Oscar–Lewis, Joseph
282	Lewis, Joseph–Lewis, Wm. I.
283	Lewis, Wm. J.–Lincoln, Thomas
284	Lincoln, Thomas A.–Linson, Lyman
285	Linson, Theo.–Livermore, Ben.
286	Livermore, Ben. W.–Loftus, Martin
287	Loftus, Martin V.–Long, Wm. H.
288	Long, William, J.–Loucks, Peter
289	Loucks, Peter B.–Lowe, Wm.
290	Lowe, Wm.–Ludwig, John
291	Ludwig, John–Lyle, Wm. W.
292	Lyles, Alexander–Lythe, Wm. C.
293	Lytle, Aaron W.–McCabe, Francis
294	McCabe, Francis–McCartney, Wm.
295	McCartney, Wm.–McClintick, H.
296	McClintick, Henry C.–McComb, John
297	McComb, John–McCormic, Touson
298	McCormic, H.–McCume, P.
299	McCume, Philip–McDonald, John
300	McDonald, John W.–McFadden, Alex.
301	McFadden, Alex.–McGinnis, Edward J.
302	McGinnis, Edward J.–McGuire, John
303	McGuire, John–McKain, James
304	McKain, James–McKibbin, James
305	McKibben, James F.–McLaughlin, James B.
306	McLaughlin, James B.–McMican, Joseph
307	McMichael, Abraham–McNeil, George
308	McNeil, George–McTigue, Michael
309	McTigue, Patrick–Maglalang, Julian
310	Maglalang, Marce–Malarkey, Dennis
311	Malarkey, James–Mangan, John
312	Mangan, John–Manuel, Marcelin
313	Manuel, Mark–Marlin, Wm. T.
314	Marline, Aaron A.–Marshall, Thomas
315	Marshall, Thomas–Martin, John
316	Martin, John–Mary, Matthew
317	Marx, Michael–Mathers, John D.
318	Mathers, John F.–Mattoon, Charles

Roll	*Description*
319	Mattoon, Charles H.–Mayer, George
320	Mayer, George–Mechling, Amos
321	Mechling, Augustus A.–Melcoon, Samuel
322	Meloon, Samuel S.–Merithew, Wm. H.
323	Meritt, Allen–Metcalf, James
324	Metcalf, James–Mickleborough, F.
325	Mickleby, Theo. A.–Miller, Anthony M.
326	Miller, Anthony W.–Miller, Henry L.
327	Miller, Henry M.–Miller, Marvin
328	Miller, May E.–Millington, Thos.
329	Millington, Wm.–Minnis, Charles
330	Minnis, Charles M.–Mitchell, Thos.
331	Mitchell, Thomas–Monaghan, Thomas
332	Monaghan, Thomas–Moody, Jesse G.
333	Moody, John–Moore, Henry H.
334	Moore, Henry W.–Moore, Wm. H.
335	Moore, Wm. H.–Moran, James
336	Moran, James J.–Morgan, Samuel
337	Morgan, Samuel B.–Morris, Samuel P.
338	Morris, Samuel P.–Morinmer, Mabel
339	Mortimer, Marcellus–Moulton, Frank
340	Moulton, Frank P.–Mullane, Wm. H.
341	Mullaney, Anthony–Munson, Fred
342	Munson, Fred–Murphy, Thomas
343	Murphy, Thomas–Myers, Geo. A.
344	Myers, Geo. B.–Nash, Charles A.
345	Nash, Charles A.–Neff, John M.
346	Neff, John S.–Nesbitt, Wm. E.
347	Nesbitt, Wm. E.–Newman, Lazarus
348	Newman, Leon–Nichols, Wilber
349	Nichols, Wilbur–Noble, Geo. W.
350	Noble, Geo. W.–Norris, Isaac
351	Norris, Isaac–Nuckles, Wm. H.
352	Nuckolls, Asa H.–O'Brien, John
353	O'Brien, John–O'Donnell, Daniel
354	O'Donnell, Daniel–Olds, Isaac
355	Olds, Isaac–O'Neal, John T.
356	O'Neal, John T.–Orr, William
357	Orr, William–Otly, James L.
358	Otman, Sylvester–Owens, Thomas
359	Owens, Thomas–Painter, Jacob
360	Painter, Jacob–Pama, Erasmo
361	Pamanyag, Vincente–Parker, Jacob W.
362	Parker, James–Parrett, Joseph
363	Parrett, Dawson A.–Patterson, Alonzo
364	Patterson, Alonzo F.–Paulter, John
365	Paulus, Abraham–Peary, John
366	Peary, John C.–Pence, Francis W.
367	Pence, Franklin–Perkins, Isa
368	Perkins, Isaac–Perry, Thos. H.
369	Perry, Thomas H.–Pettegreew, Wm.
370	Pettengail, Clark–Philipsen, Herman
371	Philipsen, One V.H.–Pick, Earle
372	Pick, Ernest–Pigott, John
373	Pigott, John–Pixley, John S.
374	Pixley, John W.–Plunket, Wm.
375	Plunkett, Abraham–Pool, Thomas
376	Pool, Thomas–Post, Joseph
377	Post, Joseph–Powell, Thomas
378	Powell, Thomas–Prentice, Geo. W.
379	Prentice, Geo. W.–Price, Timothy
380	Price, Timothy–Pruett, Daniel
381	Pruett, Daniel B.–Putnam, John J.
382	Putnam, John L.–Quino, Flavio

Roll	*Description*
383	Quino, Marcelino–Rambo, William
384	Rambo, William–Rannie, Alexander
385	Rannie, Geo. A.–Ray, John G.
386	Ray, John E.–Records, Thos. S.
387	Records, Thompson, L.–Reed, John A.
388	Reed, John A.–Reeves, Thomas F.
389	Reeves, Thos G.–Reissig, Adolph
390	Reissig, John–Reynolds, Edmund
391	Reynolds, Edwin–Rhone, Dandridge
392	Rhone, Daniel L.–Richards, John
393	Richards, John O.–Richmond, Wm. R.
394	Richmond Wm. S.–Rigby, Wm. H.
395	Rigby, Wm. H.–Rinier, Peter
396	Rinier, Samuel–Rizer, William
397	Rizer, Wm.–Roberts, Geo. F.
398	Roberts, Geo. F.–Robilliard, John
399	Robin, Alfred–Robinson, Robert A.
400	Robinson, Robt.–Robinson, Wm. F.
401	Robinson, Wm. G.–Roe, Charles
402	Roe, Charles–Rogge, Charles H.
403	Rogge, Diedrich–Root, John E.
404	Root, John E.–Ross, George
405	Ross, George–Roush, George
406	Roush, George A.–Rubin, Arcadio
407	Rubio, Charles–Rupley, Henry
408	Rupley, Henry C.–Russum, J.
409	Russum, John W.–Sabin, Charles C.
410	Sabin, Frederick–Sames, Pearl
411	Sames, William J.–Sandquist, Gustave
412	Sandra, Francis H.–Saunders, John R.
413	Saunders, John R.–Savage, Isom
414	Savage, Jacob–Schaefer, Nicholas
415	Schafer, Nicholas–Schlaich, Henry
416	Schlaich, John–Schnelzer, Francis
417	Schnemilch, Wm.–Schuler, Wm. H.
418	Schuler, Wm. W.–Scott, Charles H.
419	Scott, Charles H.–Scoville, Thomas
420	Scoville, Wallace–Sedelbauer, John L.
421	Sedello, Pablo–Sells, David L.
422	Sells, David M.–Shade, Geo. W.
423	Shade, Harry–Shannon, William J.
424	Shannon, Wm. J.–Shaw, Prince
425	Shaw, Rodney K.–Sheldon, Shepard L.
426	Sheldon, Shepard–Sherman, Chas. A.
427	Sherman, Charles A.–Shinkle, Erastus
428	Shinkle, Eugen M.–Short, John H.
429	Short, John J.–Shuttlesworth, Wm. R.
430	Shuttleton, John–Sim, Archibald
431	Sim, Archie–Simpson, James W.
432	Simpson, James W.–Siver, Robert
433	Siver, Robert–Slaughter, Wm. R.
434	Slaughter, Wm. K.–Smathers, Reuben
435	Smathers, Robert F.–Smith, Chas. G.
436	Smith, Chas. G.–Smith, George
437	Smith, George–Smith, Jacob
438	Smith, Jacob–Smith, John H.
439	Smith, John H.–Smith, John J.
440	Smith, John L.–Smith, Oscar C.
441	Smith, Oscar–Smith, Varde
442	Smith, Varius Q.–Snakle, Peter
443	Snaman Geo. W.–Snyder, James K.
444	Snyder, James L.–Soules, Francis
445	Soules, Benjamin–Speakman, Charles
446	Speakman, Charles Y.–Spickler, Benjamin

Roll	Description
447	Spickler, Chas.–Spurgeon, Jeremiah
448	Spurgeon, Jeremiah–Stanbrough, Joseph B.
449	Stanbrough, Levi–Starling, Abraham
450	Starlin, Adam–Steerman, Charles
451	Steers, Abraham–Sterling, John B.
452	Sterling, John C.–Stevenson, Wm.
453	Stevenson, Wm.–Stickle, Wm. H.
454	Stickle, Wm. H.–Stoddard, Hez.
455	Stoddard, John A.–Stork, Wm.
456	Stork, William–Strauch, Thomas
457	Strauch, Wm.–Stryhn, Louis
458	Stryke, Chas.–Sullivan, Edward
459	Sullivan, Edward–Surkant, Louis
460	Surd, Albert–Swartwood, Almond
461	Swartwood, Alonzo–Swink, Fred
462	Swink, Fred–Tallmadge, Mose
463	Tallmadge, Nenell–Taylor, Chas. E.
464	Taylor, Charles F.–Taylor, George S.
465	Taylor, George T.–Taylor, Septimus
466	Taylor, Seth B.–Temple, Palmer C.
467	Temple, Park E.–Tharp, Washington
468	Tharp, Wilber A.–Thomas, George
469	Thomas, George–Thomas, William
470	Thomas, Wm.–Thompson, Henry R.
471	Thompson, Henry R.–Thompson, Thos.
472	Thompson, Thomas–Thost, Julius
473	Thostenson, Ole–Tilford, Lewis
474	Tilford, Nicholas–Tittsworth, James
475	Tittsworth, John C.–Tompkins, Addison
476	Tompkins, Albert–Towle, Elisha
477	Towle, Ethelbert–Trask, James H.
478	Trask, James H.–Triplett, James H.
479	Triplett, James H.–Truman, Geo. W.
480	Truman, Geo. W.–Tullar, John F.
481	Tullar, John M.–Turner, Leander
482	Turner, Leander–Tyas, Jonathan
483	Tyas, Richard–Underwood, Alonzo
484	Underwood, Ambrose–Valentine, Levi
485	Valentine, Levi–Vandermark, Abram
486	Vandermark, Abram–VanMarter, John
487	VanMarter, Joseph–VanZant, Henry
488	VanZant, Henry P.–Vermillion, Marcus
489	Vermillion, Martin–Visscher, Geo.
490	Visscher, Henry–Vreeland, Benjamin
491	Vreeland, Charles–Wagner, Jasper
492	Wagner, Jeremiah–Waldron, Isaac
493	Waldron, James–Walker, Lyman
494	Walker, Lyman–Wallace, Jos.
495	Wallace, Joseph–Walter, Andrew A.
496	Walter, Andrew F.–Wandross, Mingo
497	Wands, Alburtus–Wardell, George J.
498	Wardell, Henry–Warren, Alonzo
499	Warren, Alonzo S.–Washington, Geo.
500	Washington, Geo.–Watkins, John B.
501	Watkins, John C.–Watt, Levi
502	Watt, Levi–Weaver, Geo. K.
503	Weaver, George–Weber, Adolph
504	Weber, Adolph–Weeks, David
505	Weidenhamer, Chas. H.–Welch, John
506	Welch, John–Wells, James W.
507	Wells, James–Wentzel, Samuel
508	Wentzel, Simon–West, Prima
509	West, Ralph M.–Whalen, James B.
510	Whalen, James E.–Wheelock, DeForest
511	Wheelock, Edgar L.–White, Charles
512	White, Charles L.–White, Jordan
513	White, Joseph–Whitehead, William K.
514	Whitehead, Wm. W.–Whitlock, Henry L.
515	Whitlock, Hiran E.–Whitten, Geo. W.
516	Whitten, Gilman–Wiesman, Berhard
517	Wiesman, Ferdinand–Wilcoxen, Anthony
518	Wilcoxen, Charles–Wilkerson, Gus
519	Weeks, David–Willan, Thomas
520	Willan, Charles B.–Williams, Daniel
521	Williams, Daniel–Williams, Jacob
522	Williams, Jacob–Williams, Manuel
523	Williams, Mansfield–Williams, Wm. H.
524	Williams, Wm. H.–Willoughby, Wm. A.
525	Willoughby, Wm. A.–Wilson, George
526	Wilson, Geo. A.–Wilson, Joseph
527	Wilson, Joseph–Wilson, Wm. S.
528	Wilson, Wm. S.–Winkley, Edson S.
529	Winkley, Frank H.–Wise, Edward M.
530	Wise, Edward W.–Wixson, Mengo
531	Wixson, Robert–Wolverton, Isaac
532	Wolverton, Jacob–Wood, James
533	Wood, James–Woodcock, Alexander
534	Woodcock, Almon–Woods, Patrick F.
535	Woods, Patrick H.–Wootton, Burton
536	Wootton, Daniel H.–Wright, Alexander
537	Wright, Alexander B.–Wright, Louis
538	Wright, Louis H.–Wyatt, Frederick
539	Wyatt, Garland M.–Yates, Asa
540	Yates, Aubyn Arthur–York, Dan C.
541	York, Daniel–Young, David I.
542	Young, David J.–Young, Rutledge E.
543	Young, Salathiel–Zellman, John
544	Zellman, Wm.–Zytkoskie, Edmund

Index to Mexican War Pension Files, 1887–1926. T317. 14 rolls. 16mm.

This microfilm publication reproduces an alphabetical index to Mexican War pension files, 1887–1926. These pension files are based on service performed in 1846–48. An entry in this index shows the name of a veteran; the name and class of dependent, if any; service data; the application number; and, for an approved claim, the pension certificate number and the State from which the claim was made.

Roll	Description
1	Aaron–Anderson, Aucley
2	Anderson, Charles–Brooks, James H.
3	Brooks, James M.–Cooley, Edward
4	Cooley, Horace K.–Elmore, Stephen
5	Elmore, Thomas–Griffith, Wm. A.
6	Griffith, Wm. D.–Howard, Joshua
7	Howard, Josiah–Lazenby, Robert
8	Lea, Adolphe–Memorank, F.
9	Menard, Alfred B.–Ott, Wm. H.
10	Otten, Heinrich–Robeson, Robert
11	Robey, Thomas–Smith, John
12	Smith, John–Usher, John P.
13	Ussey, Wm. J.–Wright, J. P.
14	Wright, John T.–Zexick, Wm.

Index to Indian Wars Pension Files, 1892–1926. T318. 12 rolls. 16mm.

This microfilm publication reproduces a card index to pension files relating to service in the Indian campaigns between 1817 and 1898. An entry in this index shows the name of a veteran; the name and class of dependent, if any; service data; the application number; and, for an approved claim, the pension certificate number and the State from which the claim was made.

For pension application files concerning men who were disabled or killed in Indian wars and in whose behalf no service claims were made, see the records in the "Old Wars" series. For pension applications relating to persons who served in Indian campaigns during the War of 1812, Mexican War, or Civil War, see the pension indexes relating to claims based on service in those wars.

Roll	*Description*
1	Aagard, Andrew J.–Bent, Wm.
2	Bentall, Maurice–Chalmers, James
3	Chalmers, Tom Green–Dingins, Mose
4	Dingler, John T.–Gerhardt, John
5	Gerhardt, Karl–Hines, Squire
6	Hines, Wiley–Kirk, Charles
7	Kirk, Frederick–McDonald, Samuel T.
8	McDonald, Sidney B.–Na-Te-Cli
9	Nat-O-E–Ready, George
10	Regan, Daniel–Smith, John
11	Smith, Aaron–Truckey, Nicholas
12	True, Judson E.–Zweig, Louis

Organization Index to Pension Files of Veterans Who Served Between 1861 and 1900. T289. 765 rolls. 16mm.

The index cards reproduced on this microfilm publication refer to pension applications of veterans who served in the U.S. Army between 1861 and 1917. The majority of the records pertain to Civil War veterans, but they also include veterans of the Spanish-American War, the Philippine Insurrection, Indian wars, and World War I.

The information provided here is virtually the same as that in the *General Index to Pension Files, 1861–1934,* T288. Unlike the alphabetical *General Index,* however, this index groups the applicants according to the units in which they served. The cards are arranged alphabetically by State, thereunder by arm of service (infantry, cavalry, artillery), thereunder numerically by regiment, and thereunder alphabetically by veteran's surname.

Each card gives the soldier's name, rank, unit, and terms of service; names of relationships of any dependents; the application number; the certificate number; and the State from which the claim was filed.

A list of abbreviations used in the roll listings follows:

Abbreviation	*Full name*
Art.	Artillery
Bn.	Batallion
Brig.	Brigade
Btry.	Battery
C.A.C.	Coast Artillery Corps
Cav.	Cavalry
Engs.	Engineers
Engs. & Mech.	Engineers & Mechanics
Enroll.	Enrolled
F & S	Field and Staff
Gds.	Guards
Gen. Serv.	General Service
H. Art.	Heavy Artillery
H.G.	Home Guard
Hosp.	Hospital
Ind. Terr.	Indian Territory
Indep.	Independent
Inf.	Infantry
L. Art.	Light Artillery
Mech.	Mechanic
Med.	Medical
Mil.	Militia
Mtd.	Mounted
Phil.	Philippine
Prov.	Provisional
Q.M.	Quartermaster
Q.M.D.	Quartermaster Department
Regt.	Regiment
Res.	Reserve(s)
SAW	Spanish-American War
Squad.	Squadron
SS	Sharp Shooters
Unassign.	Unassigned
Unatt.	Unattached
U.S.A.	U.S. Army
Vet.	Veterans
V.R.C.	Veterans Reserve Corps
Vols.	Volunteers

Roll	*Co., Regiment*	*Name*
Alabama:		
1	Unassign., 1 Ala. Col'd Inf.– Co. C, 29 Ala. Inf.	
Alabama–Arkansas:		
2	Unassign., 1 Ala. Inf. (SAW)– Co. A, 1 Ark. Inf.	
Arkansas:		
3	Co. B, 1 Ark. Inf.– Co. A, 1 Ark. Cav.	
4	Co. B, 1 Ark. Cav.– Co. K, 3 Ark. Cav.	
5	Co. L, 3 Ark. Cav.– Co. L, 2 Ark. Inf. (SAW)	
Arkansas–California:		
6	Co. M, 2 Ark. Inf. (SAW)– Co. E, 6 Calif. Inf.	
California:		
7	Co. F, 6 Calif. Inf.– Co. L, 2 Calif. Cav.	
8	Co. M, 2 Calif. Cav.– Co. E, 8 Calif. Inf. (SAW)	
California–Colorado:		
9	Co. F, 8 Calif. Inf. (SAW)– Co. K, 1 Colo. Cav.	
Colorado:		
10	Co. L, 1 Colo. Cav.– Btry. A, 1 Colo. Lt. Art. (SAW)	
Connecticut:		
11	F & S, 1 Conn. Inf.– Co. C, 6 Conn. Inf.	
12	Co. D, 6 Conn. Inf.– Co. B, 9 Conn. Inf.	
13	Co. C, 9 Conn. Inf.– Co. A, 12 Conn. Inf.	
14	Co. B, 12 Conn. Inf.– F & S, 15 Conn. Inf.	
15	Co. A, 15 Conn. Inf.– Co. C, 18 Conn. Inf.	

Roll	Co., Regiment	Name
16	Co. D, 18 Conn. Inf.–	
	Co. C, 22 Conn. Inf.	
17	Co. D, 22 Conn. Inf.–	
	Co. C, 27 Conn. Inf.	
18	Co. D, 27 Conn. Inf.–	Conn. Cav.
	Co. B, 1 Conn. H. Art.	
19	Co. C, 1 Conn. H. Art.–	
	Co. M, 2 Conn. H. Art.	
Connecticut–North Dakota:		
20	Indep. Btry., 1 Conn. Lt. Art.–	
	Co. I, 1 N. Dak. Inf. (SAW)	
North Dakota–Delaware:		
21	Co. M, 1 N. Dak. Inf. (SAW)–	
	Co. F, 3 Del. Inf.	
Delaware:		
22	Co. G, 3 Del. Inf.–	
	Co. C, 1 Del. Cav.	
Delaware–District of Columbia:		
23	Co. D, 1 Del. Cav.–	
	Co. A, 2 Bn., D.C. Inf.	
District of Columbia:		
24	Co. B, 2 Bn., D.C. Inf.–	
	Co. M, 1 D.C. Inf.	
Florida–Georgia:		
25	F & S, 1 Fla. Cav.–	
	2 Ga. Inf. (SAW)	
Georgia–Illinois:		
26	Co. A, 2 Ga. Inf. (SAW)–	
	Co. C, 7 Ill. Inf.	Murphy
Illinois:		
27	Co. D, 7 Ill. Inf.–	
	Co. A, 9 Ill. Inf.	
28	Co. B, 9 Ill. Inf.–	
	Co. I, 10 Ill. Inf.	
29	Co. K, 10 Ill. Inf.–	
	Co. F, 12 Ill. Inf.	
30	Co. G, 12 Ill. Inf.–	
	Co. A, Vet. Bn., 14/15 Ill. Inf.	
31	Co. B, Vet. Bn., 14/15 Ill. Inf.–	
	Co. I, 16 Ill. Inf.	
32	Co. K, 16 Ill. Inf.–	
	Co. F, 19 Ill. Inf.	
33	Co. G, 19 Ill. Inf.–	
	Co. H, 22 Ill. Inf.	
34	Co. I, 22 Ill. Inf.–	
	Co. I, 25 Ill. Inf.	
35	Co. K, 25 Ill. Inf.–	
	Co. I, 28 Ill. Inf.	Likes
36	Co. I, 28 Ill. Inf.–	McCoy
	Co. A, 31 Ill. Inf.	
37	Co. B, 31 Ill. Inf.–	
	Co. G, 33 Ill. Inf.	
38	Co. H, 33 Ill. Inf.–	
	Co. E, 36 Ill. Inf.	
39	Co. F, 36 Ill. Inf.–	
	Co. F, 39 Ill. Inf.	
40	Co. G, 39 Ill. Inf.–	
	Co. H, 42 Ill. Inf.	
41	Co. I, 42 Ill. Inf.–	
	Co. D, 45 Ill. Inf.	
42	Co. E, 45 Ill. Inf.–	
	Co. F, 47 Ill. Inf.	
43	Co. G, 47 Ill. Inf.–	
	Co. A, 50 Ill. Inf.	
44	Co. B, 50 Ill. Inf.–	
	F & S, 53 Ill. Inf.	
45	Co. A, 53 Ill. Inf.–	
	Co. K, 56 Ill. Mech. Fusilers	
46	F & S, 56 Ill. Inf.–	
	Co. H, 58 Ill. Inf.	
47	Co. I, 58 Ill. Inf.–	
	Co. F, 61 Ill. Inf.	
48	Co. G, 61 Ill. Inf.–	
	Co. G, 64 Ill. Inf.	
49	Co. H, 64 Ill. Inf.–	
	Co. F, 67 Ill. Inf.	
50	Co. G, 67 Ill. Inf.–	
	Co. B, 72 Ill. Inf.	
51	Co. C, 72 Ill. Inf.–	
	Co. K, 75 Ill. Inf.	
52	F & S, 76 Ill. Inf.–	
	Co. A, 79 Ill. Inf.	
53	Co. B, 79 Ill. Inf.–	
	— , 83 Ill. Inf.	
54	Co. A, 83 Ill. Inf.–	
	Co. H, 86 Ill. Inf.	
55	Co. I, 86 Ill. Inf.–	
	Co. B, 91 Ill. Inf.	
56	Co. C, 91 Ill. Inf.–	
	Co. G, 94 Ill. Inf.	
57	Co. H, 94 Ill. Inf.–	
	Co. B, 98 Ill. Inf.	
58	Co. C, 98 Ill. Inf.–	
	Co. H, 101 Ill. Inf.	
59	Co. I, 101 Ill. Inf.–	
	Co. H, 105 Ill. Inf.	
60	Co. I, 105 Ill. Inf.–	
	Co. B, 110 Ill. Inf.	
61	Co. C, 110 Ill. Inf.–	
	Co. K, 113 Ill. Inf.	
62	F & S, 114 Ill. Inf.–	
	Co. B, 118 Ill. Inf.	
63	Co. C, 118 Ill. Inf.–	
	Co. I, 122 Ill. Inf.	
64	Co. K, 122 Ill. Inf.–	
	Co. G, 128 Ill. Inf.	
65	Co. H, 128 Ill. Inf.–	
	Co. B, 131 Ill. Inf.	
66	Co. C, 131 Ill. Inf.–	
	Co. H, 135 Ill. Inf.	
67	Co. I, 135 Ill. Inf.–	
	Co. D, 140 Ill. Inf.	
68	Co. E, 140 Ill. Inf.–	
	Co. H, 144 Ill. Inf.	
69	Co. I, 144 Ill. Inf.–	
	Co. I, 148 Ill. Inf.	
70	Co. K, 148 Ill. Inf.–	
	Co. C, 153 Ill. Inf.	
71	Co. D, 153 Ill. Inf.–	
	Misc. Ill. Vols.	
72	F & S, 1 Ill. Cav.–	
	Co. B, 3 Ill. Cav.	
73	Co. C, 3 Ill. Cav.–	
	Co. A, 5 Ill. Cav.	
74	Co. B, 5 Ill. Cav.–	
	Co. B, 7 Ill. Cav.	
75	Co. C, 7 Ill. Cav.–	
	Co. M, 8 Ill. Cav.	
76	F & S, 9 Ill. Cav.–	
	Co. L, 10 Ill. Cav.	Lynch
77	Co. L, 10 Ill. Cav.–	McGee
	Co. G, 12 Ill. Cav.	
78	Co. H, 12 Ill. Cav.–	

Roll	Co., Regiment	Name
	Co. A, 15 Ill. Cav.	
79	Co. B, 15 Ill. Cav.–	
	F & S, 1 Ill. Lt. Art.	
80	Co. A, 1 Ill. Lt. Art.–	
	Co. D, 2 Ill. Lt. Art.	
81	Co. E, 2 Ill. Lt. Art.–	
	Co. I, 1 Ill. Inf. (SAW)	
82	Co. K, 1 Ill. Inf. (SAW)–	
	Co. G, 4 Ill. Inf. (SAW)	
83	Co. H, 4 Ill. Inf. (SAW)–	
	Co. H, 7 Ill. Inf. (SAW)	
84	Co. I, 7 Ill. Inf. (SAW)–	
	Co. K, 1 Ill. Cav. (SAW)	
Illinois–Indiana:		
85	Co. L, 1 Ill. Cav. (SAW)–	
	Co. A, 8 Ind. Inf.	
Indiana:		
86	Co. B, 8 Ind. Inf.–	
	Co. A, 10 Ind. Inf.	
87	Co. B, 10 Ind. Inf.–	
	F & S, 12 Ind. Inf.	
88	Co. A, 12 Ind. Inf.–	
	Co. K, 13 Ind. Inf.	
89	F & S, 14 Ind. Inf.–	
	F & S, 17 Ind. Inf.	
90	Co. A, 17 Ind. Inf.–	
	F & S, 20 Ind. Inf.	
91	Co. A, 20 Ind. Inf.–	
	Co. C, 22 Ind. Inf.	
92	Co. D, 22 Ind. Inf.–	
	Co. F, 24 Ind. Inf.	
93	Co. G, 24 Ind. Inf.–	
	F & S, 27 Ind. Inf.	
94	Co. A, 27 Ind. Inf.–	
	Co. G, 30 Ind. Inf.	
95	Co. H, 30 Ind. Inf.–	
	Co. C, 33 Ind. Inf.	
96	Co. D, 33 Ind. Inf.–	
	Co. H, 35 Ind. Inf.	
97	Co. I, 35 Ind. Inf.–	
	Co. H, 38 Ind. Inf.	
98	Co. I, 38 Ind. Inf.–	
	Co. F, 42 Ind. Inf.	
99	Co. G, 42 Ind. Inf.–	
	Co. H, 44 Ind. Inf.	
100	Co. I, 44 Ind. Inf.–	
	Co. I, 48 Ind. Inf.	
101	Co. K, 48 Ind. Inf.–	
	Co. G, 51 Ind. Inf.	
102	Co. H, 51 Ind. Inf.–	
	Co. K, 53 Ind. Inf.	
103	F & S, 54 Ind. Inf.–	
	Co. K, 57 Ind. Inf.	
104	F & S, 58 Ind. Inf.–	
	Co. D, 60 Inf. Ind.	
105	Co. E, 60 Ind. Inf.–	
	Co. A, 67 Ind. Inf.	
106	Co. B, 67 Ind. Inf.–	
	Co. F, 70 Ind. Inf.	
107	Co. G, 70 Ind. Inf.–	
	Co. C, 74 Ind. Inf.	
108	Co. D, 74 Ind. Inf.–	
	Co. D, 80 Ind. Inf.	
109	Co. E, 80 Ind. Inf.–	
	Co. D, 84 Ind. Inf.	
110	Co. E, 84 Ind. Inf.–	
	Co. A, 88 Ind. Inf.	

Roll	Co., Regiment	Name
111	Co. B, 88 Ind. Inf.–	
	Co. E, 93 Ind. Inf.	
112	Co. F, 93 Ind. Inf.–	
	Co. D, 101 Ind. Inf.	
113	Co. E, 101 Ind. Inf.–	
	Co. D, 118 Ind. Inf.	
114	Co. E, 118 Ind. Inf.–	
	Co. A, 128 Ind. Inf.	
115	Co. B, 128 Ind. Inf.–	
	Co. A, 133 Ind. Inf.	
116	Co. B, 133 Ind. Inf.–	
	Co. A, 137 Ind. Inf.	
117	Co. B, 137 Ind. Inf.–	
	F & S, 142 Ind. Inf.	
118	Co. A, 142 Ind. Inf.–	
	Co. A, 146 Ind. Inf.	
119	Co. B, 146 Ind. Inf.–	
	Co. I, 149 Ind. Inf.	
120	Co. K, 149 Ind. Inf.–	
	Co. G, 153 Ind. Inf.	
121	Co. H, 153 Ind. Inf.–	
	F & S & Band, 158 Ind. Inf. (SAW)	
122	Co. A, 158 Ind. Inf. (SAW)–	
	Co. M, 160 Ind. Inf. (SAW)	
123	F & S, 161 Ind. Inf. (SAW)–	
	Co. C, 1 Ind. Cav.	
124	Co. D, 1 Ind. Cav.–	
	Unassign. and F & S, 4 Ind. Cav.	
125	Co. A, 4 Ind. Cav.–	
	Co. H, 6 Ind. Cav.	
126	Co. I, 6 Ind. Cav.–	
	Co. F, 9 Ind. Cav.	
127	Co. G, 9 Ind. Cav.–	
	Co. K, 12 Ind. Cav.	
128	Co. L, 12 Ind. Cav.–	
	Btry. 1 Indep. Btry. Ind. Lt. Art.	
129	Indep. Btry.(2) Ind. Lt. Art.–	
	Indep. Btry., 20 Ind. Lt. Art. (Ind. Ter.)	
130	Indep. Btry., 21 Ind. Lt. Art.–	
	Co. M, 3 Ind. H.G. Inf.	
Indiana–Iowa:		
131	F & S, 4 Ind. T.H.G. Inf.–	
	Co. K, 3 Iowa Inf.	
Iowa:		
132	F & S, 4 Iowa Inf.–	
	Co. B, 7 Iowa Inf.	
133	Co. C, 7 Iowa Inf.–	
	F & S, 10 Iowa Inf.	
134	Co. A, 10 Iowa Inf.–	
	Co. K, 12 Iowa Inf.	
135	Unassign. and F & S, 13 Iowa Inf.–	
	Co. C, 15 Iowa Inf.	
136	Co. D, 15 Iowa Inf.–	
	Co. C, 18 Iowa Inf.	
137	Co. D, 18 Iowa Inf.–	
	Co. K, 21 Iowa Inf.	
138	F & S, 22 Iowa Inf.–	
	Co. F, 25 Iowa Inf.	
139	Co. G, 25 Iowa Inf.–	
	Unassign. and F & S, 29 Iowa Inf.	
140	Co. A, 29 Iowa Inf.–	
	Co. C, 32 Iowa Inf.	
141	Co. D, 32 Iowa Inf.–	
	Co. I, 34 Iowa Inf.	
142	Co. K, 34 Iowa Inf.–	
	Co. E, 38 Iowa Inf.	

Roll	Co., Regiment	Name
143	Co. F, 38 Iowa Inf.– Co. C, 45 Iowa Inf.	
144	Co. D, 45 Iowa Inf.– Co. M, 49 Iowa Inf. (SAW)	
145	Unassign. and F & S, 50 Iowa Inf. (SAW)– Co. L, 52 Iowa Inf. (SAW)	
146	Co. M, 52 Iowa Inf. (SAW)– Co. H, 2 Iowa Cav.	
147	Co. I, 2 Iowa Cav.– Co. H, 4 Iowa Cav.	
148	Co. I, 4 Iowa Cav.– Co. C, 7 Iowa Cav.	
149	Co. D, 7 Iowa Cav.– Indep. Btry., 2 Iowa Lt. Art.	
Iowa–Kansas:		
150	Indep. Btry., 3 Iowa Lt. Art.– Co. K, 3 Kans. Inf.	
Kansas:		
151	Co. L, 3 Kans. Inf. & Cav.– Co. B, 7 Kans. Cav.	
152	Co. C, 7 Kans. Cav.– Co. A, 10 Kans. Inf.	
153	Co. B, 10 Kans. Inf.– Co. A, 13 Kans. Inf.	
154	Co. B, 13 Kans. Inf.– Co. I, 16 Kans. Cav.	
155	Co. K, 16 Kans. Cav.– Co. I, 21 Kans. Inf. (SAW)	
156	Co. K, 21 Kans. Inf. (SAW)– Indep. Btry., 2 Kans. Lt. Art.	Longacre
Kansas–Kentucky:		
157	Indep. Btry., 2 Kans. Lt. Art.– Co. E, 3 Ky. Inf.	McKinzey
Kentucky:		
158	Co. F, 3 Ky. Inf.– Co. E, 6 Ky. Inf.	
159	Co. F, 6 Ky. Inf.– Co. D, 9 Ky. Inf.	
160	Co. E, 9 Ky. Inf.– Co. F, 12 Ky. Inf.	
161	Co. G, 12 Ky. Inf.– Co. D, 15 Ky. Inf.	
162	Co. E, 15 Ky. Inf.– Co. C, 18 Ky. Inf.	
163	Co. D, 18 Ky. Inf.– Co. K, 21 Ky. Inf.	
164	Unassign. and F & S, 22 Ky. Inf.– F & S, 28 Ky. Inf.	
165	Co. A, 28 Ky. Inf.– Co. A, 32 Ky. Inf.	
166	Co. B, 32 Ky. Inf.– Co. B, 39 Ky. Inf.	
167	Co. C, 39 Ky. Inf.– Co. K, 45 Ky. Inf.	
168	Unassign. Misc., 46 Ky. Inf.– Co. H, 52 Ky. Mtd. Inf.	Lucas
169	Co. I, 52 Ky. Mtd. Inf.– Co. A, Halls Gap Bn., Capitol Gds. Ky. Inf.	
170	Co. B, Halls Gap Bn., Capitol Gds. Ky. Inf.– Co. H, 1 Ky. Cav.	Luttrell
171	Co. H, 1 Ky. Cav.– Co. L, 4 Ky. Cav.	McClanahan
172	F & S, 5 Ky. Cav.– Co. I, 7 Ky. Cav.	
173	Co. K, 7 Ky. Cav.– Co. K, 10 Ky. Cav.	
174	Co. L, 10 Ky. Cav.– Co. K, 13 Ky. Cav.	
175	Co. L, 13 Ky. Cav.– Co. K, 17 Ky. Cav.	
176	Co. L, 17 Ky. Cav.– Co. A, 3 Ky. Inf. (SAW)	
Kentucky–Louisiana:		
177	Co. B, 3 Ky. Inf. (SAW)– Co. B, 2 La. Inf.	
Louisiana:		
178	Co. C, 2 La. Inf.– Co. K, 4 La. Corps d'Afrique Inf.	
179	Co. A, 5 La. Corps d'Afrique Inf.– Co. I, 11 La. Corps d'Afrique Inf.	
180	Co. K, 11 La. Corps d'Afrique Inf.– Co. F, 1 La. Corps d'Afrique Engs.	
181	Co. G, 1 La. Corps d'Afrique Engs.– Co. K, 1 La. Inf. (SAW)	
Louisiana–Maine:		
182	Co. L, 1 La. Inf. (SAW)– Co. E, 3 Maine Inf.	
Maine:		
183	Co. F, 3 Maine Inf.– Co. K, 6 Maine Inf.	
184	Unassign. and F & S, 7 Maine Inf.– Co. E, 9 Maine Inf.	
185	Co. F, 9 Maine Inf.– Co. B, 12 Maine Inf.	
186	Co. C, 12 Maine Inf.– Co. G, 14 Maine Inf.	
187	Co. H, 14 Maine Inf.– Co. B, 17 Maine Inf.	
188	Co. C, 17 Maine Inf.– Co. C, 20 Maine Inf.	
189	Co. D, 20 Maine Inf.– Co. C, 24 Maine Inf.	
190	Co. D, 24 Maine Inf.– Unassign. and F & S, 29 Maine Inf.	
191	Co. A, 29 Maine Inf.– Co. H & Unassign., 31 Maine Inf.	
192	Co. I, 31 Maine Inf.– Unassign. And F & S, 1 Maine Cav.	
193	Co. A, 1 Maine Cav.– Co. L, 1 Maine Cav.	Ludden
194	Co. L, 1 Maine Cav.– Co. G, 1 Maine H. Art.	McAllister
195	Co. H, 1 Maine H. Art.– Co. F, 1 Maine Inf. (SAW)	
Maine–Maryland:		
196	Co. G, 1 Maine Inf. (SAW)– Co. F, 2 Md. Inf.	
Maryland:		
197	Co. G, 2 Md. Inf.– Co. H, 5 Md. Inf.	
198	Co. I, 5 Md. Inf.– Co. K, 9 Md. Inf.	Roach
199	Unassign. and F & S, 10 Md. Inf.– Co. I, 13 Md. Inf.	
200	Co. K, 13 Md. Inf.– Co. C, 2 Md. Inf., Potomac Home Brig.	
201	Co. D, 2 Md. Inf., Potomac Home Brig.– Co. C, 1 Md. Cav.	
202	Co. D, 1 Md. Cav.–	

Roll	Co., Regiment	Name
	Co. A, Purnell Legion, Md. Cav.	
Maryland–Massachusetts:		
203	Co. B, Purnell Legion, Md. Cav.–	
	F & S, 1 Mass. Inf.	
Massachusetts:		
204	Co. A, 1 Mass. Inf.–	
	Co. D, 3 Mass. Inf.	
205	Co. E, 3 Mass. Inf.–	
	Co. A, 5 Mass. Inf.	
206	Co. B, 5 Mass. Inf.–	
	Co. E, 7 Mass. Inf.	
207	Co. F, 7 Mass. Inf.–	
	Co. K, 9 Mass. Inf.	
208	Unassign. and F & S, 10 Mass. Inf.–	
	Co. G, 12 Mass. Inf.	
209	Co. H, 12 Mass. Inf.–	
	Co. A, 16 Mass. Inf.	
210	Co. B, 16 Mass. Inf.–	
	Co. D, 18 Mass. Inf.	
211	Co. E, 18 Mass. Inf.–	
	Co. I, 20 Mass. Inf.	
212	Co. K, 20 Mass. Inf.–	
	Co. G, 23 Mass. Inf.	
213	Co. H, 23 Mass. Inf.–	
	Co. A, 26 Mass. Inf.	
214	Co. B, 26 Mass. Inf.–	
	Co. G, 28 Mass. Inf.	
215	Co. H, 28 Mass. Inf.–	
	Co. E, 31 Mass. Inf.	
216	Co. F, 31 Mass. Inf.–	
	Co. I, 33 Mass. Inf.	
217	Co. K, 33 Mass. Inf.–	
	Co. F, 36 Mass. Inf.	
218	Co. G, 36 Mass. Inf.–	
	Co. D, 39 Mass. Inf.	
219	Co. E, 39 Mass. Inf.–	
	Co. G, 42 Mass. Inf.	
220	Co. H, 42 Mass. Inf.–	
	Co. D, 46 Mass. Inf.	
221	Co. E, 46 Mass. Inf.–	
	Co. C, 50 Mass. Inf.	
222	Co. D, 50 Mass. Inf.–	
	Unassign. and F & S, 54 Mass. Inf.	
223	Co. A, 54 Mass. Inf.–	
	Co. B, 57 Mass. Inf.	
224	Co. C, 57 Mass. Inf.–	
	Co. E, 59 Mass. Inf.	
225	Co. F, 59 Mass. Inf.–	
	Unattached, 25 Unatt. Co. Mass. Inf.	
226	Unattached, 26 Unatt. Co. Mass. Inf.–	
	Co. L, 2 Mass. Cav.	Swank
227	Unassign. and F & S, 3 Mass. Cav.–	
	Co. F, 5 Mass. Cav.	
228	Co. G, 5 Mass. Cav.–	
	Co. F, 2 Mass. H. Art.	
229	Co. G, 2 Mass. H. Art.–	
	Co. I, 4 Mass. H. Art.	
230	Co. K, 4 Mass. H. Art.–	
	Indep. Btry., 13 Mass. Lt. Art.	
231	Indep. Btry., 14 Mass. Lt. Art.–	
	Co. A, 8 Mass. Inf. (SAW)	
Massachusetts–Michigan:		
232	Co. B, 8 Mass. Inf. (SAW)–	
	Co. I, 1 Mich. Inf.	
Michigan:		
233	Co. K, 1 Mich. Inf.–	
	Co. A, 4 Mich. Inf.	

Roll	Co., Regiment	Name
234	Co. B, 4 Mich. Inf.–	
	Co. H, 6 Mich. Inf.	
235	Co. I, 6 Mich. Inf.–	
	Co. G, 9 Mich. Inf.	
236	Co. H, 9 Mich. Inf.–	
	Co. C, 12 Mich. Inf.	
237	Co. D, 12 Mich. Inf.–	
	Co. E, 14 Mich. Inf.	
238	Co. F, 14 Mich. Inf.–	
	Co. G, 17 Mich. Inf.	
239	Co. H, 17 Mich. Inf.–	
	Co. C, 21 Mich. Inf.	
240	Co. D, 21 Mich. Inf.–	
	Co. A, 24 Mich. Inf.	
241	Co. B, 24 Mich. Inf.–	
	Co. K, 27 Mich. Inf.	
242	Unassign. and F & S, 28 Mich. Inf.–	
	Co. L, 31 Mich. Inf. (SAW)	
243	Co. M, 31 Mich. Inf. (SAW)–	
	Co. G, 35 Mich. Inf. (SAW)	
244	Co. H, 35 Mich. Inf. (SAW)–	
	Co. G, 1 Mich. Engs. & Mech.	
245	Co. H, 1 Mich. Engs. & Mech.–	
	F & S, 2 Mich. Cav.	
246	Co. A, 2 Mich. Cav.–	
	Co. C, 4 Mich. Cav.	
247	Co. D, 4 Mich. Cav.–	
	Co. B, 7 Mich. Cav.	
248	Co. C, 7 Mich. Cav.–	
	Co. C, 9 Mich. Cav.	
249	Co. D, 9 Mich. Cav.–	
	Co. B, 1 Mich. Lt. Art.	
	and U.S. Lancers, Mich. Cav.	
Michigan–Minnesota:		
250	Co. C, 1 Mich. Lt. Art.–	
	Co. A, 1 Minn. Inf.	Lyons
Minnesota:		
251	Co. A, 1 Minn. Inf.–	McCulloch
	Co. I, 3 Minn. Inf.	
252	Co. K, 3 Minn. Inf.–	
	Co. B, 7 Minn. Inf.	
253	Co. C, 7 Minn. Inf.–	
	Co. F, 11 Minn. Inf.	
254	Co. G, 11 Minn. Inf.–	
	Co. I, 14 Minn. Inf. (SAW)	
255	Co. K, 14 Minn. Inf. (SAW)–	
	Co. E, Hatch's Bn., Minn. Cav.	
Minnesota–Mississippi:		
256	Co. F, Hatch's Bn., Minn. Cav.–	
	Co. D, 6 Miss. Inf.	
Mississippi:		
257	Co. E, 6 Miss. Inf.–	
	Co. E, 3 Miss. Inf. (SAW)	
Mississippi–Missouri:		
258	Co. F, 3 Miss. Inf. (SAW)–	
	Co. D, 4 Mo. Inf.	
Missouri:		
259	Co. E, 4 Mo. Inf.–	
	Co. C, 9 Mo. Inf.	
260	Co. D, 9 Mo. Inf.–	
	Co. A, 14 Mo. Inf.	
261	Co. B, 14 Mo. Inf.–	
	Co. E, 21 Mo. Inf.	
262	Co. F, 21 Mo. Inf.–	
	Co. E, 25 Mo. Inf.	Fletcher
263	Co. E, 25 Mo. Inf.–	Guyer
	Co. B, 31 Mo. Inf.	

Roll	Co., Regiment	Name
264	Co. C, 31 Mo. Inf.–	
	Cos. intermingled, 37 Mo. Inf.	
265	Cos. intermingled, 38 Mo. Inf.–	Collins
	Co. I, 43 Mo. Inf.	
266	Co. K, 43 Mo. Inf.–	
	Co. E, 48 Mo. Inf.	
267	Co. F, 48 Mo. Inf.–	
	Co. E, 2 Mo. Col'd. Inf.	
268	Co. F, 2 Mo. Col'd Inf.–	
	Co. C, 5 Prov. Enroll. Mo. Militia	
269	Co. D, 5 Prov. Enroll. Mo. Militia–	
	Co. I, 9 Prov. Enroll. Mo. Militia	
270	Cos. intermingled, 10 Enroll. Mo. Militia–	
	Co. C, 44 Enroll. Mo. Militia	
271	Co. D, 44 Enroll. Mo. Militia–	
	Co. B, 69 Enroll. Mo. Militia	
272	Co. C, 69 Enroll. Mo. Militia–	
	Co. K, Mo. Engs. of the West	
273	Co. L, Mo. Engs. of the West–	
	Co. F, Cass County Mo. H.G. Cav.	
274	Co. G, Cass County Mo. H.G. Cav.–	
	Mayo's Prov. Enroll. Mo. Militia	
275	Co. Mercer, Bn. Mo. Militia Inf.–	
	Co. D, Webster County Mo. H.G.	
276	Westerberg's Indep. Co., Mo. Militia Cav.–	
	Co. I, 1 U.S. Res. Corps, Mo. Inf.	
277	Co. K, 1 U.S. Res. Corps, Mo. Inf.–	
	Co. F, 1 Bn. U.S. Res. Corps, Mo. Inf.	
278	F & S, 1 Mo. State Militia Inf.–	
	Co. C, 1 Mo. Cav.	
279	Co. D, 1 Mo. Cav.–	
	Co. F, 3 Mo. Cav.	
280	Co. G, 3 Mo. Cav.–	
	Co. D, 6 Mo. Cav.	
281	Co. E, 6 Mo. Cav.–	
	Co. C, 10 Mo. Cav.	
282	Co. D, 10 Mo. Cav.–	
	Co. F, 13 Mo. Cav.	
283	Co. G, 13 Mo. Cav.–	
	Co. I, 2 Bn. Mo. Militia Cav.	Murphey
284	Cos. intermingled, 10 Bn. Mo. Militia Cav.–	
	Co. C, 3 Mo. State Militia Cav.	Orendor
285	Co. C, 3 Mo. State Militia Cav.–	Payton
	Co. I, 5 Mo. State Militia Cav.	
286	Co. K, 5 Mo. State Militia Cav.–	
	Co. H, 8 Mo. State Militia Cav.	
287	Co. I, 8 Mo. State Militia Cav.–	
	Co. C, 11 Mo. State Militia Cav.	Loeffler
288	Co. C, 11 Mo. State Militia Cav.–	McCallister
	Co. L, 1 Mo. Lt. Art.	
289	Co. M, 1 Mo. Lt. Art.–	
	Co. G, 1 Mo. Inf. (SAW)	
290	Co. H, 1 Mo. Inf. (SAW)–	
	Co. G, 5 Mo. Inf. (SAW)	
Missouri–Nebraska:		
291	Co. H, 5 Mo. Inf. (SAW)–	
	Co. I, 1 Neb. Cav.	
Nebraska:		
292	Co. K, 1 Neb. Cav.–	
	F & S and Unassign., 3 Neb. Inf. (SAW)	
Nebraska–New Hampshire:		
293	Co. A, 3 Neb. Inf. (SAW)–	
	Co. B, 3 New Hamp. Inf.	

Roll	Co., Regiment	Name
New Hampshire:		
294	Co. B, 3 New Hamp. Inf.–	
	Co. F & S, 6 New Hamp. Inf.	
295	Co. A, 6 New Hamp. Inf.–	
	Co. C, 9 New Hamp. Inf.	
296	Co. D, 9 New Hamp. Inf.–	
	Co. B, 13 New Hamp. Inf.	
297	Co. C, 13 New Hamp. Inf.–	
	Co. E, 18 New Hamp. Inf.	
298	Co. F, 18 New Hamp. Inf.–	
	Co. I, 1 New Hamp. H. Art.	
New Hampshire–New Jersey:		
299	Co. K, 1 New Hamp. H. Art.–	
	Co. D, 2 N.J. Inf.	
New Jersey:		
300	Co. E, 2 N.J. Inf.–	
	Co. K, 4 N.J. Inf.	
301	F & S, 5 N.J. Inf.–	
	Co. B, 8 N.J. Inf.	
302	Co. C, 8 N.J. Inf.–	
	Co. K, 10 N.J. Inf.	
303	F & S, 11 N.J. Inf.–	
	Co. G, 13 N.J. Inf.	
304	Co. H, 13 N.J. Inf.–	
	Co. I, 22 N.J. Inf.	
305	Co. K, 22 N.J. Inf.–	
	Co. F, 27 N.J. Inf.	
306	Co. G, 27 N.J. Inf.–	
	Co. C, 33 N.J. Inf.	
307	Co. D, 33 N.J. Inf.–	
	Co. K, 38 N.J. Inf.	
308	F & S, 39 N.J. Inf.–	
	Co. E, 2 N.J. Cav.	
309	Co. F, 2 N.J. Cav.–	
	Co. G, 1 N.J. Inf. (SAW)	
New Jersey–New Mexico:		
310	Co. H, 1 N.J. Inf. (SAW)–	
	Co. E, 1 New Mex. Inf.	
New Mexico:		
311	Co. F, 1 New Mex. Inf.–	
	Vigil's New Mex. Cav.	
New Mexico–New York:		
312	Simpson's Indep. Mtd. Spies & Scouts, New Mex.–	
	Co. A, 5 N.Y. Inf.	Loud
New York:		
313	Co. A, 5 N.Y. Inf.–	McAuliffe
	Co. B, 8 N.Y. Inf.	
314	Co. C, 8 N.Y. Inf.–	
	Co. C, 11 N.Y. Inf.	
315	Co. D, 11 N.Y. Inf.–	
	Co. B, 16 N.Y. Inf.	
316	Co. C, 16 N.Y. Inf.–	
	Co. G, 20 N.Y. Inf.	
317	Co. H, 20 N.Y. Inf.–	
	Co. D, 25 N.Y. Inf.	
318	Co. E, 25 N.Y. Inf.–	
	Co. D, 29 N.Y. Inf.	
319	Co. E, 29 N.Y. Inf.–	
	Co. G, 34 N.Y. Inf.	
320	Co. H, 34 N.Y. Inf.–	
	Co. C, 39 N.Y. Inf.	
321	Co. D, 39 N.Y. Inf.–	
	F & S, 42 N.Y. Inf.	
322	Co. A, 42 N.Y. Inf.–	
	Co. I, 45 N.Y. Inf.	

Roll	Co., Regiment	Name
323	Co. K, 45 N.Y. Inf.–	
	Co. A, 49 N.Y. Inf.	
324	Co. B, 49 N.Y. Inf.–	
	Co. C, 54 N.Y. Inf.	
325	Co. D, 54 N.Y. Inf.–	
	Co. E, 58 N.Y. Inf.	
326	Co. F, 58 N.Y. Inf.–	
	Co. C, 109 N.Y. Inf.	Worrick
Entire 59 N.Y. Inf., also Co. G, 106 N.Y. Inf. (beginning with McNanny). See roll 340.		
327	Unassign. and F & S, 60 N.Y. Inf.–	
	Co. F, 63 N.Y. Inf.	
328	Co. G, 63 N.Y. Inf.–	
	Co. D, 67 N.Y. Inf.	
329	Co. E, 67 N.Y. Inf.–	
	Co. G, 70 N.Y. Inf.	
330	Co. H, 70 N.Y. Inf.–	
	Co. B, 75 N.Y. Inf.	
331	Co. C, 75 N.Y. Inf.–	
	Co. A, 78 N.Y. Inf.	
332	Co. B, 78 N.Y. Inf.–	
	Co. H, 81 N.Y. Inf.	
333	Co. I, 81 N.Y. Inf.–	
	Co. E, 85 N.Y. Inf.	
334	Co. F, 85 N.Y. Inf.–	
	Co. B, 90 N.Y. Inf.	
335	Co. C, 90 N.Y. Inf.–	
	Co. I, 92 N.Y. Inf.	
336	Co. K, 92 N.Y. Inf.–	
	Co. I, 95 N.Y. Inf.	
337	Co. K, 95 N.Y. Inf.–	
	Co. F, 98 N.Y. Inf.	
338	Co. G, 98 N.Y. Inf.–	
	Co. B, 102 N.Y. Inf.	
339	Co. C, 102 N.Y. Inf.–	
	Co. G, 106 N.Y. Inf.	Lyman (see roll 326)
340	Co. G, 106 N.Y. Inf.–	Mead (see roll 326)
	Co. C, 109 N.Y. Inf.	
341	Co. D, 109 N.Y. Inf.–	
	Co. F, 112 N.Y. Inf.	
342	Co. G, 112 N.Y. Inf.–	
	Co. A, 117 N.Y. Inf.	
343	Co. B, 117 N.Y. Inf.–	
	Co. I, 120 N.Y. Inf.	
344	Co. K, 120 N.Y. Inf.–	
	Co. C, 124 N.Y. Inf.	
345	Co. D, 124 N.Y. Inf.–	
	Co. C, 128 N.Y. Inf.	Lyden
346	Co. C, 128 N.Y. Inf.–	
	Co. E, 134 N.Y. Inf.	McKown
347	Co. F, 134 N.Y. Inf.–	
	Co. C, 140 N.Y. Inf.	
348	Co. D, 140 N.Y. Inf.–	
	Co. I, 143 N.Y. Inf.	
349	Co. K, 143 N.Y. Inf.–	
	Co. F, 147 N.Y. Inf.	
350	Co. G, 147 N.Y. Inf.–	
	Co. D, 151 N.Y. Inf.	
351	Co. E, 151 N.Y. Inf.–	
	Co. H, 154 N.Y. Inf.	
352	Co. I, 154 N.Y. Inf.–	
	Co. B, 160 N.Y. Inf.	
353	Co. C, 160 N.Y. Inf.–	
	Co. I, 162 N.Y. Inf.	
354	Co. K, 162 N.Y. Inf.–	

Roll	Co., Regiment	Name
	Co. I, 173 N.Y. Inf.	
355	Co. K, 173 N.Y. Inf.–	
	Co. C, 182 N.Y. Inf.	
356	Co. D, 182 N.Y. Inf.–	
	Co. D, 188 N.Y. Inf.	
357	Co. E, 188 N.Y. Inf.–	
	Co. D, 7 N.Y. Mil. Inf.	
358	Co. E, 7 N.Y. Mil. Inf.–	
	Co. H, 20 N.Y. Mil. Inf.	
359	Co. I, 20 N.Y. Mil. Inf.–	
	Co. B, 69 N.Y. Mil. Inf.	
360	Co. C, 69 N.Y. Mil. Inf.–	
	Co. E, 1 N.Y. Engs.	
361	Co. F, 1 N.Y. Engs.–	
	Co. A, 50 N.Y. Engs.	
362	Co. B, 50 N.Y. Engs.–	
	Co. B, 1 N.Y. Mtd. Rifles	
363	Co. C, 1 N.Y. Mtd. Rifles–	
	Co. M, 1 N.Y. Cav.	
364	Unassign. and F & S, 2 N.Y. Cav.–	
	Co. L, 3 N.Y. Cav.	Libeau
365	Co. L, 3 N.Y. Cav.–	McCarthy
	Co. B, 7 N.Y. Cav.	
366	Co. C, 7 N.Y. Cav.–	
	Co. C, 9 N.Y. Cav.	
367	Co. D, 9 N.Y. Cav.–	
	Co. H, 11 N.Y. Cav.	
368	Co. I, 11 N.Y. Cav.–	
	Co. G, 15 N.Y. Cav.	
369	Co. H, 15 N.Y. Cav.–	
	Co. C, 20 N.Y. Cav.	
370	Co. D, 20 N.Y. Cav.–	
	Co. B, 24 N.Y. Cav.	
371	Co. C, 24 N.Y. Cav.–	
	Co. A, 2 N.Y. Vet. Cav.	
372	Co. B, 2 N.Y. Vet. Cav.–	
	Co. E, 3 N.Y. Prov. Cav.	
373	Co. F, 3 N.Y. Prov. Cav.–	
	Co. L, 1 N.Y. Lt. Art.	
374	Co. M, 1 N.Y. Lt. Art.–	
	Co. B, 3 N.Y. Lt. Art.	
375	Co. C, 3 N.Y. Lt. Art.–	
	Co. E, 4 N.Y. H. Art.	
376	Co. F, 4 N.Y. H. Art.–	
	Co. L, 5 N.Y. H. Art.	
377	Co. M, 5 N.Y. H. Art.–	
	Co. A, 7 N.Y. H. Art.	
378	Co. B, 7 N.Y. H. Art.–	
	Co. A, 9 N.Y. H. Art.	
379	Co. B, 9 N.Y. H. Art.–	
	Co. C, 10 N.Y. H. Art.	
380	Co. D, 10 N.Y. H. Art.–	
	Co. B, 14 N.Y. H. Art.	
381	Co. C, 14 N.Y. H. Art.–	
	Co. B, 16 N.Y. H. Art.	
382	Co. C, 16 N.Y. H. Art.–	
	6 Indep. Btry., N.Y. Lt. Art.	
383	7 Indep. Btry., N.Y. Lt. Art.–	
	30 Indep. Btry., N.Y. Lt. Art.	
384	31 Indep. Btry., N.Y. Lt. Art.–	
	Co. C, 8 N.Y. Inf. (SAW)	
385	Co. D, 8 N.Y. Inf. (SAW)–	
	Co. F, 22 N.Y. Inf. (SAW)	
386	Co. G, 22 N.Y. Inf. (SAW)–	
	Co. I, 71 N.Y. Inf. (SAW)	

Roll	Co., Regiment	Name
New York–North Carolina:		
387	Co. K, 77 N.Y. Inf. (SAW)– Co. E, 1 N.C. Inf.	
North Carolina:		
388	Co. F, 1 N.C. Inf.– Misc. Vols.–N.C., Unknown Service, Unassign. recruits, Citizens Vol., some SAW	
North Carolina–Ohio:		
389	F & S, 1 N.C. Inf. (SAW)– Co. F, 1 Ohio Inf.	
Ohio:		
390	Co. G, 1 Ohio Inf.– Co. F, 4 Ohio Inf.	
391	4 Ohio Inf.– Co. E, 7 Ohio Inf.	
392	Co. F, 7 Ohio Inf.– Co. A, 11 Ohio Inf.	
393	Co. B, 11 Ohio Inf.– Co. A, 12 Ohio Inf.	
394	Co. B, 12 Ohio Inf.– Co. F, 14 Ohio Inf.	
395	Co. G, 14 Ohio Inf.– Co. I, 16 Ohio Inf.	
396	Co. K, 16 Ohio Inf.– Co. H, 18 Ohio Inf.	
397	Co. I, 18 Ohio Inf.– Co. H, 20 Ohio Inf.	
398	Co. I, 20 Ohio Inf.– Co. C, 23 Ohio Inf.	
399	Co. D, 23 Ohio Inf.– Co. C, 26 Ohio Inf.	
400	Co. D, 26 Ohio Inf.– Co. F, 29 Ohio Inf.	
401	Co. G, 29 Ohio Inf.– Co. C, 32 Ohio Inf.	
402	Co. D, 32 Ohio Inf.– Co. E, 35 Ohio Inf.	
403	Co. F, 35 Ohio Inf.– Co. E, 38 Ohio Inf.	
404	Co. F, 38 Ohio Inf.– Co. G, 41 Ohio Inf.	
405	Co. H, 41 Ohio Inf.– Co. I, 44 Ohio Inf.	Titus
406	Co. K, 44 Ohio Inf.– Co. C, 48 Ohio Inf.	
407	Co. D, 48 Ohio Inf.– Co. B, 49 Ohio Inf.	
408	Co. C, 49 Ohio Inf.– Co. B, 52 Ohio Inf.	
409	Co. C, 52 Ohio Inf.– Co. I, 55 Ohio Inf.	Love
410	Co. I, 55 Ohio Inf.– Co. F, 59 Ohio Inf.	McConnell
411	Co. G, 59 Ohio Inf.– Co. G, 62 Ohio Inf.	
412	Co. H, 62 Ohio Inf.– Co. I, 65 Ohio Inf.	
413	Co. K, 65 Ohio Inf.– Unassign. and F & S, 69 Ohio Inf.	
414	Co. A, 69 Ohio Inf.– Co. I, 72 Ohio Inf.	
415	Co. K, 72 Ohio Inf.– Co. D, 76 Ohio Inf.	
416	Co. E, 76 Ohio Inf.– Co. F, 79 Ohio Inf.	
417	Co. G, 79 Ohio Inf.– Co. I, 82 Ohio Inf.	
418	Co. K, 82 Ohio Inf.– Co. E, 86 Ohio Inf.	
419	Co. F, 86 Ohio Inf.– Co. G, 89 Ohio Inf.	
420	Co. H, 89 Ohio Inf.– Co. H, 91 Ohio Inf.	
421	Co. I, 91 Ohio Inf.– Co. D, 92 Ohio Inf.	
422	Co. E, 92 Ohio Inf.– Co. D, 96 Ohio Inf.	
423	Co. E, 96 Ohio Inf.– Co. G, 100 Ohio Inf.	
Co. D of the 99 Ohio Inf. follows Co. H.		
424	Co. H, 100 Ohio Inf.– Co. I, 104 Ohio Inf.	
425	Co. K, 104 Ohio Inf.– Co. E, 110 Ohio Inf.	
426	Co. F, 110 Ohio Inf.– Unassign. and F & S, 115 Ohio Inf.	Sharer
427	Co. A, 115 Ohio Inf.– Co. I, 120 Ohio Inf.	
428	Co. K, 120 Ohio Inf.– Unassign. and F & S, 125 Ohio Inf.	
429	Co. A, 125 Ohio Inf.– Co. I, 129 Ohio Inf.	
430	Co. I, 129 Ohio Inf.– Co. I, 134 Ohio Inf.	
431	Co. K, 134 Ohio Inf.– Co. F, 140 Ohio Inf.	
432	Co. G, 140 Ohio Inf.– Co. E, 145 Ohio Inf.	
433	Co. F, 145 Ohio Inf.– Co. D, 150 Ohio Inf.	
434	Co. E, 150 Ohio Inf.– Co. F, 155 Ohio Inf.	
435	Co. G, 155 Ohio Inf.– Co. E, 161 Ohio Inf.	
436	Co. F, 161 Ohio Inf.– Unassign. and F & S, 167 Ohio Inf.	
437	Co. A, 167 Ohio Inf.– Co. B, 172 Ohio Inf.	
438	Co. C, 172 Ohio Inf.– Co. H, 176 Ohio Inf.	
439	Co. I, 176 Ohio Inf.– Co. F, 181 Ohio Inf.	
440	Co. G, 181 Ohio Inf.– Co. G, 185 Ohio Inf.	
441	Co. H, 185 Ohio Inf.– Co. A, 191 Ohio Inf.	
442	Co. B, 191 Ohio Inf.– Co. G, 195 Ohio Inf.	
443	Co. H, 195 Ohio Inf.– Misc. & Unknown, Various Ohio Cos.	Lyons
444	Misc. & Unknown, Various Ohio Cos.– Co. A, 3 Ohio Cav.	McCaslin
445	Co. B, 3 Ohio Cav.– Co. E, 5 Ohio Cav.	
446	Co. F, 5 Ohio Cav.– Co. C, 8 Ohio Cav.	
447	Co. D, 8 Ohio Cav.– Co. B, 11 Ohio Cav.	
448	Co. C, 11 Ohio Cav.– —, 3 Indep. Ohio Cav.	
449	—, 4 Indep. Ohio Cav.– Co. L, 2 Ohio H. Art.	
450	Co. M, 2 Ohio H. Art.–	

Roll	Co., Regiment	Name
	—, 5 Indep. Btry., Ohio Lt. Art.	
451	—, 6 Indep. Btry., Ohio Lt. Art.–	
	Co. C, 1 Ohio Inf. (SAW)	
452	Co. D, 1 Ohio Inf. (SAW)–	
	Co. H, 4 Ohio Inf. (SAW)	
453	Co. I, 4 Ohio Inf. (SAW)–	
	Co. C, 8 Ohio Inf. (SAW)	
Ohio–Oregon:		
454	Co. D, 8 Ohio Inf. (SAW)–	
	Misc., Various Oregon Cos. (including some Indian wars)	
Oregon–Pennsylvania:		
455	Unassign. and F & S, 1 Oregon Inf.–	
	Co. K, 2 Pa. Inf.	
Pennsylvania:		
456	F & S, 3 Pa. Inf.–	
	Co. A, 11 Pa. Inf.	
457	Co. B, 11 Pa. Inf.–	
	Co. C, 17 Pa. Inf.	
458	Co. D, 17 Pa. Inf.–	
	Co. H, 24 Pa. Inf.	
459	Co. I, 24 Pa. Inf.–	
	Co. N, 28 Pa. Inf.	
460	Co. O, 28 Pa. Inf.–	
	Co. G, 32 Pa. Inf.	
461	Co. H, 32 Pa. Inf.–	
	Co. D, 35 Pa. Inf.	
462	Co. E, 35 Pa. Inf.–	
	Co. I, 39 Pa. Inf.	
463	Co. K, 39 Pa. Inf.–	
	Co. H, 45 Pa. Inf.	
464	Co. I, 45 Pa. Inf.–	
	Co. F, 48 Pa. Inf.	
465	Co. G, 48 Pa. Inf.–	
	Co. B, 51 Pa. Inf.	
466	Co. C, 51 Pa. Inf.–	
	Co. I, 53 Pa. Inf.	
467	Co. K, 53 Pa. Inf.–	
	Co. F, 56 Pa. Inf.	
468	Co. G, 56 Pa. Inf.–	
	Co. D, 61 Pa. Inf.	
469	Co. E, 61 Pa. Inf.–	
	Co. B, 67 Pa. Inf.	
470	Co. C, 67 Pa. Inf.–	
	Co. A, 72 Pa. Inf.	
471	Co. B, 72 Pa. Inf.–	
	Co. K, 76 Pa. Inf.	
472	Co. H, 76 Pa. Inf.–	
	Co. C, 78 Pa. Inf.	
473	Co. D, 78 Pa. Inf.–	
	Co. B, 82 Pa. Inf.	
474	Co. C, 82 Pa. Inf.–	
	Co. G, 84 Pa. Inf.	
475	Co. H, 84 Pa. Inf.–	
	Co. A, 87 Pa. Inf.	
476	Co. B, 87 Pa. Inf.–	
	Co. C, 91 Pa. Inf.	
477	Co. D, 91 Pa. Inf.–	
	Co. L, 95 Pa. Inf.	
478	Co. F, 96 Pa. Inf.–	
	Co. I, 98 Pa. Inf.	
479	Co. K, 98 Pa. Inf.–	
	Co. B, 101 Pa. Inf.	
480	Co. C, 101 Pa. Inf.–	
	Co. G, 103 Pa. Inf.	
481	Co. H, 103 Pa. Inf.–	
	Co. F, 106 Pa. Inf.	

Roll	Co., Regiment	Name
482	Co. G, 106 Pa. Inf.–	
	Co. E, 111 Pa. Inf.	
483	Co. F, 111 Pa. Inf.–	
	Co. E, 119 Pa. Inf.	
484	Co. F, 119 Pa. Inf.–	
	Co. F, 125 Pa. Inf.	Lewis
485	Co. F, 125 Pa. Inf.–	McClure
	Co. C, 130 Pa. Inf.	
486	Co. D, 130 Pa. Inf.–	
	Co. I, 134 Pa. Inf.	Folks
487	Co. I, 134 Pa. Inf.–	Hague
	Co. H, 139 Pa. Inf.	
488	Co. I, 139 Pa. Inf.–	
	Co. I, 143 Pa. Inf.	
489	Co. K, 143 Pa. Inf.–	
	Co. K, 148 Pa. Inf.	
490	Unassign. and F & S, 149 Pa. Inf.–	
	F & S, 155 Pa. Inf.	
491	Co. A, 155 Pa. Inf.–	
	Co. D, 167 Pa. Inf.	
492	Co. E, 167 Pa. Inf.–	
	Co. H, 173 Pa. Inf.	
493	Co. I, 173 Pa. Inf.–	
	Co. B, 183 Pa. Inf.	
494	Co. C, 183 Pa. Inf.–	
	Co. I, 188 Pa. Inf.	
495	Co. K, 188 Pa. Inf.–	
	Co. B, 193 Pa. Inf.	
496	Co. C, 193 Pa. Inf.–	
	Co. H, 197 Pa. Inf.	
497	Co. I, 197 Pa. Inf.–	
	Co. I, 201 Pa. Inf.	
498	Co. K, 201 Pa. Inf.–	
	Unassign. and F & S, 207 Pa. Inf.	
499	Co. A, 207 Pa. Inf.–	
	Co. G, 211 Pa. Inf.	
500	Co. H, 211 Pa. Inf.–	
	Co. C, 29 Pa. Mil. Inf.	Lowe
501	Varied, not in order, 29 Pa. Mil. Inf.–	McCarter
	Varied, not in order, 54 Pa. Mil. Inf.	Lyon
502	Varied, not in order, 54 Pa. Mil. Inf.–	McAteer
	Varied, not in order, Erie Pa. Inf.	Lytle
503	Varied, not in order, Erie Pa. Inf.–	McClelland
	Misc., Pa. Cav.	Manns
504	Varied, not in order, Mason's Bn., Pa. Mil.–	
	Co. K, 2 Pa. Cav.	
	*There is 1 Inf.: Mason's Bn., Pa. Mil.	
505	Co. L, 2 Pa. Cav.–	
	Unassign. and F & S, 5 Pa. Cav.	
506	Co. A, 5 Pa. Cav.–	
	Co. M, 6 Pa. Cav.	
507	Co. B, 7 Pa. Cav.–	
	Co. B, 9 Pa. Cav.	
508	Co. C, 9 Pa. Cav.–	
	Co. H, 12 Pa. Cav.	
509	Co. I, 12 Pa. Cav.–	
	Co. A, 15 Pa. Cav.	
510	Co. B, 15 Pa. Cav.–	
	Co. A, 17 Pa. Cav.	
511	Co. B, 17 Pa. Cav.–	
	Co. A, 20 Pa. Cav.	
512	Co. B, 20 Pa. Cav.–	
	Co. B, 22 Pa. Cav.	
513	Co. C, 22 Pa. Cav.–	
	Co. A, 3 Pa. Prov. Cav.	
514	Co. B, 3 Pa. Prov. Cav.–	
	Co. D, 2 Pa. H. Art.	Lynch

Roll	Co., Regiment	Name
515	Co. D, 2 Pa. H. Art.–	
	Co. D, 3 Pa. H. Art.	McCartney
516	Co. E, 3 Pa. H. Art.–	
	Co. B, 6 Pa. H. Art.	
517	Co. C, 6 Pa. H. Art.–	
	Co. D, Indep. Btry., Pa. Lt. Art.	Fry
518	Co. D, Indep. Btry., Pa. Lt. Art.–	Gable
	Co. H, Indep. Btry., Pa. Lt. Art.	
519	Co. I, Indep. Btry., Pa. Lt. Art.–	
	Co. L, 4 Pa. Inf. (SAW)	
520	Co. M, 4 Pa. Inf. (SAW)–	
	Co. G, 9 Pa. Inf. (SAW)	
521	Co. H, 9 Pa. Inf. (SAW)–	
	Co. A, 16 Pa. Inf. (SAW)	
Pennsylvania–Rhode Island:		
522	Co. B, 16 Pa. Inf. (SAW)–	
	Co. F, 2 R.I. Inf.	
Rhode Island:		
523	Co. G, 2 R.I. Inf.–	
	Co. A, 11 R.I. Inf.	
524	Co. B, 11 R.I. Inf.–	
	Co. A, 1 R.I. Lt. Art.	
525	Co. B, 1 R.I. Lt. Art.–	
	F & S, 1 R.I. Inf. (SAW)	
Rhode Island–South Carolina:		
526	Co. A, 1 R.I. Inf. (SAW)–	
	Co. L, 1 S.C. Inf. (SAW)	
South Carolina–Tennessee:		
527	Co. M, 1 S.C. Inf. (SAW)–	
	Co. D, 3 Tenn. Inf.	
Tennessee:		
528	Co. E, 3 Tenn. Inf.–	
	Co. A, 8 Tenn. Inf.	
529	Co. B, 8 Tenn. Inf.–	
	Co. A, 2 Tenn. Mtd. Inf.	
530	Co. B, 2 Tenn. Mtd. Inf.–	
	Co. F, 7 Tenn. Mtd. Inf.	
531	Co. G, 7 Tenn. Mtd. Inf.–	
	Co. G, 3 Tenn. Cav.	
532	Co. H, 3 Tenn. Cav.–	
	Co. C, 5 Tenn. Cav.	
533	Co. D, 5 Tenn. Cav.–	
	Co. E, 8 Tenn. Cav.	
534	Co. F, 8 Tenn. Cav.–	
	Co. C, 11 Tenn. Cav.	
535	Co. D, 11 Tenn. Cav.–	
	Co. E, 1 Tenn. H. Art.	
536	Co. F, 1 Tenn. H. Art.–	
	Co. H, 2 Tenn. Inf. (SAW)	
Tennessee–Texas:		
537	Co. I, 2 Tenn. Inf. (SAW)–	
	Co. H, 1 Tex. Cav.	
Texas:		
538	Co. I, 1 Tex. Cav.–	
	Co. M, 1 Tex. Inf. (SAW)	
539	F & S, 2 Tex. Inf. (SAW)–	
	Co. K, 1 Tex. Cav. (SAW)	
Texas–U.S. Cavalry:		
540	Co. L, 1 Tex. Cav. (SAW)–	
	Co. B, 4 U.S.C. Inf.	
U.S. Cavalry:		
541	Co. C, 4 U.S.C. Inf.–	
	Co. G, 7 U.S.C. Inf.	
542	Co. H, 7 U.S.C. Inf.–	
	Co. K, 10 U.S.C. Inf.	
543	F & S, 11 U.S.C. Inf.–	
	Co. I, 13 U.S.C. Inf.	
544	Co. K, 13 U.S.C. Inf.–	
	Co. I, 16 U.S.C. Inf.	
545	Co. K, 16 U.S.C. Inf.–	
	Co. A, 20 U.S.C. Inf.	
546	Co. A, 20 U.S.C. Inf.–	Freeman
	Co. G, 23 U.S.C. Inf.	Gurnett
547	Co. H, 23 U.S.C. Inf.–	
	Co. D, 25 U.S.C. Inf.	
548	Co. E, 25 U.S.C. Inf.–	
	Co. A, 29 U.S.C. Inf.	
549	Co. B, 29 U.S.C. Inf.–	
	Co. A, 33 U.S.C. Inf.	
550	Co. B, 33 U.S.C. Inf.–	
	Co. F, 36 U.S.C. Inf.	
551	Co. G, 36 U.S.C. Inf.–	
	Co. A, 40 U.S.C. Inf.	
552	Co. B, 40 U.S.C. Inf.–	
	Co. G, 44 U.S.C. Inf.	
553	Co. H, 44 U.S.C. Inf.–	
	Co. I, 48 U.S.C. Inf.	
554	Co. K, 48 U.S.C. Inf.–	
	Co. H, 52 U.S.C. Inf.	
555	Co. I, 52 U.S.C. Inf.–	
	Co. H, 56 U.S.C. Inf.	
556	Co. I, 56 U.S.C. Inf.–	
	Co. E, 60 U.S.C. Inf.	
557	Co. F, 60 U.S.C. Inf.–	
	Co. D, 64 U.S.C. Inf.	
558	Co. E, 64 U.S.C. Inf.–	
	Co. E, 68 U.S.C. Inf.	
559	Co. F, 68 U.S.C. Inf.–	
	Co. H, 74 U.S.C. Inf.	
560	Co. I, 74 U.S.C. Inf.–	
	Co. D, 79 U.S.C. Inf.	
561	Co. E, 79 U.S.C. Inf.–	
	Co. B, 81 U.S.C. Inf.	
562	Co. C, 81 U.S.C. Inf.–	
	Co. H, 84 U.S.C. Inf.	
563	Co. I, 84 U.S.C. Inf.–	
	Co. I, 92 U.S.C. Inf.	
564	Co. K, 92 U.S.C. Inf.–	
	Co. A, 100 U.S.C. Inf.	
565	Co. B, 100 U.S.C. Inf.–	
	Co. C, 104 U.S.C. Inf.	
566	Co. D, 104 U.S.C. Inf.–	
	Co. A, 110 U.S.C. Inf.	
567	Co. B, 110 U.S.C. Inf.–	
	Co. E, 114 U.S.C. Inf.	
568	Co. F, 114 U.S.C. Inf.–	
	Co. G, 118 U.S.C. Inf.	
569	Co. H, 118 U.S.C. Inf.–	
	Co. I, 123 U.S.C. Inf.	
570	Co. K, 123 U.S.C. Inf.–	
	Co. C, 135 U.S.C. Inf.	
U.S. Cavalry–U.S. Colored Troops:		
571	Co. D, 135 U.S.C. Inf.–	
	Unknown, U.S.C.T.	Byles
572	Unknown, U.S.C.T.–	Cabney
	Co. G, 3 U.S.C. Cav.	
573	Co. H, 3 U.S.C. Cav.–	
	Co. C, 1 U.S.C. H. Art.	
574	Co. D, 1 U.S.C. H. Art.–	
	Co. B, 4 U.S.C. H. Art.	
575	Co. C, 4 U.S.C. H. Art.–	
	Co. K, 5 U.S.C. H. Art.	
576	Co. L, 5 U.S.C. H. Art.–	
	Co. F, 8 U.S.C. H. Art.	

Roll	Co., Regiment	Name
577	Co. G, 8 U.S.C. H. Art.–	
	Co. L, 11 U.S.C. H. Art.	
578	Co. M, 11 U.S.C. H. Art.–	
	Co. F, 14 U.S.C. H. Art.	
U.S. Colored Troops–Utah:		
579	Co. G, 14 U.S.C. H. Art.–	
	Misc. Utah Mil. Cav.(some Inf., some Indian wars)	Jensen
Utah–Vermont:		
580	Misc. Utah Mil. Cav.(some Indian Wars;	
	1 Utah Home Gds. Inf.)–	Jeppesen
	Co. A, 3 Vt. Inf.	
Vermont:		
581	Co. B, 3 Vt. Inf.–	
	Co. F, 5 Vt. Inf.	
582	Co. G, 5 Vt. Inf.–	
	Co. C, 8 Vt. Inf.	
583	Co. D, 8 Vt. Inf.–	
	Co. A, 11 Vt. Inf.	
584	Co. B, 11 Vt. Inf.–	
	Co. B, 15 Vt. Inf.	
585	Co. C, 15 Vt. Inf.–	
	Co. G, 1 Vt. Cav.	
586	Co. H, 1 Vt. Cav.–	
	—, 3 Indep. Btry., Vt. Lt. Art.	
Vermont–Veterans Reserve Corps:		
587	F & S, 1 Vt. Inf. (SAW)–	
	Co. C, 4 V.R.C.	
Veterans Reserve Corps:		
588	Co. D, 4 V.R.C.–	
	Co. E, 8 V.R.C.	
589	Co. F, 8 V.R.C.–	
	Co. A, 12 V.R.C.	
590	Co. B, 12 V.R.C.–	
	Co. I, 15 V.R.C.	
591	Co. K, 15 V.R.C.–	
	Co. H, 19 V.R.C.	
592	Co. I, 19 V.R.C.–	
	Co. I, 23 V.R.C.	
593	Co. K, 23 V.R.C.–	
	Co. 18, 2 Btry. V.R.C.	
594	Co. 19, 2 Btry. V.R.C.–	
	Co. 64, 2 Bn. V.R.C.	
595	Co. 65, 2 Bn. V.R.C.–	
	Co. 115, 2 Bn. V.R.C.	
596	Co. 116, 2 Bn. V.R.C.–	
	Co. 163, 2 Bn. V.R.C.	
Veterans Reserve Corps–Virginia:		
597	Co. 164, 2 Bn. V.R.C.–	
	Co. B, 2 Va. Inf. (SAW)	Rison
Virginia–Washington Territory:		
598	Co. B, 2 Va. Inf. (SAW)–	Robertson
	F & S, 1 Wash. Ter. Inf.	
Washington Territory–West Virginia:		
599	Co. A, 1 Wash. Ter. Inf.–	
	Co. H, 2 W. Va. Inf.	McGinley
West Virginia:		
600	Co. H, 2 W. Va. Inf.–	McNally
	Co. A, 6 W. Va. Inf.	
601	Co. B, 6 W. Va. Inf.–	
	Co. F, 7 W. Va. Inf.	Lewellan
602	Co. F, 7 W. Va. Inf.–	Lightner
	Co. A, 11 W. Va. Inf.	Lyon
603	Co. A, 11 W. Va. Inf.–	Kelley
	Co. E, 14 W. Va. Inf.	Haught, E.
604	Co. E, 14 W. Va. Inf.–	Haught
	Co. D, 2 W. Va. Vet. Inf.	
605	Co. E, 2 W. Va. Vet. Inf.–	B
	Co. E, 2 W. Va. Cav.	Pine
606	Co. E, 2 W. Va. Cav.–	Porter
	Co. K, 5 W. Va. Cav.	Brown
607	Co. K, 5 W. Va. Cav.–	Broy
	—, Indep. Btry. D, W. Va. Lt. Art.	Smith
West Virginia–Wisconsin:		
608	—, Indep. Btry. D, W. Va. Lt. Art.–	Snider
	Co. F, 1 Wis. Inf.	Lovell
609	Co. F, 1 Wis. Inf.–	McCabe
	Co. K, 3 Wis. Inf.	Corbett
610	Co. K, 3 Wis. Inf.–	Cossentine
	Co. H, 6 Wis. Inf.	Hall
611	Co. H, 6 Wis. Inf.–	Harlocker
	Co. G, 9 Wis. Inf.	Dilges
612	Co. G, 9 Wis. Inf.–	Eberhardt
	Co. H, 12 Wis. Inf.	Tabor
613	Co. H, 12 Wis. Inf.–	Tabor, R.
	Co. K, 15 Wis. Inf.	Dicken
614	Co. K, 15 Wis. Inf.–	Ellefson
	Co. C, 18 Wis. Inf.	Evans
615	Co. E, 18 Wis. Inf.–	A
	Unassign. and F & S, 22 Wis. Inf.	Blood
616	Unassign. and F & S, 22 Wis. Inf.–	Bloodgood
	Co. H, 25 Wis. Inf.	Betts
617	Co. H, 25 Wis. Inf.–	Brauner
	Co. H, 29 Wis. Inf.	W
618	Co. I, 29 Wis. Inf.–	A
	Co. E, 33 Wis. Inf.	Roark
619	Co. E, 33 Wis. Inf.–	Robinson
	F & S, 38 Wis. Inf.	W
620	Co. A, 38 Wis. Inf.–	
	Co. F, 43 Wis. Inf.	
621	Co. G, 43 Wis. Inf.–	A
	Co. E, 48 Wis. Inf.	Lippert
622	Co. E, 48 Wis. Inf.–	Maresch
	F & S, 1 Wis. Cav.	Fox
623	Unassign. and F & S, 1 Wis. Cav.–	Goodrich
	Co. A, 3 Wis. Cav.	Jordan
624	Co. A, 3 Wis. Cav.–	Keyes
	Co. A, 1 Wis. H. Art.	Z
625	Co. B, 1 Wis. H. Art.–	A
	—, 13 Indep. Btry., Wis. Lt. Art.	Jones
626	—, 13 Indep. Btry., Wis. Lt. Art.–	Kappelman
	Co. H, 4 Wis. Inf. (SAW)	Z
Wisconsin–U.S. Infantry:		
627	Co. I, 4 Wis. Inf. (SAW)–	
	Co. E, 1 U.S. Inf.	
U.S. Infantry:		
628	Co. F, 1 U.S. Inf.–	
	Co. A, 2 U.S. Inf.	Boroughs
629	Co. A, 2 U.S. Inf.–	Bottorff
	Co. G, 2 U.S. Inf.	Evins
630	Co. G, 2 U.S. Inf.–	Falkor
	Co. A, 3 U.S. Inf.	Krois
631	Co. A, 3 U.S. Inf.–	Lafayette
	Co. H, 3 U.S. Inf.	Swint
632	Co. H, 3 U.S. Inf.–	Talley
	Co. D, 4 U.S. Inf.	Gunset
633	Co. D, 4 U.S. Inf.–	Habedank
	Co. M, 4 U.S. Inf.	Y
634	F & S, 5 U.S. Inf.–	A

Roll	*Co., Regiment*	*Name*
	Co. F, 5 U.S. Inf.	Cuskes
635	Co. F, 5 U.S. Inf.–	Daniels
	Unassign. and F & S, 6 U.S. Inf.	Myers
636	Unassign. and F & S, 6 U.S. Inf.–	Neal
	Co. H, 6 U.S. Inf.	Descole
637	Co. H, 6 U.S. Inf.–	Devine
	Co. B, 7 U.S. Inf.	Z
638	Co. C, 7 U.S. Inf.–	
	Co. I, 7 U.S. Inf.	
639	Co. K, 7 U.S. Inf.–	A
	Co. D, 8 U.S. Inf.	Kelly
640	Co. D, 8 U.S. Inf.–	Kelly, T.
	Co. L, 8 U.S. Inf.	Barker
641	Co. L, 8 U.S. Inf.–	Gus Barker
	Co. F, 9 U.S. Inf.	Collins
642	Co. F, 9 U.S. Inf.–	Wm. B. Collins
	Co. A, 10 U.S. Inf.	Moss
643	Co. A, 10 U.S. Inf.–	Mullin
	Co. H, 10 U.S. Inf.	Z
644	Co. I, 10 U.S. Inf.–	Abel Gow
	Co. I, 10 U.S. Inf.	Z
645	Co. K, 10 U.S. Inf.–	
	Co. C, 1 Bn., 11 U.S. Inf.	
646	Co. C, 11 U.S. Inf.–	Yeatman
	Co. K, 11 U.S. Inf.	Monroe
647	Co. K, 11 U.S. Inf.–	Moore
	Co. D, 2 Bn., 12 U.S. Inf.	Houck
648	Co. D, 1 Bn., 12 U.S. Inf.–	Phillip Houck
	Co. L, 12 U.S. Inf.–	McGehee
649	Co. L, 12 U.S. Inf.–	McGeraty
	Co. E, 13 U.S. Inf.	Pruitt
650	Co. E, 13 U.S. Inf.–	Purcell
	Supply and F & S, 14 U.S. Inf.	Swindall
651	Unassign. and F & S, Det. 14 U.S. Inf.–	Tate
	Co. F, 14 U.S. Inf.	Curtis
652	Co. F, 14 U.S. Inf.–	Fallon
	—, Cas. Det. 15 U.S. Inf.	Pettit
653	—, Cas. Det. 15 U.S. Inf.–	Petty
	Co. F, 1 Bn., 15 U.S. Inf.	Renzer
654	Co. F, 1 Bn., 15 U.S. Inf.–	Revis
	Co. A, 16 U.S. Inf.	Peyton
655	Co. A, 2 Bn., 16 U.S. Inf.–	Phatt
	Co. G, 1 Bn., 16 U.S. Inf.	Whalen
656	Co. G, 16 U.S. Inf.–	Wild
	Co. B, 17 U.S. Inf.	Z
657	Co. C, 17 U.S. Inf.–	A
	Co. K, 17 U.S. Inf.	Fuller
658	Co. K, 17 U.S. Inf.–	Gallagher
	Unassign., 18 U.S. Inf.	Sweet
659	Cas. Det., Unassign. and F & S, 18 U.S. Inf.–	Tarman
	Co. E, 18 U.S. Inf.	Simmons
660	Co. E, 18 U.S. Inf.–	Smith
	Co. L, 18 U.S. Inf.	Landas
661	Co. L, 18 U.S. Inf.–	Lavy
	Co. E, 19 U.S. Inf.	Byrne
662	Co. E, 19 U.S. Inf.–	Cahn
	Co. M, 19 U.S. Inf.	Z
663	F & S, 20 U.S. Inf.–	A
	Co. E, 20 U.S. Inf.	Findley
664	Co. E, 20 U.S. Inf.–	Fisher
	Co. B, 21 U.S. Inf.	Curley
665	Co. B, 21 U.S. Inf.–	Dakin
	Co. I, 21 U.S. Inf.	Guise
666	Co. I, 21 U.S. Inf.–	Gunselus
	Co. E, 22 U.S. Inf.	Morton
667	Co. E, 22 U.S. Inf.–	Mulcahy
	Co. A, 23 U.S. Inf.	Vale
668	Co. A, 23 U.S. Inf.–	Vance
	Co. I, 23 U.S. Inf.	Henison
669	Co. I, 23 U.S. Inf.–	Henry
	Co. B, 24 U.S. Inf.	Elliot
670	Co. B, 24 U.S. Inf.–	Ellis
	Co. K, 24 U.S. Inf.	Kyler
671	Co. K, 24 U.S. Inf.–	Larkins
	Co. G, 25 U.S. Inf.	Myles
672	Co. G, 25 U.S. Inf.–	Nelson
	Co. H, 26 U.S. Inf.	Rutherford
673	Co. H, 26 U.S. Inf.–	Sanders
	Co. L, 27 U.S. Inf.	Martinez
674	Co. L, 27 U.S. Inf.–	Maukkin
	Co. B, 29 U.S. Inf.	Benge
675	Co. B, 29 U.S. Inf.–	Bartley
	Co. E, 30 U.S. Inf.	Curran
676	Co. E, 30 U.S. Inf.–	Daily
	Co. H, 33 U.S. Inf.	Johnson
677	Co. H, 33 U.S. Inf.–	Jones
	Co. D, 40 U.S. Inf.	Thomas
678	Co. D, 40 U.S. Inf.–	Toney
	Various, 54 U.S. Inf.	Z
679	Various, 55 U.S. Inf.–	A
	Unassign. and F & S, 5 U.S. Vol. Inf.	Wanless
680	Co. A, 5 U.S. Vol. Inf.–	Adams
	Co. H, 6 U.S. Vet. Vol. Inf.	Ludwig
681	Co. H, 6 U.S. Vet. Vol. Inf.–	M
	Co. M, 3 U.S. Vol. Inf. (SAW)	Y
682	F & S, 4 U.S. Vol. Inf. (SAW)–	B
	Co. C, 9 U.S. Vol. Inf. (SAW)	T
683	Co. D, 9 U.S. Vol. Inf. (SAW)–	A
	Co. I, 28 U.S. Vol. Inf. (SAW)	Christy
684	Co. I, 28 U.S. Vol. Inf. (SAW)–	Clark
	Co. D, 32 U.S. Vol. Inf. (SAW)	Sommers
685	Co. D, 32 U.S. Vol. Inf. (SAW)–	Spangler
	Co. K, 35 U.S. Vol. Inf. (SAW)	Reed
686	Co. K, 35 U.S. Vol. Inf. (SAW)–	Riley
	Co. L, 39 U.S. Vol. Inf. (SAW)	Jordan
687	Co. L, 39 U.S. Vol. Inf. (SAW)–	Kantola
	Co. G, 43 U.S. Vol. Inf. (SAW)	Blake
688	Co. G, 43 U.S. Vol. Inf. (SAW)–	Boston
	Co. B, 47 U.S. Vol. Inf. (SAW)	Englert
689	Co. B, 47 U.S. Vol. Inf. (SAW)–	Evans
	Various, Puerto Rican U.S. Vol. Inf. (SAW)	Chacon

U.S. Infantry-U.S. Cavalry:

Roll	*Co., Regiment*	*Name*
690	Various, Puerto Rican U.S. Vol. Inf. (SAW)–	Charron
	Co. E, 1 U.S. Cav.	Bond

U.S. Cavalry:

Roll	*Co., Regiment*	*Name*
691	Co. E, 1 U.S. Cav.–	William Bond
	Co. L, 1 U.S. Cav.	Ullman
692	Co. L, 1 U.S. Cav.–	Van Houton
	Co. F, 2 U.S. Cav.	Jackson
693	Co. F, 2 U.S. Cav.–	James
	Cas. Det., Unassign. and F & S, 3 U.S. Cav.	Shadoan
694	Cas. Det., Unassign. and F & S, 3 U.S. Cav.–	Shank
	Co. F, 3 U.S. Cav.	McGovern

Roll	Co., Regiment	Name
695	Co. F, 3 U.S. Cav.–	McGowan
	Co. A, 4 U.S. Cav.	Isham
696	Co. A, 4 U.S. Cav.–	Jacobson
	Co. H, 4 U.S. Cav.	Stewart
697	Co. H, 4 U.S. Cav.–	Strusd
	Co. C, 5 U.S. Cav.	Cerrita
698	Co. C, 5 U.S. Cav.–	Chandler
	Co. D, 5 U.S. Cav.	Proffitt
699	Co. D, 5 U.S. Cav.–	Quinlan
	Co. M, 5 U.S. Cav.	Barton
700	Co. M, 5 U.S. Cav.–	Bushon
	Co. E, 6 U.S. Cav.	Thomas
701	Co. E, 6 U.S. Cav.–	Otha Thomas
	Co. L, 6 U.S. Cav.	Jamison
702	Co. L, 6 U.S. Cav.–	Janis
	Co. G, 7 U.S. Cav.	Dunlap
703	Co. G, 7 U.S. Cav.–	Dunn
	Co. C, 8 U.S. Cav.	King
704	Co. C, 8 U.S. Cav.–	Kingrey
	Unassign., Cas. Det., 9 U.S. Cav.	Brew
705	F & S, Unassign., & Cas. Det., 9 U.S. Cav.–	Brinson
	Co. I, 9 U.S. Cav.	Duncan
706	Co. I, 9 U.S. Cav.–	Danker
	Co. F, 10 U.S. Cav.	Johnson, M.
707	Co. F, 10 U.S. Cav.–	Johnson, W.
	Co. K, 11 U.S. Cav.	Z
708	Co. L, 11 U.S. Cav.–	A
	Co. C, 14 U.S. Cav.	Westivell
709	Co. C, 14 U.S. Cav.–	Wiggins
	Co. C, 1 U.S. Vol. Cav.	Hill
U.S. Cavalry–U.S. Artillery:		
710	Co. C, 1 U.S. Vol. Cav.–	Howland
	Co. A, 1 U.S. Art.	Dalton
U.S. Artillery:		
711	Co. A, 1 U.S. Art.–	Eaker
	Co. H, 1 U.S. Art.	Mangan
712	Co. H, 1 U.S. Art.–	Manhns
	Co. H, 1 U.S. Art.	Young
713	Co. I, 1 U.S. Art.–	A
	Co. C, 2 U.S. Art.	Boyson
714	Co. C, 2 U.S. Art.–	Bozi
	Co. K, 2 U.S. Art.	Knapp
715	Co. K, 3 U.S. Art.–	Murphy
	Co. C, 3 U.S. Field Art.	Painter
716	Co. C, 3 U.S. Art.–	Rivinius
	Co. L, 3 U.S. Art.	Mahoney
717	Co. L, 3 U.S. Art.–	March
	Co. F, 4 U.S. Art.	Barrick
718	Co. F, 4 U.S. Art.–	Callahan
	Co. A, 5 U.S. Art.	Z
719	Co. B, 5 U.S. Art.–	Abbott
	Co. I, 5 U.S. Art.	Kurtz
720	Co. I, 5 U.S. Art.–	Lacey
	Co. L, 6 U.S. Art.	Guy
Miscellaneous Units:		
721	Co. L, 6 U.S. Art.–	Hajek
	Various Cos., 11 U.S. Field Art.	Rumore
722	Various Cos., 11 U.S. Field Art.–	Rupp
	Various Cos., 81 U.S. Field Art.	Yuhasy
723	Co. A, 82 U.S. Field Art.–	Allen
	—, 15 Btry., U.S. Field Art.	Ziegler
724	—, 16 Btry., U.S. Field Art.–	A
	Co. 4, U.S. C.A.C.	Savage

Roll	Co., Regiment	Name
725	Co. 4, U.S. C.A.C.–	Saylor
	Co. 15, U.S. C.A.C.	Grant
726	Co. 15, U.S. C.A.C.–	Robert Grant
	Co. 36, U.S. C.A.C.	McCarthy
727	Co. 36, U.S. C.A.C.–	McHargue
	Co. 59, U.S. C.A.C.	Hammond
728	Co. 59, U.S. C.A.C.–	Edward Hammond
	Co. 78, U.S. C.A.C.	Yettaw
729	Co. 79, U.S. C.A.C.–	A
	Co. 106, U.S. C.A.C.	Joseph Conrad
730	Co. 106, U.S. C.A.C.–	Cormier
	Co. 144, U.S. C.A.C.	Yung
731	Co. 145, U.S. C.A.C.–	A
	8 Band, U.S. C.A.C.	Stretz
732	8 Band, U.S. C.A.C.–	Summers
	Brig. Band, U.S. Vols.	Hamilton
733	Brig. Band, U.S. Vols.–	Harkinson
	Co. A, 1 Bn., U.S. Engs.	Lyons
734	Co. A, 1 Bn., U.S. Engs.–	McCarthy
	Co. K, 3 Bn., U.S. Engs.	Pope
735	Co. K, 3 Bn., U.S. Engs.–	Prow
	Various, 16 U.S. Engs.	Stark
736	Co. A, 16 U.S. Engs.–	Streeter
	Co. M, 3 U.S. Vol. Engs.	Z
737	(Presidents of the U.S.) Commander in Chief, U.S.A.–	Adams
	Gen. Serv. U.S.A., Misc. groups & Unassign.	Churchill
738	Gen. Serv. U.S.A.–	Charles Churchill
	Gen. Serv. U.S.A., Serv. U.S. Cav.	Howard
739	Gen. Serv. U.S.A. & Misc.–	Frank Howard
	Unassign. U.S.A., Gen. Serv. U.S.A. & Misc.	Pickerell
740	Gen. Serv. U.S.A.–	Pickering
	2 Regt., Gen. Serv. U.S. Engs., Gen. Serv. U.S.A.	Power
741	2 Regt., Gen. Serv. U.S.A.–	James Power
	Hosp. Corps. U.S.A., Med. Dept. U.S.A.	Beckner
742	Hosp. Corps, U.S.A., Med. Dept. U.S.A.–	Beckton
	Hosp. Corps, U.S.A.	Hairrold
743	Hosp. Corps, U.S.A.–	Hake
	Hosp. Corps, U.S.A.	Newman
744	Hosp. Corps, U.S.A.–	William Newman
	Hosp. Corps, U.S.A.	White
745	Hosp. Corps, U.S.A.–	White
	Med. Dept., U.S. Vols.	Cutler
746	Med. Dept., U.S. Vols.–	Dailey
	Med. Dept., U.S.A. (nurses)	Kauffman
747	Med. Dept., U.S. Vols. (nurses)–	Keane
	Unknown U.S. Vols.	Nichols
748	Unknown U.S. Vols.–	Harns Nickels
	Miss. Gunboat Flotilla, U.S. Vols.	Josiah
749	West. Gunboat Flotilla, M.M.B., U.S. Vols. Inf., Miss. Gunboat Flotilla, U.S. Vols.–	Keating
	Ord. Dept. U.S.A.	Zalanf
750	Fin. Dept. U.S.A., Paymaster U.S. Vols.–	A
	2 Md. U.S. Vols.	Fitch

Roll	Co., Regiment	Name
751	Q.M. Corps U.S.A.–	Fite
	Q.M. Corps U.S.A.	Tarter
752	Q.M. Corps U.S.A.–	Tasker
	Q.M.D. U.S. Vols.	Rose
753	2 Q.M.D. U.S. Vols.–	Rosenauer
	Ret. U.S.A. (Indian Wars)	Bennett
754	Ret. U.S.A.–	Frank Buinett
	Ind. Scouts, U.S.A.	Black
755	Ind. Scouts, U.S.A.–	Black Hills
	Various Phil. Scouts, U.S.A.	Antonio
756	26 Phil. Scouts, U.S.A.–	Fausto Antonio
	20 Phil. Scouts, U.S.A.	Basilio Loquiao
757	38 & 39 Phil. Scouts, U.S.A.–	Lora
	B Squad. Phil. Cav. U.S. Vols.	Navarro
758	Co. B, Squad., Phil. Cav. U.S. Vols.–	Otis
	Co. E, Signal Corps, U.S.A.	Fikes
759	Signal Corps, U.S.A.–	Findling
	Various Tank Corps, U.S.A.	Clark
760	Tank Corps, U.S.A.–	Clark
	Various Units from different states, border defense–WWI	McBride
761	Var. WWI Units, border defense (Nat. Guard, U.S. Inf.)–	James McBride
	Misc. WWI units (Guards, U.S. Inf, etc.)	Bobsien
762	Misc. WWI Units (Inf, U.S. Engs., Field Art.)–	Bocateat
	Misc. WWI units (Guards, U.S. Inf., U.S. Engs., etc.)	Hendry
763	Misc. WWI units (U.S. Inf., U.S. Engs., Guards, etc.)–	Hengesbach
	Misc. WWI units (U.S. Inf., U.S. Engs., Field Art., Guards, etc.)	Maclay
764	Misc. WWI units (U.S. Inf., Guards, Field Art., etc.)–	Mares
	Misc. WWI units (U.S. Inf., U.S. Engs., Guards, Field Art.)	Szurminki
765	Misc. WWI units (U.S. Inf., U.S. Engs., Guards, etc.)–	Tabaka
	Misc. WWI units (U.S. Inf., U.S. Field Art., U.S. Engs., etc.)	Zanker

Veterans Administration Pension Payment Cards, 1907–1933. M850. 2,539 rolls. DP.

This microfilm publication reproduces Pension Office award cards that record payments to pensioners on the rolls, 1907–33, except World War I pensioners. The cards are arranged alphabetically by surname of pensioner. Cards for Indian names are arranged alphabetically and filmed under the pertinent letter of the alphabet before cards for other names beginning with that letter.

Roll	Description
1	A–Abbott, Gustavus A.
2	Abbott, H. Emory–Abeita, J. Jesus
3	Abel, Abigail–Ablitz, Pauline
4	Abner, Ellen–Acison, Mattie
5	Ackard, Elizabeth A.–Ackiss, Laucinda
6	Acklam, Benjamin–Adamowich, Andrew
7	Adams, A.–Adams, Christopher H.
8	Adams, Clara–Adams, Freeman D.
9	Adams, Gabriel–Adams, Joel M.
10	Adams, John–Adams, Lyman W.
11	Adams, McGray C.–Adams, Prudy
12	Adams, Rachel–Adams, Zylpha
13	Adamsky, Eliza–Adkins, Joshus K.
14	Adkins, Kinchen–Agey, Vernie
15	Agg, Sarah J.–Aikey, Zachariah
16	Aikin, Almira C.–Akey, Winfield S.
17	Akie, Henry–Alberts, Sarah J.
18	Albertsen, Andreas–Alcoke, William W.
19	Alcorn, Agnes–Aldrich, Eugene S.
20	Aldrich, Fanny–Alexander, Austin A.
21	Alexander, Barnard–Alexander, Kezia E.
22	Alexander, Laura A.–Alexander, Zachariah T.
23	Alexandry, Nicolos–Allbee, Sarah J.
24	Allbert, Delana–Allen, Byron M.
25	Allen, Calista E.–Allen, Elydia A.
26	Allen, Emaline–Allen, Huldah M.
27	Allen, I. Clifton–Allen, King P.
28	Allen, L. Scott–Allen, May F.
29	Allen, Mehitable–Allen, Syrous B.
30	Allen, Tabitha–Alleyne, Samuel
31	Allfie, John A.–Allison, Willinoth
32	Alliss, Albert–Alsover, Mary M.
33	Alspach, Amanda–Alumbaugh, Winifred B.
34	Alvarado, Jose G.–Amery, Mary G.
35	Ames, Aaron S.–Amlung, Hedwig
36	Ammack, Emily–Anderseck, Lorenz
37	Andersen, Albert–Anderson, Celista
38	Anderson, Chaney–Anderson, Frederieke
39	Anderson, Gabriel–Anderson, Jetty M.
40	Anderson, Joanna–Anderson, Lynn B.
41	Anderson, M. Louise–Anderson, Owen
42	Anderson, Page–Anderson, Virginia M.
43	Anderson, Walker–Andretsch, Arthur M.
44	Andrew, Abbie S.–Andrews, Gustavus
45	Andrews, Hamilton–Andrews, Ruth
46	Andrews, Sally–Angevine, William F.
47	Angie, Lugie J.–Anslyn, Minnie
48	Anson, Abraham H.–Antoszak, John
49	Antram, Elvira T.–Appleford, Willington
50	Applegarth, Adda J.–Arbor, Cynthia
51	Arbuckel, William C.–Ardric, Thomas
52	Areay, George V.–Armfield, Warren Ormthede
53	Armiger, Caroline M.–Armstrong, Frederick
54	Armstrong, Gabriela–Armstrong, Preston W.
55	Armstrong, Rachel–Arnoe, Joseph
56	Arnold, Aaron–Arnold, Joel
57	Arnold, John–Arnold, William T.
58	Arnoldi, August–Artist, Thomas W.
59	Artley, Anne E.–Ashard, William H.
60	Ashba, Daniel–Ashkittle, Nancy J.
61	Ashlan, Michael–Askey, William
62	Askie, Elsie–Athey, Wesley B.
63	Athington, Andrew J.–Atkinson, Lydia
64	Atkinson, Maggie–Atwood, Freeman
65	Atwood, George–Augur, Sarah L.
66	Augus, Jennie–Austill, George L.
67	Austin, Aaron–Austin, Isom
68	Austin, Jabez L.–Autes, William
69	Auth, Apollonia–Avery, William W.

Other Records Relating to Veterans' Claims (Record Groups 29, 94, and 407)

Special Schedules of the Eleventh Census (1890) Enumerating Union Veterans and Widows of Union Veterans of the Civil War. M123. 118 rolls.

An act of March 1, 1889, provided that the Superintendent of Census in taking the Eleventh Census should "cause to be taken on a special schedule of inquiry, according to such form as he may prescribe, the names, organizations, and length of service of those who had served in the Army, Navy, or Marine Corps of the United States in the war of the rebellion, and who are survivors at the time of said inquiry, and the widows of soldiers, sailors, or marines."

Each entry shows the following information: the name of the veteran (or if he did not survive, the names of both the widow and her deceased husband); the veteran's rank, company, regiment, or vessel; date of enlistment, date of discharge, and length of service in years, months, and days; post office and address of each person listed; disability incurred by the veteran; and remarks necessary for a complete statement of his term of service.

Practically all of the schedules for the States of Alabama through Kansas and approximately half of those for Kentucky appear to have been destroyed, possibly by fire, before the transfer of the remaining schedules to the National Archives in 1943. In a few cases, names of Confederate veterans were recorded inadvertently.

The schedules are arranged alphabetically by State or Territory, thereunder by county, and thereunder by minor subdivision.

Roll	*Description*
Kentucky:	
1	Boone, Bourbon, Bracken, Campbell, Clark, Fayette, Franklin, Gallatin, Grant, Harrison, Jessamine, Kenton, Owen, Pendleton, Scott, and Woodford Counties
2	Bath, Boyd, Carter, Elliott, Fleming, Floyd, Greenup, Johnson, Lawrence, Lewis, Magoffin, Martin, Mason, Menifee, Montgomery, Morgan, Nicholas, Pike, Powell, Robertson, Rowan, and Wolfe Counties
3	Adair, Bell, Boyle, Breathitt, Casey, Clay, Clinton, Cumberland, Estill, Garrard, Harlan, Jackson, Knott, Knox, Laurel, Lee, Leslie, Letcher, Lincoln, Madison, Owsley, Perry, Pulaski, Rockcastle, Russell, Wayne, and Whitley Counties and certain Federal, State, and local institutions throughout Kentucky
Louisiana:	
4	Orleans, Bienville, Bossier, Caddo, De Soto, Grant, Natchitoches, Rapides, Sabine, Vernon, Webster, and Winn Parishes
5	Ascension, Avoyelles, Caldwell, Catahoula, Claiborne, Concordia, East Baton Rouge, East Carroll, East Feliciana, Franklin, Jackson, Jefferson, Lafourche, Lincoln, Livingston, Madison, Morehouse, Ouachita, Plaquemines, Pointe Coupee, Richland, St. Bernard, St. Charles, St. Helena, St. James, St. John the Baptist, St. Landry, St. Martin, St. Mary, St. Tammany, Tangipahoa, Tensas, Terrebonne, Union, Vermilion, West Baton Rouge, West Carroll, West Feliciana, Acadia, Assumption, Calcasieu, Cameron, Iberia, Iberville, and Lafayette Parishes
Maine:	
6	Androscoggin, Cumberland, Franklin, Kennebec, Oxford, Sagadahoc, Somerset, and York Counties
7	Aroostook, Hancock, Knox, Lincoln, Penobscot, Piscataquis, Waldo, and Washington Counties
Maryland:	
8	Baltimore City and Baltimore County
9	Caroline, Cecil, Dorchester, Harford, Kent, Queen Annes, Somerset, Talbot, Wicomico, and Worcester Counties
10	Allegany, Anne Arundel, Calvert, Carroll, Charles, Frederick, Garrett, Howard, Montgomery, Prince Georges, St. Marys, and Washington Counties
Massachusetts:	
11	Hampshire, Norfolk, and Plymouth Counties
12	Middlesex County
13	Barnstable, Berkshire, Bristol, Dukes, Franklin, and Nantucket Counties
14	Hampden County
15	Essex County
16	Suffolk County
Michigan:	
17	Branch, Calhoun, Hillsdale, Jackson, Lenawee, Monroe, Washtenaw, and Wayne Counties
18	Genesee, Huron, Lapeer, Macomb, Oakland, Saginaw, St. Clair, Sanilac, and Tuscola Counties
19	Clinton, Eaton, Gratiot, Ingham, Ionia, Isabella, Livingston, Mecosta, Midland, Montcalm, and Shiawassee Counties
20	Allegan, Barry, Berrien, Cass, Kalamazoo, Kent, Muskegon, Newaygo, Oceana, Ottawa, St. Joseph, and Van Buren Counties
21	Alcona, Alger, Alpena, Antrim, Arenac, Baraga, Bay, Benzie, Charlevoix, Cheboygan, Chippewa, Clare, Crawford, Delta, Emmet, Gladwin, Gogebic, Grand Traverse, Houghton, Iosco, Iron, Isle Royale, Kalkaska, Keweenaw, Lake, Leelanau, Luce, Mackinac, Manistee, Manitou, Marquette, Mason, Menominee, Missaukee, Montgomery, Ogemaw, Ontonagon, Osceola, Oscoda, Otsego, Presque Isle, Roscommon, Schoolcraft, and Wexford Counties
Minnesota:	
22	Blue Earth, Brown, Cottonwood, Dodge, Fairbault, Fillmore, Freeborn, Houston, Jackson, Lac qui Parle, Lincoln, Lyon, Martin, Mower, Murray, Nicollet, Nobles, Olmsted, Pipestone, Redwood, Rock, Steele, Waseca, Watonwan, Winona, and Yellow Medicine Counties and certain Federal, State, local, and private institutions
23	Big Stone, Carver, Chippewa, Dakota, Goodhue, Hennepin, Kandiyohi, Le Sueur, McLeod, Meeker, Renville, Rice, Scott, Sibley, Swift, Wabasha, and Wright Counties
24	Aitkin, Anoka, Benton, Carlton, Cass, Chisago, Cook, Crow Wing, Isanti, Itasca, Kanabec, Lake, Mille Lacs, Morrison, Pine, Ramsey, St. Louis, Sherburne, and Washington Counties

Roll	Description
25	Becker, Beltrami, Clay, Douglas, Grant, Hubbard, Kittson, Marshall, Norman, Otter Tail, Polk, Pope, Stearns, Stevens, Todd, Traverse, Wadena, and Wilkin Counties
Mississippi:	
26	Entire State
Missouri:	
27	Jefferson, St. Charles, and St. Louis Counties and certain Federal, State, local, and private institutions
28	Bollinger, Butler, Cape Girardeau, Carter, Dunklin, Iron, Madison, Mississippi, New Madrid, Oregon, Pemiscot, Perry, Reynolds, Ripley, St. Francois, St. Genevieve, Scott, Shannon, Stoddard, Washington, and Wayne Counties
29	Audrain, Boone, Callaway, Camden, Cole, Crawford, Dent, Franklin, Gasconade, Lincoln, Maries, Miller, Montgomery, Osage, Phelps, Pike, Pulaski, and Warren Counties
30	Barry, Christian, Dade, Dallas, Douglas, Greene, Howell, Jasper, Laclede, Lawrence, McDonald, Newton, Ozark, Polk, Stone, Taney, Texas, Webster, and Wright Counties
31	Adair, Chariton, Clark, Howard, Knox, Lewis, Linn, Macon, Marion, Monroe, Putnam, Ralls, Randolph, Schuyler, Scotland, Shelby, and Sullivan Counties
32	Barton, Bates, Benton, Cass, Cedar, Cooper, Henry, Hickory, Johnson, Lafayette, Moniteau, Morgan, Pettis, St. Clair, Saline, and Vernon Counties
33	Andrew, Atchison, Caldwell, Carroll, Clinton, Grundy, Harrison, Holt, Livingston, Mercer, Nodaway, Ray, and Worth Counties
34	Buchanan, Clay, Jackson, and Platte Counties
Montana:	
35	Entire State
Nebraska:	
36	Adams, Butler, Chase, Clay, Dundy, Fillmore, Franklin, Frontier, Furnas, Gosper, Hamilton, Harlan, Hayes, Hitchcock, Jefferson, Kearney, Nuckolls, Phelps, Polk, Red Willow, Saline, Seward, Thayer, Webster, and York Counties
37	Antelope, Arthur, Banner, Blaine, Boone, Box Butte, Brown, Buffalo, Burt, Cedar, Cherry, Cheyenne, Colfax, Cuming, Custer, Dakota, Dawes, Dawson, Deuel, Dixon, Dodge, Garfield, Grant, Greeley, Hall, Holt, Hooker, Howard, Keith, Keya Paha, Kimball, Knox, Lincoln, Logan, Loup, McPherson, Madison, Merrick, Nance, Perkins, Pierce, Platte, Rock, Scotts Bluff, Sheridan, Sherman, Sioux, Stanton, Thomas, Thurston, Valley, Washington, Wayne, and Wheeler Counties
38	Cass, Douglas, Gage, Johnson, Lancaster, Nemaha, Otoe, Pawnee, Richardson, Sarpy, and Saunders Counties
Nevada:	
39	Entire State
New Hampshire:	
40	Entire State
New Jersey:	
41	Bergen, Essex, Morris, Passaic, Sussex, and Warren Counties
42	Hudson, Hunterdon, Mercer, Middlesex, Somerset, and Union Counties

Roll	Description
43	Atlantic, Burlington, Camden, Cape May, Cumberland, Gloucester, Monmouth, Ocean, and Salem Counties
New Mexico:	
44	Entire Territory
New York:	
45	New York County (in part)
46	New York County (in part)
47	Kings, Queens, Richmond, and Suffolk Counties
48	Columbia, Dutchess, Putnam, and Westchester Counties
49	Delaware, Orange, Rockland, Sullivan, and Ulster Counties
50	Albany, Greene, Otsego, Rensselaer, and Schoharie Counties
51	Fulton, Hamilton, Herkimer, Montgomery, Saratoga, Schenectady, Warren, and Washington Counties
52	Clinton, Essex, Franklin, Jefferson, Lewis, and St. Lawrence Counties
53	Cayuga, Madison, Oneida, Onondaga, and Oswego Counties
54	Allegany, Broome, Chemung, Chenango, Cortland, Schuyler, Steuben, Tioga, and Tompkins Counties
55	Genesee, Livingston, Monroe, Ontario, Orleans, Seneca, Wayne, Wyoming, and Yates Counties
56	Cattaraugus, Chautauqua, Erie, and Niagara Counties
57	Certain Federal, State, local, and private institutions throughout New York State
North Carolina:	
58	Entire State
North Dakota:	
59	Entire State
Ohio:	
60	Allen, Crawford, Defiance, Fulton, Henry, and Paulding Counties
61	Putnam, Sandusky, Seneca, Van Wert, Williams, and Wyandot Counties
62	Hancock, Lucas, Ottawa, and Wood Counties
63	Auglaize, Champaign, Clark, Drake, Greene, and Hardin Counties
64	Logan, Mercer, Miami, Montgomery, Preble, and Shelby Counties
65	Butler, Clermont, Clinton, and Warren Counties
66	Hamilton County
67	Adams, Brown, and Gallia Counties
68	Highland, Hocking, Jackson, Lawrence, Pike, Ross, Scioto, and Vinton Counties
69	Delaware, Fairfield, Fayette, and Franklin Counties
70	Knox, Licking, Madison, Marion, Morrow, Perry, Pickaway, and Union Counties
71	Ashland and Cuyahoga Counties
72	Erie, Holmes, Huron, Lorain, Medina, Richland, and Wayne Counties
73	Athens, Belmont, Coshocton, Guernsey, Harrison, Meigs, Monroe, Morgan, Muskingum, Noble, and Washington Counties
74	Ashtabula, Carroll, Columbiana, Geauga, Jefferson, Lake, Mahoning, Portage, Stark, Summit, Trumbull, and Tuscarawas Counties
75	Federal, State, local, and private institutions throughout Ohio

Roll	Description
Oklahoma and Indian Territories:	
76	Entire Territory
Oregon:	
77	Entire State
Pennsylvania:	
78	Philadelphia County (in part)
79	Philadelphia County (in part)
80	Philadelphia County (in part)
81	Chester, Delaware, Lancaster, and York Counties
82	Berks, Bucks, Lehigh, Montgomery, and Northampton Counties
83	Columbia, Dauphin, Lebanon, Montour, Northumberland, and Schuylkill Counties
84	Carbon, Lackawanna, Luzerne, Monroe, Pike, Susquehanna, Wayne, and Wyoming Counties
85	Bradford, Cameron, Center, Clearfield, Clinton, Elk, Lycoming, McKean, Potter, Sullivan, and Tioga Counties
86	Adams, Bedford, Blair, Cumberland, Franklin, Fulton, Huntingdon, Juniata, Mifflin, Perry, Snyder, and Union Counties
87	Armstrong, Cambria, Clarion, Indiana, Jefferson, and Westmoreland Counties
88	Allegheny County
89	Butler, Crawford, Erie, Forest, Lawrence, Mercer, Venango, and Warren Counties
90	Beaver, Fayette, and Greene Counties
91	Somerset and Washington Counties and certain Federal, State, local, and private institutions throughout Pennsylvania
Rhode Island:	
92	Entire State
South Carolina:	
93	Entire State
South Dakota:	
94	Entire State
Tennessee:	
95	Anderson, Blount, Campbell, Carter, Claiborne, Cocke, Grainger, Greene, Hamblen, Hancock, Hawkins, Jefferson, Johnson, Knox, Loudon, Morgan, Roane, Scott, Sevier, Sullivan, Unicoi, Union, and Washington Counties
96	Bledsoe, Bradley, Cannon, Clay, Cumberland, DeKalb, Fentress, Grundy, Hamilton, Jackson, James, McMinn, Macon, Marion, Meigs, Monroe, Overton, Pickett, Polk, Putnam, Rhea, Sequatchie, Smith, Van Buren, Warren, and White Counties
97	Bedford, Cheatham, Coffee, Davidson, Franklin, Giles, Lincoln, Marshall, Maury, Moore, Robertson, Rutherford, Sumner, Trousdale, Williamson, and Wilson Counties
98	Benton, Carroll, Chester, Crockett, Decatur, Dickson, Dyer, Fayette, Gibson, Hardin, Hardeman, Haywood, Henry, Henderson, Hickman, Houston, Humphreys, Lake, Lauderdale, Lawrence, Lewis, Madison, McNairy, Montgomery, Obion, Perry, Shelby, Stewart, Tipton, Wayne, and Weakley Counties
Texas:	
99	Anderson, Angelina, Bowie, Camp, Cass, Chambers, Cherokee, Delta, Fannin, Franklin, Galveston, Gregg, Harris, Harrison, Henderson, Hopkins, Houston, Hunt, Jefferson, Lamar, Liberty, Marion, Montgomery, Morris, Nacogdoches, Newton, Orange, Panola, Polk, Rains, Red River, Rusk, Sabine, San Jacinto, Shelby, Smith, Titus, Trinity, Tyler, Upshur, Van Zandt, Walker, and Wood Counties
100	Collin, Cooke, Dallas, Denton, Ellis, Grayson, Hill, Johnson, Kaufman, McLennan, Navarro, Rockwall, and Tarrant Counties
101	Austin, Bexar, Brazoria, Brazos, Burleson, Calhoun, Caldwell, Cameron, Colorado, Comal, DeWitt, Dimmit, Duval, Falls, Fayette, Fort Bend, Frio, Freestone, Goliad, Gonzales, Grimes, Guadalupe, Hays, Hidalgo, Jackson, Karnes, Kinney, La Salle, Lavaca, Lee, Leon, Live Oak, Limestone, Madison, Matagorda, Maverick, Medina, Milam, Nueces, Robertson, San Patricio, Starr, Travis, Uvalde, Victoria, Waller, Washington, Webb, Wilson, Wharton, Zapata, and Zavala Counties
102	Archer, Armstrong, Bandera, Baylor, Bell, Blanco, Bosque, Brewster, Briscoe, Brown, Buchel, Burnet, Callahan, Carson, Childress, Clay, Coleman, Collingsworth, Comanche, Coryell, Cottle, Dallam, Deaf Smith, Dickens, Donley, Eastland, Ector, Edwards, El Paso, Erath, Fisher, Foley, Gillespie, Gray, Hale, Hall, Hamilton, Hardeman, Hartley, Haskell, Hemphill, Hood, Harvard, Jack, Jeff Davis, Jones, Kendell, Kent, Kerr, Kimble, King, Knox, Lampasas, Lipscomb, Llano, McCulloch, Martin, Mason, Menard, Midland, Mills, Mitchell, Montague, Nolan, Ochiltree, Oldham, Palo Pinto, Parker, Pecos, Potter, Randall, Reeves, Roberts, Runnels, San Saba, Scurry, Shackelford, Sherman, Somervell, Stephens, Stonewall, Sutton, Swisher, Taylor, Throckmorton, Tom Green, Val Verde, Wheeler, Wichita, Wilbarger, Williamson, Wise, and Young Counties
Utah:	
103	Entire State
United States Vessels and Navy Yards:	
104	
Vermont:	
105	Entire State
Virginia:	
106	Accomack, Charles City, Elizabeth City, Essex, Gloucester, Greensville, Isle of Wight, James City, King and Queen, King William, Lancaster, Mathews, Middlesex, Nansemond, New Kent, Norfolk, Northampton, Northumberland, Prince George, Princess Anne, Richmond, Southampton, Surry, Sussex, Warwick, Westmoreland, York, Amelia, Appomattox, Brunswick, Buckingham, Charlotte, Chesterfield, Cumberland, Dinwiddie, Fluvanna, Goochland, Halifax, Henrico, Lunenburg, Mecklenburg, Nottoway, Powhatan, Prince Edward, Alexandria, Caroline, Clarke, Culpeper, Fairfax, Fauquier, Frederick, Hanover, King George, Loudoun, Louisa, Madison, Orange, Page, Prince William, Rappahannock, Rockingham, Shenandoah, Spotsylvania, Stafford, and Warren Counties
107	Albemarle, Alleghany, Amherst, Augusta, Bath, Bedford, Botetourt, Campbell, Franklin, Henry, Highland, Nelson, Patrick, Pittsylvania, Rockbridge, Buchanan, Carroll, Craig, Dickenson, Floyd, Grayson, Lee, Montgomery, Pulaski, Roanoke, Russell, Scott, Smyth,

Roll	*Description*
	Tazewell, Washington, Wise, and Wythe Counties, Hampton Normal and Agricultural Institute, and two Federal institutions in Elizabeth City County
Washington:	
108	Entire State
West Virginia:	
109	Barbour, Berkeley, Brooke, Calhoun, Doddridge, Gilmer, Grant, Hampshire, Hancock, Hardy, Harrison, Jefferson, Lewis, Marion, Marshall, Mineral, Monongalia, Morgan, Ohio, Pendleton, Pleasants, Preston, Randolph, Ritchie, Taylor, Tucker, Tyler, Upshur, Wetzel, Wirt, and Wood Counties
110	Boone, Braxton, Cabell, Clay, Fayette, Greenbrier, Jackson, Kanawha, Lincoln, Logan, McDowell, Mason, Mercer, Monroe, Nicholas, Pocahontas, Putnam, Raleigh, Roane, Summers, Wayne, Webster, and Wyoming Counties
Wisconsin:	
111	Milwaukee and Walworth Counties
112	Dodge, Jefferson, Kenosha, Ozaukee, Racine, Washington, and Waukesha Counties
113	Crawford, Dane, Grant, Green, Iowa, Juneau, Lafayette, Richland, Rock, Sauk, and Vernon Counties
114	Adams, Brown, Calumet, Columbia, Door, Fond du Lac, Green Lake, Kewaunee, Manitowoc, Marquette, Outagamie, Sheboygan, Waushara, and Winnebago Counties
115	Ashland, Clark, Florence, Forest, Langlade, Lincoln, Marathon, Marinette, Oconto, Oneida, Portage, Price, Shawano, Taylor, Waupaca, and Wood Counties
116	Barron, Bayfield, Buffalo, Burnett, Chippewa, Douglas, Dunn, Eau Claire, Jackson, La Crosse, Monroe, Pepin, Pierce, Polk, St. Croix, Sawyer, Trempealeau, and Washburn Counties
Wyoming:	
117	Entire State
Washington, D. C., and miscellaneous:	
118	Entire District

Index to General Correspondence of the Record and Pension Office, 1889–1920. M686. 385 rolls. 16mm. DP.

This microfilm publication reproduces a card index to general correspondence of the Record and Pension Office, 1889–1904.

Most of the microfilmed index cards refer to names of soldiers. Each card gives, in addition to the name of the soldier, the organization in which he served, the name of the person or office who made the inquiry, the subject of the inquiry, and the file number. Other cards refer to names of volunteer organizational units and of States; some subjects are also included. The records to which these indexes refer are not available on microfilm.

Roll	*Description*
1	A–Ac
2	Ad–Add
3	Ade–Alb
4	Alc–Alk
5	All–Allf
6	Allg–Am
7	An–Andi
8	Andl–Aq
9	Ar–Arm
10	Arn–Ash
11	Ask–Aul
12	Aum–Az
13	B–Bah
14	Bai
15	Bak–Balc
16	Bald–Bani
17	Bank–Bark
18	Barl–Barn
19	Baro–Bars
20	Bart–Batd
21	Bate–Baz
22	Bea–Beb
23	Bec–Beg
24	Beh–Bell
25	Belm–Benn
26	Beno–Berr
27	Bers–Bif
28	Big–Bir
29	Bis–Blae
30	Blag–Blaz
31	Ble–Boa
32	Bob–Boll
33	Bolm–Boo
34	Bop–Boui
35	Bouk–Bowl
36	Bowm–Boyn
37	Boys–Brah
38	Brai–Braz
39	Bre
40	Bri–Bris
41	Brit–Bron
42	Broo–Browl
43	Brown, A.–Brown, G.
44	Brown, H.–Brown, M.
45	Brown, N.–Brows
46	Brox–Brya
47	Bryc–Bue
48	Buf–Burc
49	Burd–Burk
50	Burl–Burn
51	Buro–Buse
52	Bush–Butm
53	Butn–By
54	C–Cald
55	Cale–Camo
56	Camp–Camu
57	Can–Care
58	Carg–Carp
59	Carr–Cars
60	Cart–Case
61	Casg–Caz
62	Ce–Cham
63	Chan–Chap
64	Char–Chet
65	Cheu–Chun
66	Chur–Clari
67	Clark–Clark, J.
68	Clark, K.–Clay
69	Cle–Clin
70	Clip–Coc
71	Cod–Cold

Roll	Description
72	Cole–Colk
73	Coll–Colm
74	Coln–Comp
75	Comn–Conm
76	Conn–Conr
77	Cons–Cook
78	Cool–Cooy
79	Cop–Corm
80	Corn–Cot
81	Cou–Cow
82	Cox–Crak
83	Cral–Craz
84	Cre–Crof
85	Crog–Crov
86	Crow–Cul
87	Cum–Curr
88	Curs–Cz
89	D–Damo
90	Damp–Darl
91	Darm–Davin
92	Davis–Davis, I.
93	Davis, J.–Davit
94	Davl–Dea
95	Deb–Dei
96	Dej–Denm
97	Denn–Desd
98	Dese–Dich
99	Dick–Dier
100	Dies–Disc
101	Dise–Doll
102	Dolm–Dorn
103	Doro–Doug
104	Doul–Drak
105	Dral–Dud
106	Due–Dune
107	Dunf–Durd
108	Dure–Dz
109	E–Eckl
110	Eckm–Ega
111	Egb–Ellio
112	Ellis–Emic
113	Emig–Epp
114	Epr–Evans, F.
115	Evans, G.–Ez
116	F–Farm
117	Farn–Faz
118	Fe–Fern
119	Fero–Finh
120	Fini–Fish
121	Fisk–Flan
122	Flar–Flo
123	Flu–Forc
124	Ford–Fort
125	Forw–Fow
126	Fox–Fran
127	Frap–Frem
128	Fren–Fru
129	Fry–Fy
130	G–Gall
131	Galm–Gard
132	Gare–Gat
133	Gau–Geop
134	Geor–Gibb
135	Gibe–Gilk

Roll	Description
136	Gill–Gind
137	Gine–Glu
138	Gly–Gooc
139	Good–Gord
140	Gore–Grag
141	Grah–Grav
142	Graw–Green, H.
143	Green, I.–Greg
144	Greh–Grim
145	Grin–Gud
146	Gue–Gy
147	H–Haim
148	Hain–Hall, G.
149	Hall, H.–Hamb
150	Hamd–Hamm
151	Hamn–Hanr
152	Hans–Hard
153	Hare–Harrio
154	Harris
155	Harrit–Hart
156	Harv–Hath
157	Hati–Hax
158	Hay–Hazi
159	Hazl–Hee
160	Hef–Henc
161	Hend–Heno
162	Henr–Herm
163	Hern–His
164	Hib–Hik
165	Hil–Hill
166	Hilp–Hl
167	Ho–Hoga
168	Hogc–Holl
169	Holm–Hood
170	Hooe–Horn
171	Horo–Hour
172	Hous–Howd
173	Howe–Hubb
174	Hube–Hugg
175	Hugh–Hump
176	Humr–Hurk
177	Hurl–Hy
178	I–Ink
179	Inl–Iz
180	J–Jack
181	Jacc–Jee
182	Jef–Jewa
183	Jewe–Johnson, F.
184	Johnson, G.–Johnson, L.
185	Johnson, M.–Johu
186	Joi–Jones, I.
187	Jones, J.–Jones, W.
188	Jones, Y.–Jy
189	K–Keas
190	Keat–Kelk
191	Kell
192	Kelm–Kenn
193	Keno–Ket
194	Keu–Kinb
195	Kinc–King
196	Kini–Kirk
197	Kirl–Knal
198	Knap–Kob
199	Koc–Krea

Roll	Description
200	Kreb–Ky
201	L–Lamb
202	Lamd–Lanf
203	Lang–Lart
204	Laru–Lawr
205	Laws–Lecl
206	Leco–Lehm
207	Lehn–Lets
208	Lett–Lewi
209	Lewl–Line
210	Ling–Llov
211	Lloy–Lone
212	Long–Los
213	Lot–Lowm
214	Lown–Luss
215	Lust–Ly
216	M–Mahn
217	Maho–Mal
218	Mam–Marg
219	Mari–Mars
220	Mart
221	Maru–Math
222	Mati–Max
223	May–McBo
224	McBr–McCi
225	McCl–McCor
226	McCos–McDi
227	McDo–McE
228	McF–McGn
229	McGo–McIl
230	McIn–McKe
231	McKi–McLa
232	McLe–McNa
233	McNe–Meac
234	Mead–Meeh
235	Meek–Merp
236	Merr–Mich
237	Mici–Miller, C.
238	Miller, D.–Miller, M.
239	Miller, N.–Milz
240	Mim–Miss
241	Mist–Molk
242	Moll–Moon
243	Moore
244	Moorh–Morp
245	Morr
246	Mors–Mous
247	Mout–Munl
248	Munn–Murp
249	Murr–Myen
250	Myer–My
251	N–Nebo
252	Nebr–Nels
253	Nelt–Newl
254	Newm–Nice
255	Nich–Niv
256	Nix–Nors
257	Nort–Ny
258	O–Odem
259	Oden–Ok
260	Ol–Oq
261	Or–Oste
262	Osth–Oz
263	P–Pan

Roll	Description
264	Pap–Park
265	Parl–Pats
266	Patt–Paym
267	Payn–Peci
268	Peck–Penm
269	Penn–Peo
270	Pep–Peta
271	Pete–Pheg
272	Phel–Pich
273	Pick–Pine
274	Ping–Pl
275	Po–Pors
276	Port–Pot
277	Pou–Pra
278	Pre–Prim
279	Prin–Pt
280	Pu–Py
281	Q
282	R–Ram
283	Ran–Rat
284	Rau–Reck
285	Reco–Reec
286	Reed–Reep
287	Rees–Rem
288	Ren–Reyn
289	Reys–Rice
290	Rich
291	Rick–Rile
292	Rili–Robb
293	Robe
294	Robi–Roch
295	Rock–Roge
296	Rogg–Rose
297	Rosh–Rov
298	Row–Ruk
299	Rul–Russ
300	Rust–Ry
301	S–Sanc
302	Sand–Sat
303	Sau–Sche
304	Schi–Schu
305	Schv–Scou
306	Scov–Sef
307	Seg–Sew
308	Sex–Shan
309	Shao–Shed
310	Shee–Shep
311	Sher–Ship
312	Shir–Shuk
313	Shul–Sil
314	Sim–Sinc
315	Sind–Slas
316	Slat–Smin
317	Smit–Smith, D.
318	Smith, E.–Smith, H.
319	Smith, I.–Smith, J.
320	Smith, K.–Smith, S.
321	Smith, T.–Snei
322	Snel–Soli
323	Soll–Spar
324	Spat–Spil
325	Spin–Stae
326	Staf–Stap
327	Star–Stea

Roll	Description
328	Steb–Steu
329	Stev
330	Stew–Stie
331	Stif–Stol
332	Stom–Stoy
333	St. P–Stro
334	Stru–Sul
335	Sum–Swap
336	Swar–Sz
337	T–Tayh
338	Tayl–Taylor, R.
339	Taylor, S.–Ten
340	Tep–Thol
341	Thom–Thomo
342	Thomp–Thompson, P.
343	Thompson, R.–Tib
344	Tic–Tl
345	To–Tos
346	Tot–Trat
347	Trau–Tro
348	Tru–Turner, E.
349	Turner, F.–Ty
350	U
351	V–Vande
352	Vandi–Vans
353	Vant–Verm
354	Vern–Vit
355	Viv–Vy
356	W–Walc

Roll	Description
357	Wald–Walk
358	Wall–Walte
359	Walth–Ward
360	Ware–Washe
361	Washi–Watr
362	Wats–Weau
363	Weav–Wed
364	Wee–Wello
365	Wells–Wen
366	Weo–Wet
367	Wev–Whis
368	Whit–White, J.
369	White, K.–Whitm
370	Whitn–Wilb
371	Wilc–Wilk
372	Will–Williams, G.
373	Williams, H.–Williams, R.
374	Williams, S.–Wilq
375	Wils–Wilson, J.
376	Wilson, K.–Winf
377	Wing–Wism
378	Wisn–Woob
379	Wood–Wood, W.
380	Wood, Z.–Woos
381	Woot–Wright, I.
382	Wright, J.–Wy
383	X–Young, C.
384	Young, D.–Yu
385	Z

cadet-midshipmen. Other variations in arrangement are explained in the pertinent roll notes.

An entry for each cadet in the academic and conduct records contains his name, date of admission, the name of the appointing official, his place and date of birth, the city or town of the cadet's residence at the time of appointment, his previous education (public or private), his religious denomination, and the name, address, and occupation of his parent or guardian. In the earlier volumes the cadet signed the record to attest to the accuracy of this information, but this procedure was discontinued with the class admitted in 1889. The academic and conduct records contain the same kind of information about conduct found in the old registers of delinquencies, in addition to weekly and monthly course grades, examination grades, and annual and semiannual examination results.

Roll	*Volumes*	*Academic Years*
Registers of Delinquencies, 1846–50, 1853–82:		
1	346	1846–50
	347	1853–55
	348	1855–56
	349	1856–57
2	350	1857–58
	351	1858–59
	352 (*Plymouth*)	1859–60
	353	*
3	354	1860–61
	355 (*Constitution*)	*
	356 (*Santee*)	1861–62
	357 (*Santee* and *Constitution*)	1861–63
4	358	1862–63
	359 (*Santee*)	*
	360 (*Constitution*)	1863–64
	361 (*Santee*)	*
5	363	*
	362 (*Santee*)	1864–65
	364 (*Constitution*)	*
6	365	*
	366 (*Santee*)	1865–66
	367 (*Constitution*)	*
	368	*
7	369 (*Constitution*)	1866–67
	370	*
	371 (*Constitution*)	1867–68
8	372	*
	373 (*Constitution*)	1868–69
9	374	1869–70
	375	1870–71
10	376	1871–72
	377	1872–73
11	378	1873–74
12	379	1874–75
	380	*
	397	*
	399	*
13	381	1875–76
	382	*
	400	*
14	383	1876–77
	401	*
15	384	1877–78
	385	*
	402	*
16	386	1878–79
	387	*
17	388	1879–80
	389	*
18	390	1880–81

Roll	*Volumes*	*Academic Years*
	n.n.	*
	391	*
19	392	1881–82
	393	*
	394	*
Academic and conduct records of cadets, 1881–1908:		
20	1	1881–82
	2	1881–84
21	4 (Pts. 1–3)	1881–85
	3	1882–86
22	5 (Pts. 1–3)	1883–87
	6	*
23	7	1884–88
24	8	1885–89
25	9	1886–90
26	10	1887–91
27	11	1888–92
28	12	1889–93
29	13	1890–94
30	14	1891–95
31	15	1892–96
32	16	1893–97
33	17	1894–98
34	18	1895–99
35	19	1896–1900
36	20	1897–1901
37	21	1898–1902
38	22	1899–1903
39	23	1900–1904
40	24	1901–5
41	25	1902–6
42	26 (Pts. 1–3)	1903–7
43	27	*
	28	*
44	29	1904–8
45	30	1904–8

Selected Records Relating to Black Servicemen (Record Groups 94, 107, and 153)

The Negro in the Military Service of the United States, 1639–1886. M858. 5 rolls. DP.

This microfilm publication reproduces compiled records published by the Colored Troops Division of the Adjutant General's Office (AGO). This compilation, "The Negro in the Military Service of the United States: A Compilation of Official Records, State Papers, Historical Extracts, etc., Relating to his Military Status and Service, from the date of his introduction into the British North American Colonies," consists principally of documents copied from published and unpublished primary sources. In addition, there are a few original documents and extracts from secondary sources that cover periods of history for which primary sources were not readily available. The volumes are part of the Records of the Adjutant General's Office, 1780's–1917, Record Group 94.

The records in the compilation are arranged into chapters corresponding roughly to 9 periods, and thereunder into sections by subject. Those sections concerned with military employment and civil status are further divided between Confederate States and United States. The contents are discussed in more detail beginning on page 4 of the descriptive pamphlet. Within each section the documents are arranged chronologically. Some editing of the documents, varying in amount from volume to volume, was done, indicating that the work was being prepared for the press and that mistakes had been made by the copyists. On the last page of the compilation there is a heading "Statistical Tables" and a note stating that the tables were too bulky to be placed with the copies of the records to be bound. Despite extensive searches these statistical tables have not been located.

Roll	*Description*	*Dates*
1	Colonial Period	
	War of the Revolution	1774–83
	War of 1812	1812–15
	War of the Rebellion	1861–62
	Census Report	
	Fugitive Slaves, Contraband of War, Laborers, etc.	
	Military Employment	
	Events, Battle Reports	
2	War of the Rebellion	1863
	Military Employment	
	Correspondence Relative to Civil Status, Labor, etc.	
	Events, Battle Reports, etc.	
3	War of the Rebellion	1864
	Military Employment	
	Correspondence Relative to Civil Status, Labor, etc.	
	Events, Battle Reports, etc.	
4	War of the Rebellion and the Reconstruction Period	1865–67, with some documents of later dates
	Military Employment	
	Correspondence Relative to Civil Status, Labor, etc.	
	Events, Battle Reports, etc.	
5	Treatment and Exchange of Prisoners of War	1866–86
	Regular Army	

Selected Documents Relating to Blacks Nominated for Appointment to the United States Military Academy During the 19th Century, 1870–1887. M1002. 21 rolls. DP.

This microfilm publication reproduces documents relating to 27 blacks nominated for appointment to the U.S. Military Academy from 1870 to 1887, apparently the only blacks nominated during the 19th century. The documents include nomination and appointment papers, correspondence, reports of examinations, consolidated weekly reports of class grades and conduct rolls, orders, and court-martial case files. No documents have been filmed that relate to the military careers of nominees following their graduation from the Academy.

Of the 27 black nominees, 21 were from Southern States. Eleven were nominated by black Members of the U.S. House of Representatives from Florida, Louisiana, North Carolina, and South Carolina. Five of the 11 were nominated by Representative Robert Smalls of South Carolina. The names of the nominees, the dates of their nominations, the Representatives who nominated them, and the congressional districts and States from which they were nominated are listed in the descriptive pamphlet.

Roll	*Description*	*Dates*
1	Charles Sumner Wilson	
	Henry Alonzo Napier	
	Michael Howard	
	James Webster Smith	
2	James Elias Rector	
	Thomas Van Renselear Gibbs	
	Henry Ossian Flipper	
	John Washington Williams	
	William Henry Jarvis, Jr.	
	William Henry White	
	Whitefield McKinlay	
	William Narcese Werles	
3	Johnson Chestnut Whittaker	
	Correspondence, Reports, Orders	
	Proceedings, Findings, and Sentence of the General Court-Martial of Cadet John B. McDonald	Feb. 8, 1877
4	Index to Proceedings and Proceedings of the Court of Inquiry in the Case of Cadet Whittaker	Apr. 9–17, 1880
5	Proceedings of the Court of Inquiry in the Case of Cadet Whittaker	Apr. 19–22, 1880
6	Proceedings of the Court of Inquiry in the Case of Cadet Whittaker	Apr. 23–May 15, 1880
7	Proceedings, Report of Facts, Conclusion, and Opinion of the Court of Inquiry in the Case of Cadet Whittaker	May 17, 18, 28, and 29, 1880
8	Letter of Transmittal, Index to Proceedings, and Proceedings of the General Court-Martial of Cadet Whittaker	Jan. 20–Feb. 11, 1881
9	Proceedings of the General Court-Martial of Cadet Whittaker	Feb. 14–25, 1881
10	"	Feb. 28–Mar. 14, 1881
11	"	Mar. 15–22, 1881
12	"	Mar. 23–30, 1881
13	"	Mar. 31–Apr. 8, 1881
14	"	Apr. 9–22, 1881
15	"	Apr. 23–May 3, 1881
16	"	May 4–12, 1881
17	"	May 13–June 2, 1881
18	"	June 3–10, 1881
	Prosecution Exhibits	Feb. 3–June 10, 1881
19	Defense and Unidentified Exhibits	Mar. 15–May 17, 1881
	Correspondence, Newspaper Clippings, and Other Documents Accompanying	1880–86

Roll	Description	Dates
	the Proceedings of the General Court-Martial of Cadet Whittaker	
20	Correspondence Accompanying the Proceedings of the General Court- Martial of Cadet Whittaker	1881–1903
21	Joseph Thomas Dubuclet John Augustus Simkins Charles Augustus Minnie Lemuel W. Livingston John Hanks Alexander Daniel Cato Sugg Robert Shaw Wilkinson Charles Young Julius Linoble Mitchell William Trent Andrews John S. Outlaw William Achilles Hare Henry Wilson Holloway Eli W. Henderson	

Documents Relating to the Military and Naval Service of Blacks Awarded the Congressional Medal of Honor from the Civil War to the Spanish-American War. M929. 4 rolls. DP.

On December 21, 1861, President Lincoln approved the congressional bill establishing the Navy Medal of Honor to be given to noncommissioned officers and enlisted men of the Navy and Marine Corps for "extraordinary bravery." A joint resolution of Congress that authorized the preparation of 2,000 Medals of Honor to be presented to noncommissioned officers and privates of the Army and the Volunteer Forces for "gallantry in action" and other "soldier-like qualities" was approved by President Lincoln on July 12, 1862.

The first Congressional Medal of Honor awarded to a black enlisted man of the U.S. Navy was announced in General Order 32, Navy Department, April 16, 1864. Not until April 6, 1865, were black privates and noncommissioned officers of the U.S. Colored Troops awarded the Congressional Medal of Honor.

The documents reproduced here consist mostly of copies of letters sent, letters received, and reports. Issuances and a small number of court-martial case files and log entries are also included. The ranks and ratings shown respectively for the Army noncommissioned officers and privates and Navy enlisted men are those held by the men at the time the medals were awarded.

The documents microfilmed for the Navy Medal of Honor winners, including parts of ships' logs, relate only to the acts of bravery for which they were cited and to the award of the medals. The documents reproduced for the Army Medal of Honor winners, however, often provide other information relating to their military service. A few documents, less than 75 years old and relating to two Army Medal of Honor winners, have not been filmed because they contain medical information, the disclosure of which would constitute an invasion of personal privacy. The documents that have not been filmed are identified in roll notes that appear at the beginning of roll 3.

Documents relating to Seminole-Negro Indian scouts who served with the U.S. Army during the Indian campaigns of the 1870s and were awarded the Congressional Medal of Honor have been included. These scouts were the descendents of blacks who married Seminole Indians in Florida and migrated to Mexico in the 1830s. In 1870 the Seminole-Negro Indians began crossing the Mexican border into Texas, settling in the areas around Fort Clark and Fort Duncan.

Roll	Description
Civil War—U.S. Colored Troops:	
1	Pvt. William H. Barnes 1st Sgt. Powhatan Beaty 1st Sgt. James H. Bronson Sgt. William H. Carney Sgt. Decatur Dorsey Sgt. Maj. Christian A. Fleetwood Pvt. James Gardiner Sgt. James H. Harris Sgt. Maj. Thomas R. Hawkins Sgt. Alfred B. Hilton Sgt. Maj. Milton M. Holland Cpl. Miles James 1st Sgt. Alexander Kelly 1st Sgt. Robert A. Pinn 1st Sgt. Edward Ratcliff Pvt. Charles Veal
Indian Campaigns—U.S. Regular Army:	
2	Sgt. Thomas Boyne Sgt. Benjamin Brown Sgt. John Denny Pvt. Pompey Factor Cpl. Clinton Greaves Sgt. Henry Johnson Sgt. George Jordan Cpl. Isaiah Mays Sgt. William McBryar Pvt. Adam Paine Trumpeter Isaac Payne Sgt. Thomas Shaw Sgt. Emanuel Stance Pvt. Augustus Walley Sgt. John Ward 1st Sgt. Moses Williams Cpl. William O. Wilson Sgt. Brent Woods
Spanish-American War—U.S. Regular Army:	
3	Sgt. Maj. Edward L. Baker, Jr. Pvt. Dennis Bell Pvt. Fitz Lee Pvt. William H. Thompkins Pvt. George H. Wanton
Civil War—U.S. Navy:	
4	Landsman Aaron Anderson Landsman Robert Blake Landsman William H. Brown Landsman Wilson Brown Landsman John Lawson Engineer's Cook James Mifflin Seaman Joachim Pease
Interim Period (1865–98)—U.S. Navy:	
	Ship's Cook Daniel Atkins Ordinary Seaman John Davis Seaman John Johnson Cooper William Johnson Seaman Joseph B. Noil Seaman John Smith Ordinary Seaman Robert A. Sweeney
Spanish-American War—U.S. Navy:	
	Fireman 1st Class, Robert Penn

Index to Publication Numbers

ORDER BLANKS CORRECTLY FILLED IN HELP TO SPEED PROCESSING OF YOUR ORDER

Microfilm publication numbers (preceded by an "M" or "T") are assigned to each microfilm publication. Please enter microfilm publication number and roll number in the proper column. As we accept orders for individual rolls as well as for complete microfilm publications, we must know which rolls you wish to purchase.

The microfilm pricing policy is described on page ix of this catalog.

Sample of Correctly Completed Form

M, T, or A NUMBER	ROLL NUMBER	PRICE
T624	1138	$20
T1270	89	$20

Additional order forms are available upon request.

MICROFILM ORDER *(Prices subject to change)*		MICRO. PUB. NUMBER	ROLL NUMBER	PRICE
TO	Cashier (NAJ)-Military Service National Archives Trust Fund Board Washington, DC 20408			
Please send me the microfilm listed in this order. Enclosed is ☐ CHECK ☐ MONEY ORDER for $ ______ or charge my ☐ VISA ☐ MASTER CHARGE				
ACCOUNT NUMBER	EXPIRATION DATE			
SIGNATURE				
FROM	Name			
	Address (Number and street)			
	City, State and ZIP Code		**TOTAL PRICE**	

NATIONAL ARCHIVES TRUST FUND BOARD

NATF Form 36 (8-79)

Due to increased printing and postage costs, the National Archives Trust Fund Board is charging individuals $5.00 for this catalog. This catalog is not produced at taxpayer expense and the $5.00 will be used to defray costs so that we can publish more microfilm subject-area catalogs. Catalogs will continue to be issued free of charge to libraries, genealogical societies, and other organizations.

(Appendix D)

A Selected Bibliography

Articles:

Aptheker, Herbert. Negro Casualties in the Civil War, Journal of Negro History, XXXII, (January 1947), pp.10-80.

Aptheker, Herbert. The Negro in the Union Navy, Journal of Negro History, XXXII (April 1947), pp.169-200.

Aptheker, Herbert. Notes on Slave Conspiracies In Confederate Mississippi, Journal of Negro History, XXIX (1944) pp.75-79.

Armstrong, Warren B. Union Chaplains and The Education of the Freedmen, Journal of Negro History, LII (April 1967) pp.104-114.

Bolster, Jeffrey W. To Feel Like A Man: Black Seamen in the Northern States,1800-1860, Journal of American History, Vol. 76, (March 1990), pp.1173-1199.

Dyer, Brainerd. The Treatment of Colored Union Troops By The Confederates,1861-1865, Journal of Negro History, XX, (July 1935), pp. 273-287.

Journal of the Congress of the Confederate States of America,1861-1864, (Washington 1904).

Langley, Harold D. The Negro In The Navy and Merchant Service 1789-1860, Journal of Negro History, LII, October 1967), pp.273-286.

McKelvey, Blake. Penal Slavery and Southern Reconstruction Journal of Negro History, pp.153-179.

Wesley, Charles H. The Employment of Negroes As Soldiers In The Confederate Army, Journal of Negro History, IV, (July 1919), pp.239-253.

Books and Pamphlets:

Berlin, Ira; Reidy, Joseph P.; and Rowland, L., Freedom A Documentary History of Emancipation 1861-1867 Series II The Black Military Experience, New York: Cambridge University Press, 1982.

Boynton, Charles, D.D. The History of the Navy During the Rebellion, D. Appleton and Company, New York: 1868. Vol.1.

Braxton Secret, Jeanette. Iverson Granderson First Class 'Colored' Boy in the Union Navy (1863-1865) (a.k.a. Grandison in later years), unpublished manuscript, 1995.

Brown, William Wells. The Negro In The American Rebellion: His Heroism and His Fidelity, New York: The Citadel Press, 1971.

Cotton, Bruce. The Civil War, Boston: Houghton Mifflin Company, 1960.

Cornish, Dudley Taylor. The Sable Arm Negro Troops in the Union Army, 1861-1865, New York: W.W. Norton & Company, Inc., 1966.

Dornbusch, Charles, E. Military Bibliography of the Civil War. Three Volumes. New York: The New York Public Library, 1961-1972.

Everhart, William C. Vicksburg, National Military Park, Mississippi, Washington D.C.: National Park Service Historical Handbook Series No. 21, 1954 (Reprint 1961).

Groene, Bertram Hawthorne. Tracing Your Civil War Ancestor, John F. Blair Publisher, Winston-Salem, N.C., 1992.

Gutman, Herbert G. The Black In Slavery and Freedom, 1750-1925, New York: Pantheon Books, 1976.

Hamer, Philip. A Guide to Archives and Manuscripts in the United States. New Haven: Yale University Press, 1961.

Hamersly, Thomas H.S. **Complete Regular Army Register of the United States:For100 Years (1779-1879).** Washington: Thomas H.S. Hamersly, 1880.

Handbook of Battles in the WAR of the Rebellion, Twenty-first Annual Encampment of the GRAND ARMY OF THE REPUBLIC AT ST. LOUIS, MO.; September 27, 1887.

Henige, David. **African Family History Oral Tradition-East Africa,** World Conference on Records, Salt Lake City, Ut.1980.

The Image of War: 1861-1865. Six Volumes. Harrisburg, Pennsylvania: National Historical Society, 1981-1984.

Jackson, Ronald Vern. **Louisiana and Mississippi1890 Special Census of Veterans,** Accelerated Indexing Systems Intern'l 225 North Highway 89, Suite #1, North Lake, Ut. 84054, 1985.

Johnson, Franklin. **The Development of State Legislation Concerning The Free Negro,** Westport, Connecticut: Greenwood Press Publishers, 1919.

Lipscomb, Anne E. & Hutchinson, Kathleen. **Tracing Your Mississippi Ancestors,** Jackson, MS.: University Press of Mississippi, 1994.

Litwack, Leon F. **Been In The Storm So Long:The Aftermath of Slavery,** New York: Vintage Books, 1980.

Lonn, Ella. **Foreigners in the Union Army and Navy,** Chapel Hill: University of North Carolina Press, 1947.

Long, Richard A. **Black Writers and the American Civil War,**The Blue and Grey Press, a division of Book Sales, Inc., 110 Enterprise Avenue, Secaucus, NJ 07094:1988.

Military Service Records, National Archives Trust Fund Board, National Archives and Records Administration, Washington, DC: 1985.

Miller, Francis T. **The Photographic History of the Civil War.** New York: Review of Reviews Company, 1911. (Reprint) Five Volumes. New York: Thomas Yoseloff, 1957.

Milligan, John D. Gunboats Down the Mississippi, United States Naval Institute, Annapolis, Maryland: 1965.

Morgan, Edmund S. American Slavery, American Freedom,The Ordeal of Colonial Virginia, New York: W.W. Norton & Company, 1975.

Nalty, Bernard C. Strength For The Fight: A History of Black Americans In The Military, New York: The Free Press,1986.

The Negro In Virginia, compiled by Workers of the Writers' Program of the Work Projects Administration in the State of Virginia, Winston-Salem, North Carolina: John F. Blair Publisher, 1994.

Nevins, Allan Robertson; Wiley, James, I.; Bell, I. Civil War Books: Two Volumes. Louisiana State University Press, Baton Rouge, LA.

Newman, Ralph & Long, E. B. The Civil War, Vol. II., The Picture Chronicle of the Events, Leaders and Battlefields of the War, Grossett & Dunlap, Inc., New York: 1956.

Oubre, Claude F. Forty Acres and A Mule: The Freedmen's Bureau and Black Land Ownership,Baton Rouge:Louisiana State University Press, 1978.

Quarles, Benjamin. The Negro In The Civil War, New York: DaCapo Press, Inc., 1953.

Rogers, J.A. Africa's Gift To America, The Afro-American in Making and Saving of the United States, Civil War Centennial-1961, Helga M. Rogers, 1270 Fifth Avenue, New York, N.Y.

Ross, Joseph B. compiled by, Tabular Analysis of the Records of the U.S. Colored Troops and Their Predecessor Units in the National Archives of the United States, Special List. No. 33, National Archives and Records Service, GSA, Washington: 1973.

Schweitzer, George K. Civil War Genealogy, George K. Schweitzer, 7914 Gleason Road, C-1136, Knoxville, TN 37919, 1980.

Sellers, John R. Complied, Civil War Manuscripts, Library of Congress Manuscript Division, Washington, 1986.

Sloan, Irving J. ed., The Blacks in America 1492-1977 A Chronology & Fact Book, New York: Oceana Publications, Inc., 1977.

The Union Army: A History of Military Affairs in the Loyal States, 1861-1865. Eight Volumes. Madison, Wisconsin.: Federal Publishing Co., 1908.

Valuska, David. The African-American in the Union Navy:1861-1865, New York: Garland Publishings, Inc., 1992.

Ward, Geoffrey C., with Burns, Ric, & Burns, Ken. The Civil War, New York: Alfred A. Knopf, Inc., 1990.

Wharton, Vernon Lane. The Negro In Mississippi 1865-1890, Harper & Row Publishers, 1965.

Wilson, Joseph T. The Black Phalanx, Salem, New Hampshire: Reprinted by Ayer Company Publishers, Inc., 1992. American Publishing Co., Hartford, Conn. 1890

Wilson-Reagan, Charles & Ferris, William, Encyclopedia of Southern Culture, New York: Anchor Books, 1989, Vol. 2.

Woodson, Carter Godwin. Free Negro Owners of Slaves In The U.S. in 1830, Westport, Connecticut: Negro Universities Press, 1924.

Wright, Donald R. African Family History Through Oral Tradition-West Africa, World Conference on Records, Salt Lake City, UT., 1980, Series 901.

Index of Topics

www.ingramcontent.com/pod-product-compliance
Lightning Source LLC
Chambersburg PA
CBHW060357090426
42734CB00011B/2170
9780788406720